PEYTON'S PASSING

TO HELL & BACK

Courtney Pottebaum

Battle Press
SATELLITE BEACH, FLORIDA

Peyton's Passing
To Hell & Back

Copyright © 2021 by Courtney Pottebaum

All rights reserved. No part of this book may be used or reproduced by any means, graphic, electronic or mechanical, including photocopying, recording, taping or by any information storage retrieval system without the written permission of the publisher except in the case of brief quotations embodied in critical articles and reviews.

ISBN: 978-1-7374-9913-8 (SC)
ISBN: 978-1-5136-8430-7 (eBook)

LCCN: 2021913659

First Edition

Table of Contents

Preface 5
Introduction 9
Every Parent's Nightmare 15
Peyton Passes 33
The Fight Begins 53
We've Been Waiting 65
Another Hoop 97
The Clock Keeps Ticking 121
Somebody Knows Something 157
The First Holidays Without Him 167
One Year Later 187
Our Rainbow Baby 197
The Big Day 203
I Felt Him 209
Another Blessing 211
Please, Not Again 221
Tayden Passes 247
Do I Stay? 263
HOLY Crap! 287
A Big Sign 309
Nobody Told Me This 331
A New Chapter 357
Transition 371
Happy 1st Birthday To Our Special Boy! 387
Resources That Helped My Spiritual Awakening 427

Preface

These writings are pieces of my personal journal entries after the death of both of my sons. My first son Peyton died in January of 2012 from non-accidental head injuries when he was 6 months old while attending an in-home daycare. My second son Tayden died in April of 2015 from complications of Down Syndrome. My spiritual awakening began in December of 2015. While going through grief I was given so many books by wonderful people trying to help me. These books, while well intentioned, were hard for me to connect to. They tended to be very 'rose colored' and in that place of despair, I just couldn't connect. The very common message was to 'find God and be grateful and happy'. For me, I just couldn't get there from the deep dark place that I was at. My hope in publishing some of my 'raw' journal entries is that it will give someone else hope that they are not alone and that their grief is not 'abnormal', as I often felt. My objective in this writing is to be as transparent as possible as that is what I needed during those times. For the sake of real connection I have left these writings raw and as unedited as possible.

It is possible that I may offend you with what I say from the perspective I was at. When we are hurting our thinking is not always the clearest, optimistic and it's often very selfish in nature. It is our body's way of trying to protect and guard itself from any other damage and threats. As we often hear, "Hurt people, hurt people" (Yehuda Berg) and during my time of grief I was no exception to that saying. Due to the grief and trauma, I often had very strong opinions or reactions to people, events and situations in my life. Please know that these entries and feelings are not necessarily how I feel in this present moment. I have done much healing and much inner work and many of my strong feelings or opinions don't resonate with me anymore. But again, in an effort to be transparent I had to include ALL of it to show the true nature of the journey. I have purposely kept these entries minimally edited. There will be incorrect punctuation, run on sentences, improper word usage and so forth. These journals are "human" and in real time and none of us or our lives fit perfectly into a square box.

My story is also to explain what happened to me spiritually along my path, not in an attempt to sway any of you in your personal beliefs. I have the utmost respect for the individual freedom to choose what we each believe. For me, there have been incredible events that have happened once I was able to connect and resonate to what I believe. Hope and healing is possible and that is my wish for ALL of us, no matter your level of trauma.

Please also know that in an attempt to protect everyone I have changed the names and identities of everyone in my entries except those in our immediate family.

Also know that the views, perspectives, beliefs and opinions expressed here are mine, and mine alone. It must also be noted that all parties involved are presumed to be innocent until proven guilty in a court of law.

I will be sharing some personal spiritual messages from one of my very gifted daughters. Some may wonder why I am sharing these personal messages from a 'minor'. We have taken much time in pondering whether to include her messages as a form of trying to protect her. With much consideration and insistence from her we have included them to normalize having 'spiritual gifts'.

I also feel it's important to set a 'loving boundary'. There may be people who read our story and experiences and either don't believe it, don't agree with it or both. These people may be able to do and show this in a civil manner. There may be other people that don't believe and don't understand our experiences and they may send "hate" and ill intentions. People that mostly operate in positive emotions have a high vibration of energy they "put out" to those around them. Those that operate mostly in negative emotions have a low vibration. People that vibrate with a low vibration tend to be triggered by those that encompass a higher vibration; that is a normal human phenomenon. Please understand, we have done so much work on our vibrations, therefore, we cannot lower our vibrations to those who encompass ill intentions toward us. If someone is triggered by something they read from me, rather than do anything from a place other than love towards us, it would be much more beneficial to them if they took that energy and reflected what inside of them needs to be transmuted back to love. A negative response from someone else says more about their vibration than it says about us. We all have a right to our own beliefs and opinions. We can have ours, all the while allowing others to have theirs. I respect you, no matter what.

I also need to provide a 'Trigger Warning' as topics such as death, murder, miscarriage, reincarnation, God, spirituality, abuse, suicide, infant death, and newborn death are all mentioned. If you feel that reading about any of these topics might trigger you in an unhealthy manner or cause yourself undo suffering, then please DO NOT read this. I do not want to cause harm to anyone. AT the same time, if you are triggered, maybe this is an opportunity for you to dig deep and deal with any un-dealt trauma inside of you. Again, my intent is to connect to people that are hurting, in pain, struggling to function and those that have felt the utmost of life's "blows". I SEE you, I GET you and sometimes life is really hard. If I can give you just a tiny bit of hope, then all of my struggles were completely worth it. ***YOU ARE NOT ALONE.***

"This is how it started... My son was killed and initially everyone was a suspect."

Introduction

I am married to my post high school sweetheart. We dated for five long years before getting engaged, then married a year later by a judge, as I was too practical to want to spend money on a wedding dress or a party. I wanted that money to go towards our "life", a house for our soon to be family to live in, our own home. Jeremiah and I both graduated from good colleges. He received a Bachelor of Arts in physical education and I received my Master's degree in counseling. Jeremiah and I never left our home area, we were content. We were proud of our roots and wanted nothing more than our "someday family" to be surrounded by the family that we were surrounded by growing up. Jeremiah and I always felt that we didn't care about being rich or having fancy things. We just wanted our own family and we wanted to live comfortably. We wanted to provide for our children.

Growing up I was always the 'type A' person who believed in planning life out. You know the saying "an anxious child becomes an anxious adult", yeah that was me… always me. I did things the "right" way. I tried to be genuinely nice, overly concerned about others and expected the utmost from myself in all areas of life. I planned everything. I genuinely believed that the goal to happiness was mapping out the "right way" to do things. Get married when we were "ready", start having children when we were "ready", structuring our budget so we didn't buy anything until we were "ready". Don't get me wrong, we weren't saints. But, at the end of the day I always knew what I wanted. I would go to college, then to graduate school, get married, buy a house, get dogs, get a good job, get a reliable vehicle, and start to have children. Just two though… two kids sounded perfect and my goal was to have one of each by the time I was 30. There was a lot of planning to do in order to make this plan work out the "right" way.

In November of 2007 we found out we were pregnant! A few months later we found out it was a girl and Jeremiah immediately claimed the opportunity to name her Trinity. My pregnancy was relatively uneventful until July 13, 2008. I was lying in bed and all of a sudden my water broke 5 weeks early. We grabbed our bags and off to the hospital we headed. Trinity entered this world stubbornly at approximately 3:01 p.m.! She had some problems initially breathing so she was immediately taken to the NICU unit where she stayed and got stronger. Jeremiah and I were in love to say the least. She was beautiful and precious. As she grew her "loud" personality kept us on our toes. She always let us know what she wanted. She was always very loving, busy and social. She was also often sick with some cold or ailment. She had numerous ear and strep infections. She had two sets of tubes, tonsils out, adenoids out and was on antibiotics numerous times. She was terribly colic until six months of age and in her early months of life was diagnosed with "reflux". As a baby our couches were lined with towels as her projectile vomiting covered everything. There were days I would arrive at work without noticing the vomit that she had left on my work shirt. The best gift we were ever given was a box of "shop rags" from Menards by a family member. In taking care of Trinity you constantly needed new clean rags to clean up her projectile vomit.

After Trinity's first two full years, Jeremiah and I decided we were ready for an addition to our family. Trinity was so social and we thought it would be a punishment to her not to offer her a sibling. So, we tried to get pregnant...

In June of 2010 we "tried" to get pregnant and a couple of weeks later we were. It seemed like it had all been the way it should be because we planned it out. In the end of August I felt like something was different with this pregnancy. I was about eight weeks along and not showing at all. In fact, I had even lost weight. I was the lightest I had ever been since my freshman year of high school. That was weird... I was eating and doing everything the "right way". One day after using the restroom I noticed some spotting. I wasn't too concerned as I knew this was normal for some women to do in early pregnancy. A couple of days later at one of my doctor appointments I mentioned that this had happened and just to be safe he ordered a sonogram. Jeremiah and I were in the small room receiving the sonogram and noticing that the technician knew something that we did not. She was hesitant, and careful... too careful of what she said to us. I knew at that moment that it was something bad. That night our doctor called us to confirm that in fact the baby was not vital and that he felt it was best to let a miscarriage happen naturally. I waited for the next five days, until I couldn't wait anymore. Nothing was happening and I just couldn't bear the idea of carrying around a dead baby. I was just going back to school, one of the busiest times of the year and I just couldn't sit and wait. I called my doctor and begged for a D&C so that I could start the journey of closure. My plan to get pregnant in June and have our second baby in March so I could have more time off to breastfeed and be with my baby didn't really work out...

After the loss of our baby Jeremiah and I were devastated. We didn't understand why this happens, but also understood it was relatively common. We decided that we couldn't "plan" getting pregnant. I mean, we had planned everything else out in our life, but had learned that babies were something that we could not. We decided that we would just let it happen if it were to happen. We weren't going to "try" to get pregnant, but we weren't "not" trying either. Whatever happened, happened, which was a relatively new concept to embrace.

In November of 2010 we got pregnant! In the beginning of the pregnancy I had morning sickness more than I ever had with our daughter. I was so hungry as well. I just had this feeling… I think it is a boy. I never expressed my thoughts as I didn't want to get Jeremiah set on a boy or a girl. Obviously, we both would be happy with either but, I know that deep down Jeremiah would be very ecstatic if it was a boy. A boy to play sports with, to hunt with, to bond with. Halfway through the pregnancy we received the news that it was a "BOY". We were so ecstatic, now we just hoped that he would be healthy. My pregnancy went on great. I was so huge! My belly was so much bigger than with Trinity. Due to my water breaking early specifically called, Premature Rupture of the Membranes, at 35 weeks while carrying Trinity, I was put on p17 shots. They are progesterone shots that are given once per week to keep the waters from breaking early. We wanted to keep this baby in as long as we could. In the last weeks of pregnancy every day/week counts towards bringing a healthy baby into the world. Jeremiah and I always wondered if Trinity's chronic issues had anything to do with her arriving early. We were determined that I would do whatever I had to try and keep this baby inside me to 'cook' longer. At 35 weeks I started having contractions and for the next two weeks started receiving shots to try and suppress the contractions. I wanted nothing more than to have a healthy, happy baby.

Finally, at 37 weeks, on July 23rd, 2011 at 7:00 a.m. my water broke and off to the hospital we went! Peyton James Pottebaum was delivered via C-section. Peyton was a gorgeous baby and a true "boy". I can't explain how exactly but he just looked "all boy", whatever that means. He was gorgeous and had cute chubby cheeks, 7 lbs. 8.5 oz. What a big baby for me to carry! His delivery went great and he was very healthy. His personality spoke early on... he was happy, content, easy going and healthy. The next few months were so easy and enjoyable. Peyton loved being in my arms and selfishly I loved it. I loved that he wanted me so much. I looked forward to feeding him, holding him, changing him, bathing him. I loved the relationship that was developing between Trinity and him. She loved her "Peyton Brother James". I got so many pictures of them together. She was such a good, perfect big sister. Peyton adored her... he just stared at her and smiled at her. Smile, that is what he did *all* the time! He was so happy, he loved life. He loved to watch Trinity dance and they had developed their own special bond. As a parent it was the most amazing feeling to see your children interact and love each other. They were both so little, that is what made it so special. Two special innocent little angels!

Every Parent's Nightmare

Tuesday, January 17th, 2012

We headed off to work like we do every morning. Jeremiah drops the kids off at daycare and I pick them up. My day at work was typically out of the ordinary. See, I am a school counselor. Our job description isn't exactly etched in stone. There is no template or document that states "this is what you do and only what you do". As a counselor you do a bit of everything. By nature, we are helpers and we "help" any way we can. We become the "mediums". We try to piece everything all together all for the purpose of helping kids in an academic setting.

During the day I scheduled a doctor appointment for our 3.5-year-old daughter Trinity. She had started this heavy cough in the last two days and seemed increasingly irritable. She had only been off of antibiotics for the last couple of weeks due to an ear infection and possible strep infection. With our luck with Trinity I figured we'd better play it safe and get her to the doctor thinking that something probably didn't get cleared up from before.

I picked Trinity and Peyton up from daycare and proceeded to take Trinity to the doctor for an afternoon appointment. She was feeling miserable... icky cough, crying, extremely tired. While in the waiting room of the doctor's office Trinity vomited all over the floor but did manage to get some in the trash can! Dr. Ford examined her and concluded that she had another ear infection in the same ear that was previously infected a couple of weeks earlier. I talked to Dr. Ford about Trinity's susceptibility to getting a lot of sickness. He ordered for her to have a test run the next afternoon to check for something related to her body's immunity.

While driving home I noticed a welt under Trinity's bangs on her forehead. Trinity explained that the daycare provider's son had taken a toy and hit her on the head and in the back. I wasn't overly upset as I understand that kids do hit each other sometimes. Quite frankly, Trinity had hit him before so I didn't think it would be right to get too upset about him hitting her.

Wednesday, January 18th, 2012

I met Jeremiah at one of the hospitals to have Trinity's blood drawn for testing. Jeremiah and I were prepared for *"World War 10"* with Trinity but she did awesome! She took the finger prick like a champ, bribing her with the candy and balloon helped I am sure. The kids and I headed home and Jeremiah headed to a late afternoon appointment. Me and the kids arrived home approximately 4:15 p.m. and I started my normal nightly routines. Keeping Peyton in his car seat I let the dogs out and got Trinity situated. I always tried to get her situated first, and then devote my time to Peyton. Luckily, he was such a content baby that this would work. I fed Peyton... Gerber, stage 2 oatmeal cereal with fruit. I gave him a little bottle and then put him in his jungle swing. I had put a roast in the crockpot in the morning and proceeded to dish up our plates and we ate in the living room. I sat on the floor next to Peyton in his swing. After Jeremiah got home I told him I was ready to bathe the kids, so he helped me get them in the bathtub with me. In the bath Peyton got excited while lying across my lap and kicked off the right side of the tub, which caused his head to bump into the left side of the tub ever so slightly. His eyes got big, as he was startled... but he never cried or fussed. After bath time Jeremiah took him out of the bath and entertained him on the bed while I finished bathing Trinity. The rest of our evening routine went like clock-work.

As bedtime approached I brought Peyton in the bed with me and interacted with him. I talked with him, smiled with him, and giggled with him. I was so in love with my baby boy. Eventually he started acting tired like he was ready for bed so I propped a pillow under my left arm, held him, and gave him his bottle. He ended up falling asleep. The TV was on so I just watched it and held him. It was so weird, normally, as soon as he fell asleep I would take him into his crib. But for some reason I had this lingering feeling that I just wanted to sit with him and hold him, enjoy him, just be with him. It was so precious. He slept peacefully and nestled into me. He was so warm and smelled so good, my perfect baby. I was so lucky to have such a perfect baby boy. After some amount of time I decided I needed to get him to his crib. After putting him in his crib I went back to our room and got myself ready for bed. Trinity ended up getting up once through the early part of the night. Around Peyton's normal time, usually 1-3 a.m., he awoke and I changed him and then gave him another bottle. He took this and fell back asleep and I walked him back to his crib. Shortly after getting Peyton back down Trinity stirred again. Lately her sleeping was so weak because her reflux had been acting up and for some reason she was having many nightmares. I remember next I was lying towards Jeremiah and heard Trinity crying ... when I looked at the clock it was 5 a.m. I was so tired from already getting up with her and Peyton and requested that it was Jeremiah's "turn".

Thursday, January 19th, 2012

The alarm went off at its usual time around 6:15 a.m. We hit snooze like two times; this was normal as we knew our alarm was 10-15 minutes fast and would hit snooze knowing we *really* had time. Upon getting up I told Jeremiah that I felt so "ill". I was cramping and when I went to the bathroom I had diarrhea. My head was throbbing and my throat was sore and scratchy. I knew then that whatever had caused Trinity to have an ear infection was now hosting my body! Mixed in with the bathroom issues I decided I would stay home ill. I went downstairs and logged on to our online absence system for the school district. In the mornings Jeremiah always got Trinity ready and I would get Peyton ready. For a moment I contemplated keeping the kids home with me, but after mentioning it to Jeremiah we decided it would be best for me to send them to daycare. Trinity was now on antibiotics and feeling better than the last previous days. There were a few times in the past where if I was feeling sick I would keep the kids home with me just so they wouldn't have to go to daycare. But as a mom, it's hard to take care of yourself while you're still caring for them. I took the car seat upstairs to Peyton's room. I rolled him over and he was so warm. He stretched big and gave me this huge smile. I took off his jammies as they were wet from his reflux through the night and from the pee leaking from his diaper. I changed his diaper and dressed him in new jammies. I placed him into his car seat and put a hat on him. I buckled him in and tucked a blanket around him. I put the "cozy cover" over the seat and turned the handle bars up so I could carry him downstairs to the kitchen. Jeremiah carried the bag and Trinity out to the truck. He came back for Peyton and gave me a kiss goodbye. Peyton smiled so big, and so happy as I said goodbye to him.

I had no idea this would be the last time I would ever interact with him. There are so many moments now that I wish that for that split second I had kept the kids home with me. I never dreamed anything would ever happen to my children...

Jeremiah left the house with the kids approximately 6:40 a.m. to drive them to daycare. I went back upstairs and showered as I still had night sweats from the pregnancy with Peyton. I changed into new jammies and went back to sleep in our bed. I was so tired and out. Next thing, I am awoken to my phone ringing down in the kitchen. I didn't even try to get up as I thought it was probably just my work needing something. But then it started ringing again. My initial thought is that it was Jeremiah calling to check on me, which he often did if I was home sick. I got up and went downstairs to check my phone. I didn't make it in time for the call but checked and saw that it was our daycare provider both times that had called. This struck me as odd as she never called. I quickly called back and couldn't get through as it rang busy. After a few more attempts I was finally able to get through. She answered and was hysterically crying saying that "Peyton wasn't breathing and to please come get him" and then she hung up. Next thing, her husband Brett calls and says that Anna called him at work hysterically crying saying the same thing. He said he called 911 to be safe and asked me what hospital to have Peyton taken to. I told him I was home sick so that it would be 20-25 minutes for me to get there and that I would have Jeremiah paged out of school. I told him to call me when he got to his house, as he was at his work. I ran upstairs, threw sweats on and ran out of the house. I frantically drove and called Jeremiah but of course, he didn't answer as he was teaching. I called my dad as I knew he would answer, he was retired. I told him there was an emergency, something to do with Peyton not breathing and that I needed Jeremiah to call me but didn't know his school's phone number as I didn't have it memorized. My dad called back a little while later. I didn't know but he called Jeremiah's school for me so when I called they had already been given a message to have him call me. When Jeremiah called me he asked what was going on and that he was really scared. I told him I didn't know but that Anna called and said that Peyton wasn't breathing, that 911 was called and he would be taken to one of the hospitals, so to go there. Brett called me back and explained that the fire fighter wanted to talk to me. The firefighter said that Peyton was breathing and that they would transport him to the hospital. He asked if Peyton had any allergies and if Peyton was on any medicine. I continued driving and at some point Anna called again. I couldn't understand her as she was crying and English was not her most fluent language but knew that she was crying and heard her say " I'm sorry" and assumed she meant "sorry" that this was happening, whatever was happening. I remember telling her "thank you for calling me" and hung up. Upon arrival at the emergency room the doctors and nurses were all around

Peyton trying to get him to breath. They ended up having to sedate him to be able to intubate him. The ER doctor felt that based on Peyton's recent diagnosis he may have had a mucus plug blocking his lungs which caused him the inability to breathe. He said it was rare but could happen. Peyton had been diagnosed with RSV in the end of December/beginning of January and had been on nebulizer treatments for his lungs. We were no longer doing the treatments as Peyton had recovered but the doctor's initial diagnosis made sense to us considering his recent history.

Jeremiah and I felt so helpless... Here was our little boy laying on a table with all of these people working on him and there was nothing we could do. It was terrifying. He would cough and fight all of the tubes, which is why they had to sedate him. After some time, the doctors tried him off the ventilator and just on forced oxygen and he was able to breathe on his own. I talked with Brett, the daycare provider's husband and asked what had happened. He said he didn't really know but that Anna said something about feeding him carrots baby food and then giving him a bottle. He said something about her being in the kitchen doing something with breakfast and she heard Peyton fussing. He said she went to check on him as he was in his car seat and she was worried that some of the other kids were messing with him. Then he explained that she realized that he wasn't breathing...That is when she called me and then Brett. He called me and then 911. He explained that he and an officer from school were the first to arrive at his house. Upon arrival the officer gave Peyton two rescue breaths and Peyton started to cry. It seemed that Brett only knew "bits and pieces" of what had happened, which made sense since he was at work when all of this transpired.

After a pediatrician from our doctor's office talked with the ER doctor, they made the decision to keep Peyton at the current hospital and have him transferred to the PICU unit for observation. While in the PICU unit Peyton wasn't coming out of the sedation but still breathing on his own. The pediatrician questioned what had happened and we explained that we weren't with him, that he was at daycare and that all we knew was that he quit breathing. He seemed curious and explained that it would be helpful if we could gain additional information. I called Brett at approximately 12:51 p.m., who happened to be at home with Anna and asked him to ask Anna what had happened. English was not her native language, although she spoke it fairly well, and since I needed such important information, I had called Brett to help translate. He translated this time that Anna heard him gasp from the other room and went in and noticed that he wasn't breathing and that she moved him to the floor and started doing CPR on him. She said he opened his eyes which is when she called me and then Brett who called 911. After getting off of the phone I went back to Jeremiah to explain what they said who urged me to call her back to get more of a storyline, as by now we still weren't really given a "story". Approximately 12:57 p.m. I called Brett back and explained that I didn't really understand and that the doctors needed to know exactly what had happened so that they knew what tests to run on Peyton... This time Anna explained that Peyton's head went back and forth, his eyes rolled back, his body got stiff, then clammed towards his center, and then his body went limp and went unconscious. This is when she started CPR...

I went back to the doctors and explained what she told me this time. They said this helped and that it sounded like he had a seizure and that the next question was "Did the respiratory distress cause the seizure?" or "Did the seizure cause respiratory distress?" And if it was a seizure first, why did he have a seizure? The doctors talked and ordered a CT scan. I remember the pediatrician asking if we felt comfortable with our daycare provider or if we trusted her. Up to this point we had no reason not to trust her. Our daughter had gone to Anna since she was 8 weeks old. Upon ordering a CT scan one of our more familiar pediatricians arrived in Peyton's room to get up to date on his situation as she was on call for the night shift. They wheeled Peyton away for the CT scan...

Anna had sent me three text messages through the day at the hospital asking about 'how the baby is'? Nice words huh? How is the baby? I was so offended... his name is "Peyton." She had cared for him for 3.5 months and she didn't use his name... how impersonal... how distant... how weird. I never responded to her text messages because Jeremiah and I were starting to realize that something very bad had happened and that this all didn't make sense. How could he just stop breathing? What happened at her house? Was there some tragic accident and she was scared to say what had happened? Did she do something to our dear baby boy? Did one of the kids at her house do something to Peyton? How did she **NOT** know? What was she hiding and why was she hiding it?

Upon bringing Peyton back from the CT scan, Dr. Topete urgently came into the room and explained that she wanted the other family to leave the room and just talk to Jeremiah and me. She explained that this was very serious and that Peyton had a fractured skull and a large subdural hematoma in his brain. She said that they were calling Children's Hospital in Omaha to see if they could get him transferred down there for care. She informed us that she would need to call the Department of Human Services (DHS) and report that he had a fractured skull. We completely understood as we are mandatory reporters. Dr. Topete asked us where Trinity was and we explained that she was still at daycare. Dr. Topete looked at us and firmly stated, "You need someone to go get her now." Jeremiah's mother volunteered to go pick her up. While standing next to Peyton as he lay in the bed, I remembered that last night in the bathtub he had bumped his head on the left side of the tub while lying across my lap. I walked over to Dr. Topete and asked if this could have been what caused the fracture in his skull. She explained that "No" this couldn't have been the cause. The doctors decided that they would need to do emergency surgery to Peyton's brain to remove the large blood clot surrounding his brain before he was air-transported to Omaha for fear that he wouldn't make it on the way there if they didn't. *What, for fear that he wouldn't MAKE it?*

The nurses loaded Peyton up and wheeled him down to get prepped for the emergency craniotomy by Dr. Hahn. We walked down with them. I'll never forget, as we came to the elevators the nurses were going to take Peyton on one and have us go down in another one. Peyton looked back at us with his big blue eyes as if he knew he was leaving us. I'll never forget this moment. He had not been responsive to us this whole day but for this moment he opened his eyes and looked back at us. *I believe he was saying "good bye."* He knew we were there and he knew he was leaving us. *I'll never forget...*

While Peyton was in surgery the police interviewed Jeremiah and I separately. They interviewed me for a lot longer. The detective that questioned me made comments that bothered me. They were "grilling" me about the events that took place the evening before in our home and that morning. I explained very detailed to them that everything the night before and the morning of worked like clockwork, as it did every morning.

While I was getting interviewed by the detectives the neurosurgeon had just come out of surgery with Peyton. He explained that he took a piece of Peyton's skull out and cleaned out the blood clot. He said that he also repaired a vein that was split open and that the injury was on the occipital part of the right side of his head. He explained that Peyton would be life flighted to Omaha next. Jeremiah and I went to a room together and wept after meeting with Dr. Hahn. To be honest I don't know if we truly comprehended the severity of Peyton's injuries even at that time. We were so overwhelmed and still trying to catch up to what had all transpired. *What in the hell had happened to our baby boy?* We then pulled ourselves together so that I could get back and finish my interview with the detectives. They continued to drill me about anything and everything.

I was notified that Peyton was out of surgery and in the recovery room and left my phone with the officers to look through while I went to see my boy.

Upon entering the recovery room, I noticed that Peyton was so pale white. His head was bandaged with white dressing and he laid there on the bed looking lifeless. The Omaha flight team was now there and they were all working on Peyton trying to get him stable enough to be able to transport him in the chopper. Finally, they allowed us to say good-bye and loaded him into the chopper to be flown to Omaha. We stood outside. It was so cold, so bitterly cold. We stood there and shivered and watched as our son was loaded into a helicopter and flown away.

Two of my fellow school counselors volunteered to drive us back to our home to get our bags packed and drive us to the hospital two hours away. They were our angels that night. Jeremiah and I were so blind-sighted, so at a loss for words. What had transpired in these last 15 hours that had gotten us to be driving to Omaha at 10:30 at night while our son was being flown in a helicopter above? *How did this happen? What in the hell had happened to my son?*

Jeremiah and I arrived at Children's at around 12:30 a.m. on Friday morning. When we arrived Jeremiah's older sister was already at the hospital to greet us. We met the doctor working at the time of Peyton's arrival. The doctor said that he hadn't had time to look at Peyton's chart but wanted to know what had happened to him. We explained everything that we did know but that most of it we didn't know. The doctor looked so puzzled and explained that Peyton was in very bad condition. He kept saying that in different ways like he was trying to prepare us. I finally asked what he was suggesting and he stated that "Your son is very, very sick and that he may not survive." He explained that on the chopper ride Peyton started to bleed profusely and that the team had been working on him nonstop since he arrived two hours earlier. I asked the doctor if this could have been done by a child at daycare. Trinity had come home a couple of days earlier with a couple of welts from the daycare provider's son. Maybe a kid could have struck him with a toy in the head? The doctor looked at me and speculated that the only way a child could have done this was if they had taken his head and slammed it into the ground. He said that at this point it appeared to him to be the equivalent of being dropped 5-6 feet.

Jeremiah and I just broke down. What in the hell had happened to our precious baby? How could he have left our home in perfect condition and an hour and a half later he had sustained a life-threatening injury? How can Anna supposedly not know anything but that he just stopped breathing? Clearly this didn't make any sense. **What in the hell did she do to our dear Peyton? And, HOW could she do something to our dear Peyton?** Maybe it was some tragic accident. Surely, we have gone to her for 3.5 years and we would know if she was capable of something like this? Wouldn't we? There would have been signs, right? But, we saw none... Was this a tragic accident?

We asked the doctor what we should do. Do we stay the night in the hospital? Our sister volunteered to get a hotel room. At this point we weren't allowed in Peyton's room as he was in critical condition. The doctor suggested we try to get a little sleep as he said the next couple of days would be long and hard. Around 3 a.m. we checked into a nearby hotel. I tried to sleep, even a little sleep. I might have gotten an hour or two, but not much. Seriously, how could we sleep? I was awoken and screaming from a terrible nightmare except I quickly realized it wasn't a nightmare. Around 7 a.m. I got out of bed and broke down in the shower... "*Please dear God, please save my baby boy. Please heal my dear Peyton. Please let him fight through this. I would give anything to snuggle with him again. Please don't take him from me.*"

Friday, January 20th, 2012

We arrived back at the hospital around 8 a.m. Upon arrival we met with the specialist doctor, Dr. Brightford who would be working on Peyton that day. He was very blunt and direct with us that Peyton was in very bad condition. He said that there was a good chance he may not survive and if he does he would be severely disabled. Jeremiah and I swallowed that, we could deal with him being severely disabled, as long as he survived. Dr. Brightford explained that his goal for that day is just to try and get Peyton "stable". He said at this point he wasn't even stable enough for scans or anything. Peyton was losing a continuous flow of blood and they were constantly giving him more. He was hooked up to all kinds of machines and tubing. There wasn't a limb on his body that didn't have some sort of tubing hooked up to it. It was such an overwhelming site, to see our little baby hooked up to all of this "stuff" fighting for his life. *This was so unfair. Peyton was perfect, happy, and innocent. What part of this made any sense?*

During the morning I received a phone call from The Department of Human services asking if Trinity could be interviewed with the Child Advocacy center in Sioux City. I called my mother in law and asked her to take Trinity there to be interviewed. I made sure to ask the DHS professional, "Please don't scare her."

Jeremiah and I spent the day in Peyton's room breaking down, trying to be positive, and talking and touching our baby trying to give him the power to pull through this tragedy. I prayed that God would fix him. *"Please save my baby boy. Please heal him. I would do anything."* Throughout the day our family members slowly started arriving at the hospital.

Nobody knew what to say and really, how could they? There were so many things that we didn't understand or know at the time. Just speculation. Everyone would tell us "it will be ok", "he will get through this". And really, I believed them. He may come out of this disabled but it didn't matter as long as he lived.

Towards the late afternoon a doctor who specialized in child abuse performed a special examination on Peyton. She was a pediatrician who specialized in the specific signs and symptoms of detecting child abuse and led the abuse team in Omaha. She had an eye doctor perform an examination using an ophthalmoscope to look through Peyton's eyes to see if the doctors could see what type of trauma his brain had endured. Jeremiah and I were not allowed in the room while she did her examination but afterwards she and the hospital social worker met us in a conference room to go over her findings. Dr. Sutherland began by asking us to describe how we ended up in Omaha. She asked us to recount to her what had happened the night before and the morning of Peyton's needing care. Again, we recounted everything that we had already said to the other doctors, DHS and the police investigators. Then it was Dr. Sutherland's turn. She told us that Peyton had severe retinal hemorrhaging. She said that it was one of the worst cases she had ever seen. She said that based upon her examination she believed that Peyton was "violently, traumatically shaken". *What?* I then asked, "If he was shaken how did he get a fractured skull?" She said that he was likely struck against a hard surface. *What??? I can't believe this??* I said back to her, "So you're telling me that Anna shook him and then struck his head against something?" She made a note to say that, "No, she wasn't saying it was Anna but that it was someone in that household." Anna would have been the only adult in the household. *How could this be? My poor baby was hurt, hurt badly. My innocent, precious baby was hurt by someone I have trusted for 3.5 years. How could she have done this? Why would she have done this?* Peyton was so happy, so easygoing, and so perfect. Dr. Sutherland had used the phrase "shaken baby/impact syndrome". She made a point to mention that Peyton's retinal hemorrhaging was one of the worst cases she had ever seen. How could someone hurt my baby boy? I just couldn't believe it. I asked if it was possible that one of the children could have done this. She was **extremely confident** that a child could **NOT** have done this. She said this was done by an adult. Dr. Sutherland suggested that we could tell our close family but that we shouldn't tell anyone else due to police investigations. I lost it. I started bawling. My insides were a mess and hollow.

Please let this be a very bad nightmare. Jeremiah and I sat there and bawled. How could our daycare provider hurt our baby? There's no way, is there? I mean, I would have known if she was possible of this, wouldn't I? Could this just have been an accident? Did she snap? I just can't believe it. This can't be real.

That late afternoon my in-laws brought Trinity to Omaha. While we were up with Peyton our family members kept Trinity occupied and sheltered from any of the sadness that was happening above. I believe that Trinity thought we were all there together having some sort of party or sleep over. She had no idea that her world would be drastically changing.

Throughout the last two days I noticed I was becoming so physically weak. Much of that I'm sure is because mentally I was so distraught, but I also hadn't eaten in two days. I was still feeling ill from whatever cold or virus my body had picked up. My only focus was on Peyton. I didn't need to eat or sleep, just be there for Peyton. I wanted him to know I was there. I was talking to him and watching him. Watching for any sign of hope…

Late into the evening Peyton did show some neurological function. He moved his right foot, moved a couple of fingers, and his eyelids moved ever so slightly. Dr. Brightford seemed very happy about this. It meant that things were still working, even if barely. There was still some connection. Dr. Brightford made sure to give Jeremiah and I the parent "talk". Basically, explaining that in order to be there for Peyton we had to take care of ourselves. He said that we needed to eat, try to sleep, and so on. He said that he has had parents that he had to check into the ER because of physical exhaustion. He said, "This is not the 50 yard dash", "This is a marathon". He made sure to say that, "There will be a long road ahead, months, and months". We needed to preserve our energy the best we could. We were only on day two of what sounded like many.

PEYTON'S PASSING

Our family that was now in Omaha decided to get adjacent hotel rooms so that we could all be located near one another. We headed back to the hotel and tried to get a bite to eat. Literally, a bite to eat. We showered and tried to nestle down. Most importantly we hugged and nestled with Trinity. We had not interacted with her since she and her brother left for daycare on Thursday morning. As we lay in the bed that night with Trinity between us, I inquired about her "visit" with the lady earlier that afternoon. She called this person her "lady friend" and said that they played with some toys and talked. She said she told the lady that her, "Peyton's brother James was sick with a bad cough and taken to the hospital so that the doctors could make him better." I then asked her what had happened to Peyton while they were at Anna's house. Trinity got very quiet and scared. This was so odd to me because she was never quiet and never afraid to tell me anything. She clearly didn't want to talk about this, but then, she mentioned that "Anna drop Peyton on the carpet by the fireplace." We sat there with our mouths open. Trinity mentioned a fireplace, and Anna does have a fireplace. We never mentioned anything about Anna's fireplace. *How could Trinity make that up? She had to have seen this happen. Oh God, what did she see? Why was she afraid to tell me about what happened?* And then I realized... Peyton was taken by ambulance at 8:45 a.m. but Trinity wasn't picked up from Anna's until 3:30 p.m. because we were all led to believe that Peyton's issues were all a breathing issue. What did Anna say to Trinity? Did Anna talk to Trinity and tell her to be quiet? Did she threaten her? Why was Trinity so scared? Trinity knew that what she saw was bad. My poor girl witnessed Anna do something horrible to her baby brother, her best friend. Trinity knew it was wrong.

As a mother we often have these feelings about our kids. We have this "sixth sense" ability when it comes to our children. We can tell things that are going on with them that they can't verbally explain to us. It is part of being a mother, it starts when they are babies. We learn what our children need and how they need it without ever being "told" what those things are. We know our children better than anyone else. As Trinity was talking to us I knew that she "saw" what happened. I also knew that Trinity was very, very scared. I wondered if she had told the investigators any of this in her interview earlier. I just had this feeling that she probably did not. She was terrified to tell me so I'm sure she wouldn't talk to anyone else. But I hoped she had, I hoped that Trinity had told them exactly what she had said to me.

Saturday, January 21st, 2012

Jeremiah and I had left the hospital the night before pretty confident that Peyton was going to pull through this. I had even called Peyton's bedside nurse through the night just to check on his status. His nurse seemed pretty positive and said that there were no major changes, just the normal small changes. I never realized but those small changes were changing all of the time since Peyton's surgery. These small changes when pooled together added up to large changes. The doctor had made a statement the day before that there would be no way to update us with all of Peyton's changes and what was happening all of the time. (Blood loss, blood pressure, heart rate, chemical levels, and so on). So many changes all of the time...

We arrived that morning at the hospital around 9 a.m. or so as we were waiting on family to arrive from the airport. We actually tried to eat breakfast at the hotel before we arrived. We were feeling pretty positive about Peyton's progress the night before. When we arrived Dr. Brightford was waiting for us. He looked miserable and tired. You could tell that he had been working, and trying, and not sleeping. He told us that he was getting ready to get off of his shift, but he felt he needed to talk to us before he left. He felt that it was important that we talk to him since we had dealt with him the day before. I started to become scared. There was a clear urgency in his voice, a sad, clear urgency. He went on to inform us that he was so tired and had been doing everything he could to keep Peyton going. He stated that he was exhausted and he was sure we were even more so. He said that through the night Peyton's neurological functions had stopped and that he felt that Peyton "had already gone to heaven". He felt that Peyton may be brain dead and that this morning's CT scan confirmed that there were parts of Peyton's brain that were already dying. *WHAT???*

We had left the hospital the night before with such hope. We saw our baby boy move his foot and his fingers. I wouldn't have left his side if I thought he was leaving us. Dr. Brightford stated that he wanted us to hold on to a small bit of hope but that today would entail testing to confirm if there was any movement in Peyton's brain. He stated that he needed to be realistic with us and he was. He said that for a hospital to confirm a patient as "dead" they would need to allow 12-24 hours and numerous neurological tests to confirm this. He prepared us that this is what Peyton would be undergoing all day.

I can't believe this has happened. Is my baby boy really gone? *Dear God, please show us some sign that Peyton is still here and still fighting to come through this. Please allow my son to live. He is perfect and precious and innocent. Please don't take my baby.*

Jeremiah and I met with family to disclose the new information. We wept as we told our family and yet we were trying to "hold it together". I now look back and think "why were we trying so hard to be strong?" Maybe because it was easier to "hope" that there must have been some terrible accident that she was covering up; then to have to admit that someone we have trusted for 3.5 years has intentionally/unintentionally killed our baby. Jeremiah and I clung to each other in the hospital. We whispered together that Anna had taken our little boy and that we would not allow her to destroy the rest of the family we have left. We told each other that we would try not to get angry. As a counselor I know that anger can destroy people. It makes them bitter, distrusting and miserable to be around. I do not want that for Jeremiah and I. We are not those people and I don't want to become that. But truthfully, it's a battle every day to get up and NOT let the anger overtake me.

Through Saturday the doctors that monitored Peyton continued to treat him and respond to any changes that they would normally do. But deep down we could tell, the look on their faces was defeat. They did a good job of trying to be optimistic to us as they did each of Peyton's tests. Jeremiah and I were there for all of them; all of them but two that is, because we weren't allowed in the room for those. During each test I sat at the edge of the seat hoping that maybe this time there would be some sign of life. I clung to the hope that maybe God would hear me and answer my prayer. Just maybe he could spare my little boy, but test after test came back negative. Peyton's body lay there so lifeless. His body was horribly swollen from all of the fluids that had been pumped through him. He didn't look like my baby Peyton and truthfully I wanted to believe that he was really in a deep sleep; unfortunately he was. A sleep he would never wake from.

Peyton Passes

To conclude the day of testing Peyton underwent a blood flow scan. This is where they inject dye into the brain to see if there is any movement in the brain. If there is not then this is indicative that there is no longer life. We were warned that even if it came back that there was some movement that still wasn't a guarantee that there was "life". As an outsider to medicine it is easy to believe that all medical science is so precise and that there are medical explanations for all medical issues. Unfortunately, we learned that sometimes this is not always the case. After the nurses returned Peyton from the brain scan test we were informed that he failed the test and there was no movement. Dr. Rodriquez said tearfully, "I'm so sorry". He explained that there would be one more neurological test done. And again, this test came back negative. Both doctors looked at us with tears in their eyes and sorrowful faces and expressed their deepest condolences. This was the final answer..no more hoping... no more begging God to save him. Our dear Peyton was dead. My precious, sweet, innocent, perfect, beautiful baby boy was dead.

I just can't believe it. This can't be real. This isn't really happening. This must just be an awful, terrible nightmare. I am numb, I am in shock, I am hysterical, and I hurt so deeply. Dear God, why my baby? Why did you take my baby? Why my dear Peyton? What did he do to deserve this? What did I do to deserve this? How can this be? I just can't believe this. My happy, happy baby boy is gone.

Jeremiah and I took turns holding him. The nurses pulled a recliner up to his bed and let us hold him for as long as we wanted. Everything was still hooked up to him. I couldn't snuggle with him like I usually did. His little tongue stuck out of his mouth because of the tubes in his mouth. He was so lifeless and limp. His head, neck and body were so swollen. I kissed him over and over. I touched him everywhere as I knew this would be the last time I had to touch him. His perfect chubby feet. His chubby thighs and calves. His cheeks, his adorable full cheeks. I think I kept hoping that just "maybe" the doctors had missed something. Just maybe my little boy would start coughing or a finger or toe would move. Maybe I just needed to hold him longer, show I longed for him deeper, and convince God that I needed him more. But my baby boy was gone, gone forever.

Our family took turns holding Peyton. This was such a time of despair, disbelief and shock. Everyone wept. Jeremiah and I now had to deal with the fact that Trinity had to be "told" about the death of her special brother. *Oh God, I am so scared. How do we tell her? She won't be able to understand. Hurt me, put me in despair but please God don't put my baby girl through this pain. I now have to talk to her about the death of her brother. Please help me, I don't know if I can do this.*

The Pastor helped us to speak with a gentleman who was the hospital's "Child Life" specialist. He is an expert in talking to kids about death. Jeremiah and I had no idea what to say or how to say it. So, he talked with us. He told us what to say and how to say it. What would we do without him? It was time to talk to Trinity. We brought her in a room and started to explain, with the help of the specialist that, *"Baby brother Peyton James had gotten a bad boo-boo on his head. The doctors worked on his body really hard but his body quit working. And because his body quit working he lost his breath. And because he lost his breath, he died. Peyton has died and he is never coming back. Mommy and daddy are really sad."* She just looked at us. She was so confused, so at a loss for words. She didn't understand what we were talking about. She had no idea what death was about. The specialist asked if she wanted to see a picture of her brother and she said yes. He showed her a picture of Peyton on his cell phone. To her, I am sure it looked scary. He asked her if she wanted to go see him and she said yes. We picked her up and took her in to say good-bye to her brother, her best friend. Jeremiah held her, she was scared. All of the bandages and tubing was overwhelming I am sure. She didn't want to touch him. I think she thought he was sick, and that she would "get it", "get this death". My heart just crumbled. This was the last time my two special babies would be together. *Dear God, how is this fair?* Soon enough Trinity couldn't take anymore. The Pastor led us in a group prayer. Even though we prayed I was so hurt. *How am I supposed to pray to him when he took my child?*

Family was then escorted out of the room. Jeremiah and I needed to be with Peyton alone. We needed to lay with him, talk to him, touch him and let him know that we dearly loved him. We needed him to know we were broken and aching. We needed to lay with him one last time, snuggle with him one last time and share our love with him one last time. We created him out of love for each other and we were going to "say goodbye to him" together. We lay on the bed with him and we sobbed, and sobbed, and sobbed. God had blessed me with such a beautiful baby boy and then taken him from me. *What is the purpose of this pain?* It was like some cruel joke. It was now our cruel reality. I don't know how long we lay with Peyton, but it wasn't long enough.

Dr. Rodriquez came into the room and asked if we wanted to be with him while Peyton was unhooked from the ventilator. There was no question in my mind. I was there from the beginning and I would be there until the end, the very end. Dr. Rodriquez unhooked some tubing and shut off the breathing machine. Peyton's chest no longer raised... he turned blue immediately. It started in his hands, feet, lips and face. So, this is what death looks like? I didn't know it could look so bitterly sweet. Here was my beautiful baby... "Dead". He turned cold very quickly. This was the end, the real end. The room was so quiet. I didn't realize how in the short time we were at Children's how I'd been at ease with the humming sound of the ventilator. It had brought me some type of comfort. As long as it was on we still had our boy. We attempted to say "good-bye" one last time, multiple times. Each time we got to the door to leave we just broke down and ran back to his bed. We couldn't leave him. We never dreamed we would be leaving without him... None of this was in our "plan". Finally, we gathered our things and decided that we weren't ready, but that we had better leave now or the hospital staff was never going to get us out of his room. I looked back, one more time, the last time.

We hugged Peyton's nurses and Dr. Rodriguez and thanked them for their tedious effort to try and save our son. The doctors and nurses at Children's were these amazing guardian angels. They worked so tirelessly and they never stopped. They just kept going, until God wouldn't let them go any farther. Once God took over there was nothing more they could do.

We went back to the hotel that night. There was such heaviness in our hearts. There was nothing we could do or say to truly see the big picture, our new reality. We decided to post on our social networking site that our baby boy had passed. I couldn't believe we were typing this factual statement. I know that "life happens", but I never thought it would "happen" like this. Never, ever.

Photo Credit @Lola's Hope

Sunday, January 22nd, 2012

We left the hotel and stopped by Children's to pick up a mold that the chaplain had made of Peyton's hand and foot. I opened up the box to view them. They were so identical to his feet and hands, down to every detail. Every line, every crease. The chaplain would never know the depths of gratitude I would have to him for making these for me. These are the only "real" items I have left of him.

Jeremiah and I left the hospital to drive home. It was a quiet ride. What was there really to talk about? As we drew closer to home I started to have this panicking feeling in my stomach. How could I walk into my house and see all of Peyton's things and know that he was no longer here? I was so scared to go to the place that has been my sanctuary. Upon entering our house I prepared myself to "deal" but as I walked in I noticed that somebody had already been there. I didn't see Peyton's bottles, his formula, his toys, or his clothes. Upon initial arrival there was no sign that this house had previously been filled with baby things. I later learned that my mother had gone to the house to put things away for me. God Bless Her.

The Next Few Days

The next few days were spent with the 'drop-bys' of friends, family and community members. They brought food, drinks, cards, feeding utensils, comfort and condolences. We were so lucky to have so many people that cared about us. The hard part is that we were so numb and deep down really hadn't yet acknowledged that this was our reality. We were just going through the motions.

We decided on the funeral home and the next few days consisted of all the details of Peyton's services. I don't know what we would have done without my husband's parents. They just stepped up and offered to do all of the contacting and arranging for us. I can never repay them for this. I couldn't have done it. A co-worker of mine had once said to me that everyone takes a role during the passing of a loved one. She was right. All of our family took this unspoken beautifully orchestrated role. Nobody talked but somehow everybody knew what to do for us. *Maybe this was God's way of saying, "I am trying to take care of you."*

A couple of days after being home Jeremiah and I received a phone call from the detectives and they wanted to know if anyone was at our house. He explained that they needed to do some walk-throughs and take some pictures. We were busy at the funeral home but explained that our family was home and would let them in. Jeremiah and I tended to Peyton's arrangements. Once arriving back home the police investigators were still "working". I don't know exactly what they were doing but they were going room to room and investigating each room very detailed. I truly felt that we were on some sort of CSI episode. It also struck me as odd... Why were the detectives combing through our home when Peyton acquired his injuries at daycare? Something wasn't adding up...

The detectives asked us to go downtown to the station to do an interview with them. Detective Johnson stated that there were so many distractions at the hospital. We agreed to the interview, anything to help them gain information on our baby boy. I knew quite a few of the officers that were at our house. The city we live in is small and Jeremiah and I were both very social in the community. That was the weird part. I never thought I would be someone that they were investigating. I was so naive. At the time I didn't realize this is what they were doing. One of the female investigators asked to talk to me. First, she gave me a hug and I asked her, "nobody is talking to us, can you tell us what is going on?" All of a sudden she distanced herself. She became cold and explained that Detective Johnson was going to talk to us at the station.

Jeremiah and I headed down to the station willing and ready to help them so that they could find out what happened to our baby boy. We had no idea we were walking into an interrogation. They immediately split us up and put us in different rooms. There were two detectives with us in each room. They read us our rights and explained that everything would be videotaped. *What was happening? Is this just procedural?* I watched NCIS and when Mark Harmon did this he was doing it to someone he thought had done something wrong. *OH GOD, do they think we did something to our son? Please tell me that is NOT what is happening?*

And so the interrogation continued... The detectives asked me to recount what had happened leading up to Peyton being taken to the hospital. It doesn't take much to get me to talk. I talk a lot, sometimes too much. I wear my heart on my sleeve. I am an open book and have never been afraid of someone knowing or caring how I was feeling or thinking. I am a detailed person. So, I proceeded to give a detailed recount of what had transpired the night before and the morning of Peyton being taken to the hospital. The detectives really switched how they talked to me, this was a true interrogation. They started out nice but now they were doing anything they could to get me to trip up. I kept explaining and explaining and was getting frustrated because I didn't feel like they were listening to me. They kept asking me to "re-tell" certain things. It made me feel like, 'am I not explaining this good enough?' Later I learned this was all purposeful. They were trying to trip me up or uncover some certain uncertainty. But, there wasn't one. I can retell the events and timelines that lead up to Peyton initially being taken to the hospital. There was nothing to hide. The detectives just kept pressing. The female detective explained that she had little ones and she understood what it was like to go without sleep. She said, "Maybe you were so sleepy and you accidentally dropped him. Maybe you fell asleep. Maybe you accidentally ran into a door." *What in the hell was she saying?* I replied back firmly, "Tori, NO that didn't happen. NONE of that happened. When Peyton awoke in the middle of the night to eat I fed him and walked him back and placed him into his crib. I never fell asleep, I never dropped him, I never ran into a wall or door." Wow, they were really searching. This made me even sadder, as this clearly meant they didn't have a clue about what happened to my baby boy. At one point in the interrogation I made the comment that I was depending on them to find out what had happened to my baby boy.

The detectives had a point of drilling me about why I was on Zoloft. They asked what I was like when I wasn't on it and was I diagnosed "postpartum". *Are you kidding me?* I had been on Zoloft for 8-9 years; since I was in college. I had anxiety, I worried, I planned but Jesus I wasn't some nut job. That is how they made me feel. I was insulted and also felt it was so typical for them to question me and drill me because of me being on Zoloft. I snapped back, "Really, maybe if Anna was on it, this wouldn't have happened!" I was probably the most stable one because I was on it. Couldn't they see this? In my mind I felt like they thought it was me; that I had hurt my son. My stomach was becoming so upset, so nauseous from this idea. I was very numb and calm for much of my interrogation. After four days of nothing but crying there comes a time when there is nothing left; except numbness. The investigators made a point of questioning why I stayed home from work the morning of Peyton's issues. I explained that I was having stomach issues and felt very ill. I explained that Trinity had been sick and now I had whatever it was. I angrily asked the detectives, "Why did Anna call me and then her husband who ended up calling 911? Why didn't Anna call 911? Even if I had been at work that morning what in the hell was I supposed to do when I was 10 minutes away?" They said nothing but just stared at me. I didn't start crying until the detective leaned toward me and got angry and asked, "Why aren't you angry? What if Anna had snapped and done this? Aren't you angry with her? What do you want done to her?" I just started bawling. I just kept saying, "I don't know, I don't know. I am the parent and I have no idea what happened to my child." This was all too much. I understand that their job is to 'break' people. But, emotionally, I was already broken times one hundred. I had nothing to hide, my tank was empty. I was broken as of four nights ago when my son died.

After hours of interrogation the detectives decided to let us go. They seemed frustrated that they didn't 'get anything.' No shit, we weren't the ones they needed to look at. I made a point of saying to the lead detective that he talks/acts like my son is an object; he is my baby boy. The detective stated that 'this is what he had to do, but know that he was crying on the inside.' Whatever that means. Did they really want to find out what happened to Peyton or did they just want someone to pin it on and close the case? Unfortunately, I felt it was the latter.

On the way home from the police station we were both so numb. What in hell did we have to just go through and why? We are the victims, obviously they didn't think so. This was like something you watch on TV or read about, not something one ever dreams they will go through. It was so brutally rough and mean. Jeremiah explained that they didn't really interrogate him. They bull-shitted with him about sports and being married. What??? They questioned him about why I was on Zoloft and what I was like when I wasn't on it. Seriously, his interrogation consisted of the detectives trying to get information about me. Why couldn't they ask me? I'm an open book; I'd tell them anything they want to know. I couldn't believe it. Clearly, I was a suspect in the death of my dear Peyton. *Are you kidding me? Are these detectives idiots? Why can't they see that Anna's series of events or lack of them didn't make any sense?*

When I walked into our house with family waiting, I just broke down. I was so emotionally and physically exhausted. That was the second worst thing I had ever been through in my entire life. I landed in my father's lap and sobbed. I am 30 years old and wanted nothing but to be held by my father. *Please daddy, make this better. Please fix this for me, as you have with everything else in my life.* But he couldn't. He just held me and wept with me.

The next morning, I woke up and felt as if I were too dying. And truly, I didn't care if it meant that I got to hold my baby again. I was so dehydrated, so weak. I couldn't even get out of bed. Jeremiah carried me to the shower and I just sobbed. I was so skinny and lethargic. I couldn't stand up, so I just sat in the bottom of the shower. I hadn't really eaten in a week and it was taking a toll on my body. I was maybe 100 lbs. A week ago I was 110 lbs. Truthfully, I didn't really have the 10 lbs. to lose. But I did, and now my body was paying for it. Jeremiah tearfully stated, "Please eat Courtney, I just lost my son and I don't want to lose you too."

Throughout the last few days since arriving from Children's we had been working with the funeral home and cemetery on planning Peyton's services. We were struggling with being able to plan the exact days for his services as his body had not yet been returned to Sioux City from the autopsy and the coroner's officer couldn't confirm exactly when it would be back. Peyton's body was taken to have his autopsy done by pathologists who have worked on cases/infants such as Peyton. This brought me some peace that maybe these specialists could find out what had happened to my son. Even though the child abuse pediatrician had given us a pretty good idea of what that was, we still longed for the final autopsy. To us, the autopsy was the final say so to speak. And so, we clung to it.

Thursday, January 26th, 2012

The day of Peyton's prayer service was exactly one week from him being taken to the hospital for respiratory distress. Late in the morning the funeral director from the funeral home said that he was done working on Peyton and that he would give us the opportunity to see Peyton in private before the showing later that night. Jeremiah and I jumped at the opportunity and rushed to the funeral home.

Jeremiah and I sat on a couch in a dimly lit room. The funeral director walked into the room holding our baby boy and ever so gently placed him into my arms. *Oh God, my dear baby boy.* He was so cold, and heavier than I remember. My poor baby looked like a precious baby doll. He wore a Bear's sleeper that his aunt had given him for Christmas. He wore a Bear's hat that covered all of the injuries to Peyton's head from the surgery and autopsy. I lifted the hat to look. Jeremiah looked away in disgust. But, I had to look. I had to know what his head looked like. I had to know everything I could, this was my baby. Up until this all transpired, I was the only one that had known everything about him. His body was so cold and the tears from my eyes continually shed over his face and cheeks. I was afraid I would smear the make-up they used on his face. My tears were dripping all over his face, a symbolism of him and I being one. I just wanted to get up and take him home and be with me forever. I couldn't believe this was my poor baby, that this was real. I held him, caressed him, kissed him, loved him, wept over him, tried to suck up these last memories with him. Jeremiah held him. To see my big strong husband with his 'awaited for' baby boy have their last moments together was cruel and agonizing. I took Peyton again and I stood up and rocked with him. This movement was so natural, so peaceful. It was what we did for the last 6 months before bed. This was our time; my time to enjoy him. Some amount of time later we decided to put him in his casket. This is something no parent should ever have to do. We lay him in his new physical home. We had it decorated gorgeously, a Bear's blanket, his favorite rattle and a couple of stuffed animals; only the best for our baby. The pastor in Omaha gave me two matching heart shaped necklaces, one for Peyton, one for me. I lay his necklace around his little neck and chest. At least we would have some constant link together. I wanted to crawl inside the casket next to him and secretly I begged God to take me with him.

Jeremiah and I traveled home and began the chore of making sure everything was "ready" for Peyton's prayer service. Truthfully, we really didn't have to do much. Our family took their roles and everyone had something they did. My step-mom got flowers and frames with pictures arranged and my sisters made a board for him with pictures of him all over it. My sisters also helped me put together Peyton's baby book. I hadn't even started this yet. I thought I had time and thought that I would start it while we were on spring break in April. I had to have his book done now, a tribute to him. I wrote this letter to him the day of his prayer service:

My Precious Baby Boy

"I can't believe you are gone... You have been my special, perfect, absolutely adorable baby boy. Peyton James you were so special and you made me so happy and fulfilled as a mommy. Secretly I loved that you just wanted me. You made me glow, you gave me life. I couldn't wait to see you grow up, to crawl, to walk, to talk, to say mama first :) Everything about you was perfect, your big blue eyes, your chubby legs and feet, your gorgeous complexion, and your huge smile. You loved life and you have taught me more about life in the short 6 months that I was blessed with you. You hardly got upset, you were just happy to "be". You loved to be held and snuggled and you just loved your family. You adored your sister Trinity. Her small world is crashing down without you. You were her special "Peyton brother James". She loved to perform for you and protect you. She asks nightly, "When is baby brother coming home?" My heart breaks every time she asks this. How does a 3.5-year-old little girl understand the concept of death? To be honest, I don't know if I truly do myself. One week ago our household worked like clockwork. I woke you up in the morning, I changed you, I buckled you in your car seat and daddy loaded you up in the truck to go to daycare. An hour and a half later I got a frantic call that you weren't breathing. Baby boy, what happened to you? I can't imagine that someone could hurt my dear Peyton. How? You were precious and innocent and so perfect. Every morning I wake up believing this has been a terrible nightmare and hope that I have finally awoke. But, quickly reality hits and I realize that this tragedy is real. I know that there are so many people that are praying for our family; praying for you. I can't help but ask God why? Maybe he knew how perfect you are and he just had to have you to himself. The mommy in me hopes that he can dote on you the way I would. All I wanted is to make you happy. As daddy once said, "Anything for a happy baby". Our world revolved around you and Trinity. You are what we have waited for, our family finally felt complete. We had Trinity; we were

blessed with you; so lucky to have one of each. Our family truly felt complete; you made it feel that way. I don't know how I can go on without you? I can't fathom what our new normal must be but I am terrified of it. Baby boy, I love you so much. Thank you for blessing our family. I am so in love with you. I love you so much and feel so lost without you. Please help guide mommy, daddy and Trinity and save a spot for us next to you.

We'll love you forever, my sweet baby boy."

How can a parent write a goodbye letter to their child? It is unnatural and so unreal. There is nothing I could say to him to bring myself peace. The only way I could ever have peace again is to have him in my arms.

That afternoon as Jeremiah and I got ready we were so slow moving and so quiet. I think we both moved slowly hoping this would "stall" the pain we were about to endure. Upon arriving at the church we looked around at the commons area which was filled with all of the frames and pictures we had gotten ready for Peyton. I had so many pictures of Peyton and Trinity. She was such a proud big sister. Jeremiah and I needed to approach the casket and so we did. Very slowly, very calmly, very sadly. *Oh Dear God, my Peyton lay here so beautifully, so tragically. I can't believe you took him from our family. I can't understand this and I don't know how to go on without him.* Jeremiah and I sobbed and sobbed some more.

I have often heard that in times of tragedy it can often tear couples apart. But, that's not what happened to Jeremiah and I. It was like we were magnets that instinctively drew so close to each other. We held each other up and clung to each other for dear life, literally dear life.

People started arriving and quickly a lot of people started arriving. This evening was so incredibly hard. We are so indebted to all of the people that showed up on behalf of our dear Peyton. Many didn't know what to say and those that did seemed to hurt along beside us. It was hard to hear all of the condolences and have nothing to say back. I didn't know what to say to anyone or even how to say it. I'll never forget her message. Dr. Topete, Peyton's doctor, showed up and came up to me and hugged me. She said, "I'm sorry I couldn't save him. He isn't hurting anymore; we are the ones hurting." God Bless her for being there and comforting us spiritually. As one of the initial doctors to work on Peyton while he was at the hospital I have a feeling that she knew Peyton's grim prognosis. She came on shift after Peyton had already been lying in the hospital crib for 6 hours and 11 minutes. As he lay there his brain continued to bleed making his prognosis even worse. Throughout this time we all believed based on the given story that Peyton had suffered a lung issue. I wished that Dr. Topete's shift had been earlier in the day. She was aggressive and was the one who did the CT scan of Peyton's head. Maybe if she was on earlier and had found out the injury earlier, Peyton would still be here. That's the problem, we'll never know. All we can do is speculate and wish and do the "what if?"

The prayer service was beautiful, as sadly beautiful as it could be for a parent to bury their son. The entry to the church was decorated with frames and pictures of Peyton everywhere. My sisters made a big board filled with pictures of Trinity and Peyton together, her favorite "Peyton Brother James". There were flowers beautifully set around the atrium of the church. In the sanctuary at the front of the church was Peyton's little, white casket. There were so many flowers sent by so many people. The flowers covered the stage of the church. There was a giant screen behind the casket that played a continuous role of pictures of Peyton and our family. The pictures were accompanied by a soft, beautiful piano melody. In the small white casket there lay my precious, sweet, innocent baby; my precious, sweet, innocent Peyton. He lay there quiet, still. He was dressed in his Bear's attire and wrapped in a Bear's blanket from the waist down. He would never know how desperately his daddy wanted him to be a Bear's fan with him. They would watch football every Sunday, they would play sports together, and maybe someday they would go to a game together. But no, this was just a dream now. This reality breaks my heart. I have my daughter who I can bond with, shop with, talk with as she gets older. But Jeremiah, who waited so long for his special boy, will never get those opportunities with his son. Those days are now gone. Jeremiah doesn't express that but I know that is what he thinks. In Peyton's casket was a couple of stuffed toys and his favorite rattle. There was no need for them in our house anymore. They were always with him and needed to leave with him as well. My step-mother had made a wreath made of baby bath toys. It was gorgeous and perfect. I had Peyton's baby book lie on a counter in the atrium for anyone to view. On the last page of his book I had written him a good-bye letter and left it in there for anyone to view. I needed people to understand how bad I hurt and I didn't think I could verbally express that.

Peyton looked so swollen laying there in his casket. His swollen head lay on a Bear's pillow that my mother-in-law made for him in the days leading up to the service. Peyton looked like a little doll, not like my cuddly baby. His hands were so cold, so chubby, so perfect. His little lip had a cut from all of the tubes that were in his mouth. His right cheek was bruised from the pressure of the tubes against his baby soft cheek. His eyes were more sunk in than normal, or maybe it was his head was more swollen than normal. I kept caressing his hands, trying to hold them one more time. I kissed his lips over and over... so cold, so stiff. My tender baby was gone.

There were so many people that came to express their condolences to our family. I don't remember much of the conversations. There were a few times I remember being asked to "sit down" as I was physically overtaken with emotion and I couldn't stand. Nobody knew what to say and really, I didn't want anyone to say anything. *Just hold me, love me, cry with me, pray with me and beg God to heal this broken family.*

PEYTON'S PASSING

Towards the end of the service Pastor Jay led the service with some prayers and inspirational words. One thing I hold on to every morning is Pastor Jay's message of, "you just need to get through one day at a time." As he spoke to the congregation I watched up above on the screen as all of our family pictures played on. Did God know when he blessed us with Peyton that we would only have him for a short time? Why would God bless me with such a perfect baby and then rip him away from me? The entire service was so overwhelming and so bitter...

Trinity was at the prayer service; she played mostly out in the atrium and was entertained by everyone there. At one point, Jeremiah and I felt we needed to offer her the opportunity to say goodbye to her brother. Jeremiah picked her up and we took her up to the casket. She clung to Jeremiah not sure of why her brother was laying in this thing. She kept saying he was sleeping and asking if Peyton was sick. She just didn't get it. How can one explain it well enough to a 3-year-old? This was agonizing for me as I thought of the many years down the road where I would re-tell her about her last viewing of her baby brother. Trinity made comments to me that night that "Anna hit my baby brother really hard in the head, she shake him really hard and drop him on the carpet. Anna was really naughty to my brother Peyton." *Dear Lord, how can Trinity make this up?*

We left that night exhausted and so empty, there was nothing to say. Many times this night I begged God to take me to be with my baby. But angrily, I still awoke the next morning...

Friday, January 27th, 2012

We woke up in the morning dreading this final day, Peyton's funeral. The service was scheduled for 10:00 a.m. We were to be at the church at 9:00 a.m. to have a private viewing "good bye", but me being me, I was late and didn't get there until 9:30 a.m. My legs felt like concrete blocks and no matter how much I tried to move faster I just couldn't.

The service was well orchestrated by Pastor Jay. He gave a beautiful sermon and talked very real to our friends and family. The church was decorated the same way we left it the night before. Two of our good friends were the pallbearers, which I'm sure is something they never imagined they would be for dear Peyton.

After the service we drove out to the cemetery for Peyton's graveside service, and then the family was invited down to his actual plot. We had the option of viewing them putting Peyton's casket into his plot. Of course, I had to do this. I had to know where he would end up and I needed him to know I was there until the very end, until they laid him into the ground. I walked up to the hole that now held my dear Peyton and prayed that this earth would protect him. *I can't believe I am burying my special, precious, perfect baby boy. Why in the hell has this happened? God please make "her" pay for what she has done to my son.*

We made it back to the church for a small, simple luncheon. Many of our family and friends were there. At one point I looked back and noticed that the high school girls' volleyball team was there and they were all surrounding Jeremiah in a group hug. He was in the middle and breaking down and the girls came together and hugged him. Jeremiah was normally the big, strong coach but now, he desperately needed these girls to hold him up… and they did without him ever uttering a word. *"Dear volleyball girls, Thank you from the bottom of my broken heart."*

The Next Few Days

The next few days entailed the packing of my family. They had been home with me for one of the longest weeks of my life and it was now time for them to go home. I was terrified for them to leave me. Who would Jeremiah and I lean on? We hadn't done laundry or cooked or cleaned ever since we got back from Omaha. But now, we would have to learn how to pick ourselves up and do what needed to be done. I knew my family had to get back to their lives but selfishly I wanted them to stay with me, hurt with me so that I didn't have to hurt alone. One of the most surreal feelings is that of the rest of the world continuing on like normal, while ours is sadly, agonizingly standing still. Everyone else continues to do what they've always done, but we do not. There is nothing normal about our new life.

Over the next couple of days Jeremiah and I talked about when we would go back to work. We were so worried about taking too much time off but really, I think we were afraid to stay home and think too much. For the next week home that is what we did. We thought, and thought and thought. We were used to being busy, but being home seemed to push us down further into this depression. Each day it became easier to lose interest in normal interesting things. Jeremiah decided he needed to get back to work, he needed to be kept busy. I wasn't really ready to go back but I also knew I couldn't stay home alone. I was emotionally at a place where I didn't trust myself to be home alone.

We started Trinity in her new daycare that week and that was really hard. We tried to be excited for her but really, I didn't know who the separation anxiety was worse for, her or me. That was something I wasn't prepared for, the separation anxiety I had from leaving her. I knew she would go through that but I did as well. Her first day at school after she was dropped off to her classroom I stood outside and cried. I tried to leave but I couldn't. The last time I left my children one of them wasn't returned to me. How would I ever be able to trust anyone again? I didn't let her see me. I didn't want to make it harder on her. But it took everything I had not to run in there and take her back home with me. Deep down I knew she needed this. She needed to find a new routine and be around other kids who could help distract her.

The Fight Begins

March 2012

From the start Trinity's daycare teachers started expressing to me that she was talking to them about what the former daycare provider had done to her baby brother. I had asked the teachers to please document anything that was said to them. What I didn't realize is that Trinity would start to talk about it all of the time, to anyone that was willing to listen. Trinity would say very consistently, "Anna hit Peyton in the head like this (demonstrating... sometimes too hard and then I would say, "Trinity please don't hit yourself in the head"... and under my breath I would mumble, "that would not look good right now with what our family is going through"), then she would say that Anna "shake him really hard, threw him on the floor or dropped him on the floor". How can a 3.5-year-old little girl make something like this up? There is no way. She knows what she saw and she isn't emotional about it. She states this so 'matter of fact' like. Sometimes she will end by saying, "Anna was really naughty and I yell at her to stop being mean to my Peyton". At this point in writing it has been 9 weeks since this traumatic event occurred. Trinity is still talking and now she is talking more than ever. There is no way that if this was just a 'story' she could remember this. I believe that what she is saying is fact. There's no way a 3.5-year-old little girl could gather that without seeing it. She is the only witness but nobody will listen to her because they consider her 'unreliable'. Trinity is seriously traumatized and nobody is listening or talking to her. It is so sad to me that as a society we insult the intelligence of children. They know more than we give them credit for.

The detectives had called me the morning of Trinity's first day of school. Detective Johnson pressed on that they would like Jeremiah and I to do polygraph tests. I explained that we were probably ok with doing them since we had agreed earlier, but that we wanted to run it by our lawyer just to make sure it was ok. All of a sudden the detective's demeanor changed, he became somewhat angry and said, "Are you telling me not to talk to you anymore? I don't want this to turn in to something where we are communicating through your lawyer." I started bawling and expressed that "I didn't know what I was telling him. I didn't know who to trust anymore and that we are good people and love our children. Our children have been our life and I don't understand why this is happening." Then I asked him, "Can you tell me one thing? Is Anna still sticking to the story that Peyton just stopped breathing?" The detective replied back, "yes she was". I sobbed more and explained that I didn't understand and that I hope he understood how hard the interrogation was on me. I explained that I wasn't eating, wasn't sleeping. The detective asked if I was seeing anyone and I explained that I wasn't but that I know I needed to be. The detective sounded annoyed that I had mentioned talking to my lawyer and told me to call him if and when I was ready to do the polygraph.

When I got off of the phone with the detective I just broke down more. Why do the detectives need Jeremiah and I to do polygraph tests? We have been so cooperative and told them everything we know. It made me sad as obviously the detective still wasn't sure "who" hurt our dear Peyton, which only means that they viewed us as suspects. I am so angry and hurt at the thought of this. How can they not see? There is so much that doesn't make sense. How can they not see right through her? I feel the worst I have ever felt in my life and I am terribly devastated that focus is still on Jeremiah and me. From the beginning Jeremiah and I have been very open to do a polygraph. I was the one who volunteered it in my interview with the officers. Jeremiah and I really didn't know anything about polygraph tests but we were afraid of how emotionally unstable we have been. Would it be a good idea for us to take them in this state or wouldn't it matter? Clearly, we didn't have a clue about any of this legal stuff and truthfully, we've never needed to. At this point we don't trust anyone. We have had a trusted 'friend' kill our baby and an investigative team that is viewing us as suspects. I feel like my life is being taken away from me piece by piece and all I can do is stand by and watch it diminish.

That afternoon I had a meeting with my lawyer to go over the case thus far. When we had gotten back from Omaha I had contacted our lawyer to run this all by him as we were already questioning how to pursue a civil suit. We had no idea that we may actually need him to defend ourselves. The first thing my lawyer said to me was that Jeremiah would need to have his own lawyer. He then explained to me that he wasn't going to let me take the polygraph test. He explained that he didn't think all of this trauma and loss had 'hit me yet' and he felt emotionally I couldn't handle it. I told him all about my interview and interrogation with the detectives and he was appalled at how they treated me after just losing my baby boy. He then went on to tell me that I was done talking to the detectives as I emotionally couldn't handle it anymore. He felt I needed to focus on myself and grieve the loss of my son and let him deal with this other part.

In that initial meeting with my lawyer he kept telling me not to talk to anyone, not to research things on my computer, and so forth. I was so confused. Why couldn't I do any of these things? I didn't have anything to hide. I was coming to him because the detectives scared the shit out of me. I didn't know what to do. It was one of my family members that mentioned that lawyers have to defend all types of people and that they probably have had to sometimes defend people they know are guilty. So, to be safe they tell everyone not to talk. But, that isn't me! As I've said a million times during this event, "If I hurt one of the stray cats that I fed I would be a mess, let alone my dear baby!"

Just like that my constant communication with the detectives stopped. I heard no more, I said no more. Now the only thing I could do was wait; wait and pray that somebody would be able to gain answers. This part has been the hardest part of my life. The 'waiting'; it was days, then weeks, now months. How can this take so long?

While waiting, we have also been faced with the fact that now the true 'grieving' takes place. Jeremiah and I stayed home for two weeks but like I said earlier we went back to work after that as emotionally/mentally staying home any more would have led to some serious depression and for me, worse. We knew that we needed to function for Trinity and we needed to try and 'pick ourselves up'. As a counselor I am very familiar with the grieving process. I talk to kids all of the time about grief and the five stages of grief. I know that one goes through denial, anger, bargaining, depression and acceptance. I genuinely believed that they happened in a linear fashion, one step at a time. I was so WRONG. My grief has been so up and so down, so unpredictable, so fluid. One moment I am extremely depressed and hopeless. The next minute I think "ok maybe I can do this" and then the next minute I am so angry, hateful and revengeful. My grief is all over the board and now 9 weeks out I am still *all over the board*.

Our fathers have been the 'hound-dogs' in the family. They have been calling the investigators once a week since Peyton's passing. Once they turned it over to the District Attorney our family has been calling him as well. They have also been calling the state death investigator and checking in once per week. They have become our "voice". Now that Jeremiah and I have lawyers and aren't supposed to talk to anyone, there needed to be someone else to have that communication for us.

Even if we could talk to people the bottom line is that really, we couldn't. We are just trying to function every day, every moment. There is no way we can think logically enough to inquire about the right things, whatever those things are. The case has been so "hush-hush". I am terrified of this. I feel it could mean that they don't want her to flee or that really, they don't have anything and they're afraid of announcing that for fear of push back from our family or the public. As Peyton's mother I have suddenly grown angry and very "hard". I want 'justice' for my son. I want Anna to be held accountable in some shape or form. I am Peyton's advocate and he needs me to tell the world his story. He needs me to bring him the justice he deserves. It's so weird to say that word "justice" because really to us, there could never be justice. The only thing that could make this any better is to have our dear Peyton here, here in my arms. But, that will never happen again, not for a very long time. The only thing that brings me peace at night is trying to believe that if Anna is not served justice on this earth that she will be in heaven or hopefully lack of it for her.

Our days now are very moment to moment. One second I think maybe I can function and be "ok" but really I'll never be "ok" again. For the rest of my life I will carry this hollow, empty longing for the baby that was taken from me. I never knew I could ever feel pain like this. It is this pain that aches so badly and no matter what I do, what anyone else does or says, it just remains. It hides so deeply in my tissues that no matter what I try it goes dormant, only to surge out again at an unforeseen time.

Mornings and nights are extremely hard for our family. They are the times when we had routines but now those normal routines have been replaced with new, un-normal ones. The newness is so saddening and so empty. We wake up in the morning feeling absolutely exhausted from a lack of sleep. We try to sleep but we are so emotionally and physically exhausted that we can't even do that. The first thought in my mind is "has this just been a really bad nightmare?" But, I open my eyes and look around the room, *"No... this is really my life."* This is the hand of cards I was dealt and I will never understand why. My next thought is that I really can't do this. I don't want to "try" anymore. I want to give up. *Dear God, "you win", you have exhausted all of my energy to be.* But then I hear Trinity and I know that I have to function for her. We have to get up and we have to "try" for her. Without her I don't know if Jeremiah and I would still be here.

When we first came back from Children's in Omaha the day after Peyton passed, Jeremiah asked a family member if he would stop at our house and get all of Jeremiah's guns. We were so devastated and depressed. I would like to believe that Jeremiah and I would never 'take our own lives'. But the depression that takes over, the pain that is never-ending. It makes one wonder what it would feel like not to hurt anymore? I was taught growing up that it is against God's will to take one's own life, and I know that I wouldn't be in Heaven if I did. All I want is to be in Heaven holding Peyton. There are times when I hurt so badly and I just want the hurting to stop. I now understand why those individuals with terminal diseases sometimes just wish to die. When you hurt so bad for so long all you want is for it to stop. *What is the point in continuing to live when you know it will continue to get worse?* Sometimes, you just need the pain to stop. I have begged God to take my life every night since Peyton died. For some torturous reason, I am still here. *And no matter how hard I beg he still hasn't taken me.*

One of the layers of trauma is the betrayal I feel from Anna. She was my friend, my kids' second mother, and someone that I deeply trusted. How could she have intentionally, or unintentionally, hurt my son and then lied by omission? How can she sit back and watch us go through this and not offer the very information we need for closure? *How can you be so heartless? How can one be so cruel?*

I have talked to so many people through the loss of Peyton. Jeremiah and I have some amazing friends and family. We have had so many people send us cards and condolences for the loss of Peyton. There are so many people that I don't even know. We have had people that have lost children send us cards with their cell phone numbers in them in case we ever want to talk. That's one thing I am learning, it's like this small group of people that have lost children. It is not common and so when it happens those who have gone through it are so welcoming for you to join it to try and comfort you. But, this isn't a group I would ever have wished to belong to.

In the beginning I had some people say to me, "In times of tragedy it does show you that there are some good people out there." In the first weeks after Peyton's passing I would have told you to 'shut the hell up'. But now nine weeks out, I do understand what these people are saying. As I mentioned earlier people have reached out to our family in so many ways. People have brought food, given us money for funeral expenses and medical bills and hosted events for us. Last weekend an adult competitive volleyball group in Sioux City held a tournament in a nearby town for Peyton. It was called, "Play for Peyton" and it was a benefit to help with all of our expenses. The tournament started at 9:00 a.m. and it didn't get over until 8 pm. It was a great tournament and Jeremiah's team even won the competitive league. Normally I don't go to any of his tournaments as with kids it would be hard to watch them and watch him play. Being that this one was for Peyton I so desperately wanted to be there. Trinity came with me and she ran and played the entire day. She had so much fun, as did I. Here were these amazing people doing something that they loved all in an attempt to raise money for our family. We will forever be indebted to them for all of their help for our family.

Part of my new routine involves getting off of work and going to the cemetery. I go visit Peyton's grave about every day. When I get off of work I long to go see him, to talk to him, to cry and pour out all of my feelings to him. I desperately want him to know how I miss him. Maybe if he knows how much I miss him he'll truly understand how much I loved him. I get to the cemetery and I go sit by his plot on the ground. His marker is not in yet so I have decorated it with solar lights and a decorative heart. Jeremiah's sister and mom decorated it with Easter eggs. Every symbol is a reminder that I won't get to do those things with him. When I get to the cemetery I usually "lose it". I try to be as strong and productive as I can when I'm at work. By the time I get to the cemetery my ducts are full and I can no longer pretend that I am "ok". I bawl and I talk to him about how much I miss him. I tell him how perfect he was for our family and we are so incomplete without him. I talk to him about how Trinity is having such a hard time and she asks where her "Peyton brother James" is? *Dear God, that question from her is so hard to answer every day, every time.* Sometimes I read to Peyton what I have written down thus far. I want him to know I am fighting for him the best way I can. I am trying to be professional and hope that the legal system will do what's right. I sit next to Peyton and I cry about all of the things I will never get to do with him. I cry about all of the things that I got to do with him but will never get to do again...

I had an appointment earlier this week with one of my doctors who is amazing. I saw her often when I was pregnant with Peyton. I had made this appointment with the idea of getting my IUD taken out. While I was in the waiting room I started to get this panicky feeling. I remembered that the last time I was there was with Peyton and a lady telling me how I had such a beautiful baby boy. He was beautiful. I kept myself together the best I could while in the waiting room but when I got into an exam room, I lost it. Tears streamed down my face and I explained to the nurse how it all came flooding back. She expressed her condolences and I just started telling her everything. Tears welled up in her eyes as I told her all about everything we'd gone through with Peyton. My doctor came in next and explained that I didn't have to re-tell everything as the nurse had talked to her, but I wasn't done talking. I kept talking and talking, maybe because I knew that my conversations with them were confidential. I could finally talk to someone and so I did. My doctor started crying. She listens and she is so honest. Finally, we started to talk about the reason I was there which was getting my IUD taken out. My doctor looked at me and said, "I don't want to take it out right now. I don't think you are ready. Your body is going through so much physically and emotionally. I want you to be at the best place you can be when you get pregnant again". Then she said, "I am worried that you are trying to replace Peyton". I assured her that, "there was no way I could ever replace Peyton". I would hurt the rest of my life for him. I knew Jeremiah wanted me to get the IUD taken out and inside I was worried as I had always said that I wanted to have two children by the time I was 30 and guess what, I am 30. My doctor went on to explain that if I wasn't at my best and got pregnant again and went through another miscarriage, she feared it would be too much to handle. Deep down I knew everything she was saying was right. I wasn't ready. How could I ever be ready?

That is an interesting concept. Ever since the passing of Peyton, Jeremiah has been very adamant that he didn't want to pressure me but that whenever I was ready he would like to get pregnant again. He has since expressed to me that he would love to have two more children. He has explained that because of the passing of Peyton he has realized what is really important in life. Sometimes I wonder if God allowed this to happen because he didn't think we were devoted enough to him or that we didn't appreciate the small things? Maybe I question this because I feel like we have been punished except I don't know what we did. Our son was taken from us and we don't know why.

Since losing Peyton I struggle with what God's role in our life and world is. Does God have this plan for all of us for some extent or purpose? Or does God only know what is going to happen and because there is sin in the world things do happen, but that he offers Heaven for those that have lived a worthwhile life? I am so perplexed as to what I think. I just don't know. I wish I knew. It is harder for me to accept that this was his entire plan. At the same time I find myself trying to make meaning out of this tragedy. *What am I supposed to learn or gain from losing my son?*

Trinity is struggling every day. She asks about her brother all of the time. She still doesn't understand that death is permanent. She thinks he is coming back from this "death". I wish he was but unfortunately

I have to explain to her again that Peyton is never coming back. She gets very angry and acts out. She cries a lot. She talks a lot about what Anna did to her brother. It has been nine weeks and Trinity still talks about what she saw Anna do to her brother. A 3.5-year-old couldn't remember a story this long unless the story is what they saw for fact, bottom line.

I opened Peyton's door today. I was cleaning and decided that I should really open his door. It has been nine weeks and I had only been in his room two times, the last being four weeks ago. I stood in the hallway and paced from room to room. I want to open his door but I am so scared, so sad to see that it will be empty. I finally turned the handle on the door and even though his room was full of all of his stuff it was so quiet, so empty, so undisturbed. The room smelled like my baby boy Peyton. In his crib lay some of the items from his services and the wreath that my step-mother had made for him. His baby book lay in there as well with items that were normally in his diaper bag. His changing table was stacked full of clean blankets and diapers. His floor was covered with all of his baby toys, jungle gym, swing, glider, bath tub, and clothes. His dresser was still stocked full of clothes that would now be too small for my Peyton if he were still here. His humidifier was still filled with the water that was used nine weeks ago. By now the water had turned dark from the country sediment. Clothes and jackets still hung in his closet. What would I do with all of his things? I couldn't move them or touch them. I never wanted to have to change his room. As long as I left everything the "way it was" I felt like a part of him was still here.

I'll Lend You for a Little Time a Child of Mine

"I'll lend you for a little time a child of mine,
He said.
For you to love the while he lives and
mourn when he is dead,

It may be six or seven years, or twenty-two
or three.
But will you, till I call him back, take care of
him for me?

He'll bring his charms to gladden you, but
should his stay be brief,
You'll have his lovely memories, as solace
for your grief,

I cannot promise he will stay, since all from
earth return,
But there are lessons taught down there I
want this child to learn.

I've looked the wide world over in my
search for teachers true,
And from the throngs that crowd life's lanes
I have selected you.

Now will you give him all your love, nor
think the labor vain,
Nor hate me when I come to call to take
him back again?

*I fancied that I heard them say: Dear Lord,
Thy will be done!
For all the joy Thy child shall bring, the risk
of grief we'll run.*

*We'll shelter him with tenderness: we'll love
him while we may,
And for happiness we've known forever
grateful stay.*

*But should the angels call for him much
sooner than we'd planned.
We'll brave the bitter grief that comes and
try to understand."*

Edgar Guest

We've Been Waiting

Monday, March 19th, 2012

I arrived home from work after picking Trinity up from daycare. We pull into the drive and notice that Jeremiah is parked in the driveway just sitting in his truck. Upon further investigation I notice that he is reading something. He is very concentrated and doesn't even notice us walking up to the truck. He looks up and mentions that we got the autopsy in the mail. What!!!? Our long awaited document that we have hoped for two months will bring our family the answers needed. I wanted so badly to rip it from Jeremiah's fingers and start reading through it desperate to find the answers we have waited for. As we walk into the house Jeremiah hands it over to me and I start to physically tremble. My stomach is so upset, my head feels heavy, and I feel like I might pass out. I may be holding the one document that proves what we have learned our babysitter did to our dear Peyton. Jeremiah goes downstairs to do his workout and of course, Trinity is clung to my side. I am so happy to see her but I so desperately want time to read and focus on this document. And then I feel so utterly horrible for wanting my "own" time. I would give anything to have moments with Peyton again and I never wanted to take for granted my moments with Trinity, even now. I start to read through the autopsy. My fingers and hands are trembling. I turn through the pages as fast as I can hoping to find the cause and manner of death. Finally I do and I stare. It says for cause of death, *head injuries* and for manner of death, it says *undetermined*. WHAT??? What do you mean UNDETERMINED??? HOW??? This has been the long awaited document that is supposed to give us all the answers. I feel so helpless...

Dear God, I have been patient for two terribly long months. I have been respectful to all of those professionals that are "supposed" to be handling this. I have been as respectful as I can to the person that did this. I haven't slandered her as much as I have wanted to. God PLEASE help me. I try to do what you ask. If you can't do it for me, dear God, please speak for my baby boy Peyton. I am trying to help him. I am trying to speak for him.

I start to read through the autopsy, which is almost impossible to do without the internet handy or a medical dictionary. On the second page it lists all of Peyton's pathological diagnosis. There are so many terms that I have never even heard of. Immediately I start googling the internet to define some of these clinical words. I spent this entire evening combing through the autopsy trying to understand what it is saying to me. I end up staying up until 12:00 a.m. this night. The whole time I am thinking I need to go to bed. I am so tired, but I can't stop. I won't stop for my baby. I have to understand what all of this means. I research word, after word, after word.

After all of my hours researching I am able to confirm that all of Peyton's brain injuries are the same injuries reported in the most severe cases of "Shaken Baby Syndrome or Non-accidental head trauma". Dr. Sutherland was right. She knew what she saw. She knew that this is what had happened to Peyton. Why and how could I ever have doubted her? She investigates child abuse for a living; of course she was originally right. I guess deep down, up until the autopsy, I kept hoping that I was missing something. It is so traumatic to realize and admit that my child was killed.

My dear, perfect, precious baby was killed by a trusted friend. I will never know why I had to bury my son. How can Anna remain silent knowing she has committed a murder? Doesn't she have a conscience? How can she wake up in the morning? How can her husband not see through her? What made her snap and attack my innocent baby? My son couldn't have been the trigger, there is no way. He was easy going, calm, and he almost never cried. He would fuss but nothing dramatic. Peyton was genuinely perfect. I have said this so many times but he was the baby that any mom would have wanted. He was so "easy". So desperately I want Anna to pay for what she has done to this family. She has shattered us. This is a letter I have written her:

"Anna,

I don't know exactly what to say to you or how to say it. I never thought I would lose a child, nor did I ever foresee that my baby boy would have been killed by a good friend. Anna, what exactly did you do to my dear son? How could you do it? How? I trusted you for 3.5 years with my family, my babies. I thought I knew you, I thought you were a good person, I thought you genuinely cared for my children and our family. I had no idea I was taking my children to a killer. Even if you were originally afraid to say what you did, why couldn't you have given some indication of head trauma? My son could've at least had a chance if we had known to look at his head. You took so many lives away that morning. You have left our family so terribly devastated. How can you sleep at night? I hope your conscience, if you have one, eats you alive from the inside out. I hope it slowly, miserably eats away at you until it takes everything you have wanted away from you. I want you to hurt like we do, feel the pain that I do. I had to bury my son and I have no idea why. I had to bury my son not truly knowing how he died. You deserve to go to hell, you deserve to lose everything you have. Often I am afraid of running into you around town, for fear that if and when I do, something bad would happen. I want to think I'd be as professional as I could and look away. But really, how could I just look away from my son's killer? You have traumatized Trinity. For the rest of her life she will have nightmares about what she witnessed you do to her brother. You are so sick, so delusional, and so unstable. You may be able to "fake" it to your family but the rest of us know what you did to Peyton. You hurt him very bad, you lied by omission, and then you let him die. I hope Peyton's death haunts you for the rest of your life. I hope it consumes you and you crumble to pieces. God knows what you did, he knows you murdered my son. You could have made another choice. You didn't need to take "it", whatever it was, out on my dear Peyton. You will pay the rest of your life for that "choice". Please take the fast track to hell. We all know what you did."

Epic

"Hell was created not for mankind, but for Satan and his angels....

Hell is not God's intention for mankind. But remember--he gave us free will. He gave us a choice."

John Eldredge

Adventures in Orthodoxy

"The person who disbelieves in Hell doesn't really believe in Heaven either. He believes in oblivion. He desperately hopes that he'll cease to exist after death. He hopes he'll get away with it after all."

Dwight Longenecker

March-ish 2012 Continued
(I am struggling to use dates)

Upon talking to our family member tonight he mentioned that he had talked to the state death investigator. He said that the death investigator mentioned to him that he had sent a request 2-3 times to the police investigators asking for some of their reports. He said that they have given him "nothing" and that they have not been cooperative in helping. Why have they been this way? Why wouldn't they communicate with the state on this matter? Could they really be trying to cover up Peyton's death for the sake of "saving one of their own"? In the beginning we were afraid of this because of Brett's brother, Anna's husband, being a police officer. Brett also works for the court system. But now, after learning this I can't help but wonder. Are they trying to cover this up?

They don't know who I am. I could never just roll over and let them cover up my son's death. Never, ever.

Upon talking to my lawyer at this last visit he mentioned that Jeremiah and I may be ready to take a private polygraph. He asked if I was ok with it, and of course I am. He said that he didn't want us to take it early in the beginning as we were so dreadfully emotional. That's the weird thing. Jeremiah and I are still "emotional" now, just in a different way. We don't overtly show it as much; not because we don't want to but because we are so physically dried up that the tears no longer run. Now, it stirs so much deeper. It is this aching that can never be fixed. It is this new constant "stomach ache". No matter what happens or what doesn't that "ache" will never go away; that much I am sure of. I don't know if the overtly aching or the silent aching is worse for a polygraph. The bottom line is we want to do the polygraph; we have nothing to hide. We want to show the world that we don't know what happened to our son and hope that it is the convincing that the County Attorney needs. I hope this is all he will need in order to move forward in charging her. As my father said later this week, it is the county attorney's job to prosecute, it is the jury's job to convict. I just hope that this is really not a small town 'cover up' of their own. I would like to believe we live in a city that employs better people than that but then again I took my children to a killer without ever knowing it. I guess anything is possible.

My lawyer also mentioned the idea that worst comes to worst, if nothing was happening with the county attorney even after we pass our polygraphs that we go to the media and issue a press statement. He said that by passing the polygraph he can forward that on to the county attorney and say, "Here, the family has done everything you have requested. You have had four people take the polygraph and three have passed. The one that failed was the one alone with the child at the time of injury. It is decisively clear who did this." Ok well maybe he didn't say it exactly like this but in my mind this is how I picture he would say it. My lawyer seemed hesitant about the idea of going to the media. He said "I need to prepare you that when we do that there could be some negative pushback. There could be some people that really think that Jeremiah and you did this. They could question why you stayed home that day and make comments about you being on medication. People could start treating you differently in the community or say things to you." I replied back to him that, "I have no trouble saying to anyone that the reason I stayed home is because I had horrible cramps and diarrhea, not to mention a horrible headache and sore throat. I'd tell anybody that I was prescribed Zoloft for anxiety and that I had been on it for 8-9 years since I was in college." I explained to him that, "You don't really know me that well. By nature I am an emotional fighter. I may not come across as it, but inside I fight for what I believe is right. I can't let somebody do this to my child and walk away free." I just felt like deep down he still questioned everything I had said to him. I suppose lawyers are lied to everyday. Everyone they talk to 'never did anything wrong.'

I am at this point where I am becoming more hardened, more unconcerned about what people think about me, more persistent that the 'right' thing be done. As I have lately been caught saying, "I could give two fucks about what someone I didn't know thought about me". That's the thing, I care VERY much what my family and friends think but other than that, I don't. I believe that as Peyton's mother I have a duty to speak for him, as clearly no one else is. My baby is looking down at me and I want to make him proud. I want him to look down and proudly protest that "she is my mom". Part of this fighting is also realizing when it could affect the rest of the family we have left. It's like it is this perfect balance between loving and mending, and yet holding firm to speak for the unspoken.

Today Trinity came to church with me. This is somewhat rare as usually I go by myself. Jeremiah doesn't often go with me and I don't pressure him or make him feel guilty. I want him to go when he truly wants to go. To be honest, I have always enjoyed going by myself. Ever since Trinity was born, Sunday morning church was the one time that I had alone. It has become a sort of meditation for me and through the last four years this new discovery of God has emerged. Don't get me wrong, Jeremiah would let me go do anything I wanted at any time, but my hobbies are hobbies that I can do at home; make jewelry, watch NCIS or Intervention, go for walks or runs. I don't really like belonging to organized leagues or teams. I am more of an independent participant. I like to do things when I feel like it. I like to take my coffee into the sanctuary and sit and listen and meditate to the music.

I really like the church we have found. I like that the pastor preaches strictly from the bible. Growing up I never really learned about the bible and when I would be in church I would have no idea what the priest was talking about. I would do the motions not really understanding "why". The whole notion just doesn't fit me. I am completely a "why" person. I want to know the "why" of everything. I like that the pastor at this church talks about real world events and encourages us to be better human beings. He doesn't act like he's on some pedestal and usually incorporates his own miss-doings into his sermons. I respect that he doesn't expect one to be perfect. I like that he also says the uncomfortable things that most don't want to say nor does anyone want to listen to. Those are the 'topics' that we should talk about. In my opinion those things that make us more uncomfortable are usually the topics most in need of discussing.

Trinity did so good for me at church. I tried to get her to go into one of the play rooms while I attended the service but she didn't want to leave me. I brought her in with me and she did great. She kept asking me if Peyton was up there, meaning in the front part of the church. I forgot but the last time she was at church was for her brother's funeral. I reassured her that no Peyton wasn't up there and she got very sad, very sad. She looked up at me and said, "Mom I miss my brother Peyton. Where is he? When is he coming home?" I could tell that she was so disappointed. Earlier I wondered why she wanted to go to church with me so bad, but now I realized that she had wanted to come in hopes of seeing Peyton, as this was the last place she saw him. She started crying and I held her so tight. *Dear God, do you see what I do every day? Do you see how I have to console my other child? Please hold me up. I need your strength in moments like these. Please take her pain away. I don't care about me, I will take all the hurt that you need me to carry but please, please don't make her feel this sadness. She feels things that no 3.5-year-old little girl should ever know about.* Trinity and I sat there crying...

Sweet Child

"God made a sweet child
A child who never grew old,
He made a smile of sunshine
He molded a heart of pure gold.

He made that child as close to an angel
As anyone ever could be,
God made a Sweet Child
And He gave that dear child to me.

Then God saw His wonderful creation
Growing very tired and weak,
So He wrapped the child in His loving arms
And said, "You my child I keep."

*But now my Sweet Child is an angel
Free from hurt and pain,
I'll love you forever, until we meet again.*

*So many times I have missed you
So many times I have cried,
If all my love could have saved you
Sweet Child you never would have died."*

Author Unknown

I've had so many people give me hugs and tell me how strong we are for enduring this. That is the thing, we didn't have a choice. Trust me, if we did Peyton would still be here. We didn't have a choice in any of this and tragically we have to pick up everything piece by piece and hope that while putting it back together that in the end it will still fit. The hard part now is that there is so much sadness. There is nothing to look forward or get excited for. Everything now is a fight. Every day we wake up fighting to make it through one more day. We fight to maintain our composure while at work. We fight when we talk to coworkers and friends as we try not to break down hysterically as anyone purposely or not asks us "How are you?" Really, what we want to say is, "How the fuck do you think we are?" We fight every night we get home to establish new routines. We fight every time Trinity talks about missing her brother Peyton James. We fight every day, all the time, every time. That's all that we do is fight. Nobody gave us a choice. To date, nobody is willing to fight in our place.

My Child's Name

"Go ahead and mention my child,
The one that died, you know.
Don't worry about hurting me further,
The depth of my pain doesn't show.

Don't worry about making me cry,
I'm already crying inside.
Help me to heal by releasing the tears that I try to hide.

I'm hurt when you just keep silent,
Pretending he didn't exist.
I'd rather you mention my child,
Knowing that he has been missed.

You asked me how I was doing,
I say "pretty good" or "fine."
But healing is something ongoing,
I feel it will take a lifetime..."

Author Unknown

Shortly after Peyton's passing I had a good friend say to me that she hates the saying that, 'God only gives us what we can handle'. She always hoped that God would see her as weak so that he didn't give her anything to worry about. And then she said, "Why should someone be punished because they are strong?" I have thought of this so much. It is true. I have had so many people tell me that they think we are so strong. Why are we punished for being strong?

This weekend it was extremely nice outside, around 80 degrees and sunny. Trinity and I spent much of the weekend outside around the house in our swimsuits. I made sure to cover her from head to toe in sunscreen, but I neglected to douse myself and now I am paying for it. We were so productive. I mowed, pulled weeds, cleaned the deck, cleaned daddy's grill, and planted new plants. I got so much done in a short period of time. That is the thing. I had all of this time that I shouldn't have had. I should have been interrupted to change a diaper, or to make a bottle, or to entertain Peyton. But, no matter how much I hoped to hear him cry or whimper I heard nothing.

The Cord

"We are connected
My child and I,
by An invisible cord
Not seen by the eye.

It's not like the cord
That connects us 'til birth,
This cord can't been seen
By any on Earth.

This cord does it's work
Right from the start,
It binds us together
Attached to my heart.

I know that it's there
Though no one can see,
The invisible cord
From my child to me.

The strength of this cord
Is hard to describe,
It can't be destroyed
It can't be denied.

It's stronger than any cord
Man could create,
It withstands the test
Can hold any weight.

And though you are gone
Though you're not here with me,
The cord is still there
But no one can see.

It pulls at my heart
I am bruised..I am sore,
But this cord is my lifeline
As never before.

I am thankful that God
Connects us this way,
A mother and child
Death can't take it away!"

Author Unknown

End of March-ish 2012

The other night I lay down in bed with Trinity. Lately she has been having nightmares all of the time. We try to lie down in her bed with her to get her to go to sleep but then sometime through the night she ends up coming into our room begging to sleep in our bed with us. This breaks my heart. It's like she is having these recurrent nightmares that won't leave. Is my poor baby girl having nightmares about what she saw happen to her brother? How could she not? It angers me that even in her sleep she can't escape this tragedy.

Dear God, why has this massive, blunt, direct and isolating tragedy happened to our family? Why did this happen to my baby out of all the babies in the world? Why was my baby chosen to be a victim? Not that this should ever happen, but why our family?

As I lay with Trinity she tossed and turned and tried to find any reason to not go to bed.

Suddenly, very seriously she rolled over and said, "Momma I miss my Peyton James."

I said, "Oh honey, I know you do. Mommy and daddy miss Peyton so much too."

She then says, "Momma I saw it. I saw what Anna do to Peyton James. She hit him in the head like this (demonstrating) and she shake him (demonstrating) and she throw him (demonstrating)."

I say, "Oh Trinity I know you did and I'm sorry you had to see that. I wish mommy could have been there so you wouldn't have to have seen that. I wish I could have been there to protect you and Peyton."

Trinity softly says, "Momma it's not your fault. I try to save him. I try to save Peyton James. I yell at Anna to leave my baby brother alone. I tell her she's being naughty."

I sadly state, "Trinity I know you tried to save him and you did everything you could to protect Peyton, but Anna was naughty and there was nothing you could have done. You were the best big sister to Peyton."

And then she says, "Momma where is Peyton?" This is so hard. I naively thought early on that each day would get easier, but I was wrong. There have been so many people that have told me that every day will get easier. But, they have been wrong too. Each day for me gets worse. I can "fake it" better. I can go to work and act "normal" and then leave and turn into a hysterical mess. I can "fake it" at home during the evenings while playing with Trinity or talking to Jeremiah. I can even try to "fake it" in my sleep. But, the deep, irreversible reality is that there is this never-ending, terribly devastating pain that consumes my soul. I feel that as each day continues to go by and nothing is done with the investigation a part of me is slowly chiseled away.

I have this new sad reality. There was so much that died with the passing of my son. I don't know if I will ever be the same. I believe I am forever changed. I was proud of who I was. I was proud of how I looked at the world, people, and how I truly felt emotion. I feel that part of me is gone, or hiding so deeply, so terrified to show the world she exists. I have this new distrustful outlook. I feel so negative and skeptical of life itself. *What is the purpose of life?* Why are we put on this earth and put through the test of life before we can actually live? I have so many questions that will never be answered. I feel so hopeless for myself, my mind, my emotions, my friends, and my family. I am so saddened by the loss of the old me. *Will I ever find that part of me again or is she lost forever?* I hope my friends and family can accept the new me. The new bitter, me.

This is something that I also never would have thought about. But, I can tell a part of Jeremiah has disappeared as well. He has been talking about quitting coaching volleyball. He has so much guilt about missing the first three months of Peyton's life because he was gone coaching. He has said, "If I had known we would only be blessed with him for 6 short months I wouldn't have coached. I would have spent every second with my son." He talks about realizing what is important and that he has realized he just wants to be with his family. Trust me; there are always times in the season when I wish he wasn't coaching because it puts much of the family tasks on me. I often count the season down, week by week. But, I can't imagine him NOT coaching. Jeremiah loves coaching. He loves working with the girls. He loves the sense of accomplishment it brings him. I would never expect nor ask him to stop. I knew this when I married him. I understand where his guilt is coming from, but I just am terrified of him making a life changing decision and then resenting it later.

Trinity is different. She is often sad and cries a lot about the loss of her brother. She is going through a separation anxiety where she is afraid to be away from Jeremiah or me for a moment. She is especially afraid to be away and she wants confirmation that anytime I leave her I am coming back for her. *Dear God, please allow your guardian angels to follow her, look over her, and protect this child. She is so traumatized and scared. Please take away her anxieties, her nightmares, and calm her gentle mind. Please give her peace that brother Peyton is now safe. Please God, help me to take care of this child.* I am trying my best not to show my devastation, my hollow core. But, she is so smart and I know she can sense my sadness, she can see through my "fake-ness". I always believed that you had given us a handful like Trinity as you felt we could handle her, but now I know that you gave us a daughter as strong as she is, as you knew we would need her to keep us up.

> *"Loved with a love*
> *beyond telling,*
> *Missed with a grief*
> *beyond all tears."*
>
> Author Unknown

I believe even the dogs can sense the loss of Peyton. They no longer get to try and help clean off his face that was full of baby food. It's like they go room to room searching for him. They are so "on guard" of our family. It's like they have sensed that something bad has happened and they are trying to protect us.

The other night I attended my first night of the "Compassionate Friends" group, which is for parents who have lost a child. The group meets the last Wednesday of every month at one of the hospitals. I haven't gone until now because of how we have been directed not to talk about anything to anybody. Over the past couple of weeks I am "past" that not talking about anything crap. Why do we have to remain silent when we didn't do anything wrong? I want to fight for my son. I want Anna to pay for what she has done. I want my son to look down from heaven and say proudly, "That is my mom. She is the best mom." I want Peyton to look down and be proud of me. I want him to know that I am fighting for him. I am his mother and that is my job. I swore to take care of him from the moment I conceived him. And I did that, and I will do that. I will take care of him until the end. I will take care of him as long as I can. I cared for him while he lived and I will care for him while he's dead. I will forever fight for my son.

> *"Dear Lord, I would have loved to have held my babies on my lap and tell them about you, but since I didn't get the chance, would you please hold them on your lap and tell them about me?"*
>
> Author Unknown

Attending the support group did help some but I also had to face some ultimately harsh realities. Me being me, even though I am trying not to, I still am tempted to "plan" things. I found myself looking at my calendar thinking ok it is almost April now. Maybe in a couple of months I'll feel like this or that. And, maybe in a year I'll feel like this or that. But, that's the thing, I think this is my new feeling and it will never change. I asked the group, "When will I get to the point that I can open his door and go into Peyton's room for any length of time?" The group just bowed their heads. They couldn't give me that reality. For some of them they lost their child nine years ago and they still can't comfortably be in their loved ones room. I guess I was hoping for a time table, some type of direction for lengths of time my pain will last. The sad reality is that my pain will last forever. There was a couple there who have attended the group since they lost their teenage daughter in the 1980's. I was only four then and

Peyton's seed didn't even exist. But, as they talked they still wept and the anguish still held their heart so closely. Maybe the group will be beneficial for me. If anything, I will talk with people who have somehow continued to live even though their life was taken.

Even while at the group and listening and relating to people who lost a child like I did, I still felt so incredibly isolated. I have the grief and devastation of losing my son, my family, myself and I relate to all of these peoples' pain. But, I also have this sense of true victimization. My child was killed by a trusted friend of mine and this person may just get to walk away without any consequence. My son was murdered and we are truly victims and we are given no sympathies from the justice system. What is so terribly wrong with our justice system? How is it that people who are not guilty are convicted of crimes, yet people who are guilty are never held accountable? And we wonder why we have a society like we do... Isn't it a red flag that something is so wrong with how we punish? When I hear people brag about the United States I am proud to exist in America. But, my new harsh reality is that is it really that much better? How could our legal system be changed to better serve the citizens of our country? What do we need to do differently so that innocent people are never convicted and guilty people are always convicted? As a society and country where is our sense of accountability? Screw the politics... The elections..... The popularity... What happened to doing what is right at the right time?

I have had these theories in my mind. From the information I have gathered I have learned that the county attorney is the official that doesn't want to prosecute Anna, not the police force. If this is the case I am sure it is because he doesn't want to have to work for a case. He wants it cut and dry. He wants to know he will win a case before he ever enters the courtroom. It seems that he only cares about politics and having a 'winning' record of case wins; even if that means ignoring the most important. It seems he only cares about winning and getting elected. It's not about doing what is right. As my father said, "It is the prosecutor's job to prosecute, the jury's job to convict." I have thought about that concept often. What if they did 'try' her and the jury still ended up finding her 'not guilty' because they didn't feel like they had enough evidence to convict her. I could still swallow that. At least in a small way she would have to go through some sort of accountability. The blame in some way would be shone unto her. I could live with myself knowing that I did everything I could to defend and speak for Peyton. I could look up above and tell him I've done everything I could.

I have always been a fighter, not in a physical sense. But, emotionally I have always been a fighter. I have always believed in speaking the truth whatever that is. It's interesting how one can so naturally be like this but after undergoing all of this emotional distress be leveled down to feeling so weak.

I think about Anna all of the time. What was going on in her mind? What stress was she under that she took it out on my dear Peyton? How could she snap? How can she continue to lie knowing she is destroying an entire family? Doesn't she have a conscience? Does she have nightmares about what she did to my son? How can she live with herself? How can she live with herself knowing she is a murderer? What mental instability exists in her mind? **How didn't I notice it?** *Dear God, please let her dream of hell every night for the rest of her life.*

Jeremiah and I are feeling like the county attorney isn't willing to follow through with anything concerning this case. We feel they are hoping that this will all disappear, that we will stop asking questions; that we will just 'move on'. What he doesn't know is that we don't have the capability to do that. We don't have the ability to just roll over and take it. I can't do that. Our lawyers have agreed to allow us to do a polygraph test next week, as we aren't as emotional basket cases as we originally were. I want our lawyers to take our positive polygraphs and bombard the county attorney with our positive results and question that there have been three individuals that have passed the polygraph and one that has failed and she just happens to be the one that was with the child at the time of injury. I want to pressure him to move. If he still won't move forward then move ahead with the media and explain to the public the resistance from their special elected officials. His mission statement on his website states that he is there to protect the abused and neglected children of the community. Make me sick, really?! I have no problem stating that to the media. Grow some balls, do what you know is right. Stand tall and pursue. Quit being a chicken shit.

Part of my advocacy for Peyton is researching all of the time. I am on the internet all of the time researching as much as I can about brain injuries. I know that is also bad to do but nobody is saying anything so I am left to find the answers myself. My boss jokes about how "just ask Dr. Courtney", and seriously, I can't read enough. I keep reading, keep clicking, keep searching for the answers that the prosecution needs. I decided to write to Dr. Sutherland, who diagnosed Peyton as 'Shaken & Struck' in Omaha, and explain to her our situation and frustration. I attached a copy of the autopsy and DHS report in hopes that the child advocate in her will view them. I want to know if she still believes that Peyton's symptoms would have been immediate. To me, she is the missing link. If she is willing to state on the stand that yes, this was traumatic enough that his symptoms would have been immediate, maybe the prosecutors would finally charge Anna. If Dr. Sutherland was willing to state this Anna could be held accountable. I wrote this letter in hopes that Dr. Sutherland will respond. So again, we wait. That's all we have done, is wait. Here is the letter I wrote Dr. Sutherland:

Tuesday, March 20th, 2012

Re: Death of Peyton Pottebaum

Dr. Sutherland,

I don't know if you remember our family but I hope you do. On Thursday night, January 19th our baby boy Peyton Pottebaum was life flighted to Children's in Omaha from St. Luke's Hospital in Sioux City, Iowa.

We received a phone call from our day care provider at 8:30 a.m. on Thursday, January 19th, 2012 (90 minutes after our children had arrived at daycare) saying that our son wasn't breathing. Three weeks prior Peyton had been diagnosed with RSV but had recovered and so his respiratory distress was initially determined by the ER doctor to be from that. Upon later examination that day, after Peyton lay in the hospital for approximately 6 hours and 11 minutes, a CT scan was ordered and Peyton's pediatric doctor found a fractured skull and a subdural hematoma. An emergency craniotomy was done on Peyton and he was life flighted to Children's where they tried to keep him stable. On Friday afternoon, January 20th my husband, Jeremiah, and I met with you as you had just done the examination through Peyton's eyes. We explained how we ended up in Omaha, unfortunately much of it we didn't know. We were told by his daycare provider that he just "stopped breathing". You explained to Jeremiah and I that you believed that Peyton was "violently, traumatically shaken" due to the hemorrhage in his eyes that you saw. I asked you how he would have acquired a fractured skull if he was shaken and you stated that most likely he was struck against a hard surface. I then asked you how soon the symptoms would have started once the injury had taken place. Your response was "immediately". When you talked to us you mentioned the term "Shaken Baby Impact Syndrome". You also mentioned that Peyton had one of the most severe cases of retinal hemorrhaging you had ever seen.

This is why I am writing to you.... Jeremiah and I dropped off a happy, healthy baby boy a little before 7:00 a.m. on January 19th, 2012 and 90 minutes later we received a call that he wasn't breathing with no indication of head trauma. To date, the daycare provider is adamant that nothing happened and that he just stopped breathing. Our 3.5 year old little girl is talking about what she "saw" all of the time and is clearly traumatized. I started her in play therapy four weeks ago. She has been telling us and her teachers at school that, "Anna hit Peyton James in the head, she shake him really hard and then she throw him on the carpet; (Not necessarily always in that order). I asked her school teachers to document what she says to them so that the investigators hear it from someone else besides just her family. Our family is so devastated.. We finally received the autopsy report, but it lists his manner of death as "undetermined".

All of this has been so traumatizing and we are feeling like the Sioux City investigators and the Woodbury County Attorney will not move ahead with charging our former daycare provider as they have made the statement to a family representative that there were "four adults within contact of Peyton in a 24 hour window". Anthony Logan, SME Investigator, has told our family representative that Sioux City has been uncooperative in releasing police records to them which makes it difficult to list his manner of death.

The county attorney supplied our family representative with the two medical journal studies that indicate time frames for onset of symptoms of an injury like this to an infant. In the Starling report it states the symptoms would be immediate and in the Gilliland study it says severe symptoms could take up to 24 hours to display but that the child wouldn't be acting normally. Obviously, Jeremiah and I know that nothing happened to our dear Peyton under our watch and we also know that "something" happened at the daycare pro-

vider's home. Peyton was acting normally the morning of his injuries and was happy and smiling and even the daycare provider and her husband initially stated this in the DHS report. Peyton ate well the night before and the daycare provider fed him carrots the morning of, which he later threw up in the ER room at the hospital.

I am feeling so helpless and hopeless. I want to fight for Peyton... I want someone to be held accountable for what they have done. It is **not o.k.** that someone can do this to my child and then just walk away from this. Have you had experience in cases like Peyton's? What would you advise us to do to advocate for our son? Dr. Sutherland, we lost our baby boy, our 3.5 year old is traumatized, and I can't fathom that the person responsible for this may just get to walk away. It terrifies me that she could do this again to another child.

I have attached the DHS report, as well as the autopsy. Do you feel confident in your original statements concerning how you believe Peyton was injured and that his symptoms would have been immediate? As my daughter was the oldest at the daycare that morning our only evidence is medical testimonial.

Any information you could provide would be very much appreciated. Thank you for doing what you do.

Courtney Pottebaum (Peyton's mom)

1-555-555-5555

This feeling of having to advocate for your dead son because no one else is willing to, makes me sick to my stomach. The hard part for me right now is that Jeremiah and I are clearly dealing with this in our own ways. This is really hard. I am the one who is actively fighting for Peyton. I am not saying that Jeremiah isn't, but I am the one researching, copying, writing letters, coming up with game plans on how to advocate next. Jeremiah on the other hand seems more removed. He sits back and rides the waves. I'm not saying that he doesn't care like I do, because he is terribly devastated about the loss of his son. But, he's not fighting as overtly like I am or maybe it's not consuming him like it is me. He made the comment to me last night that he wants to have other children. I know he wasn't trying to offend me, but this little part of me was panic stricken. I don't want my dear Peyton looking down at me wondering how I could replace him or move beyond him. There are these little moments in time that I think about being pregnant again, about carrying another precious baby. But, those moments are few and far between. Really, the only baby I can think about is Peyton. He was the baby I wanted, he was the baby I had, and he is the baby I constantly dream of. He was my perfect, waited for baby boy. For me, I don't know if I can carry another baby again until I am void of this agonizing pain. But, will that be ever?

04-01-2012

This morning I decided not to go to church. I knew it was supposed to be sunny and gorgeous out so I wanted to spend time outside with Trinity. When the weather is nice out that is what Trinity and I do; we spend our days consumed with the sun and outside projects. We got up this morning and went to get breakfast and then stopped at Target to get Trinity some Spring/Summer clothes. I normally get all of her things at a large indoor rummage twice per year, but it won't be for another two weeks and it's been in the 80s and 90s. On the drive into town Trinity got very sad, very quiet and whimpered that she missed Peyton James and that Anna is naughty. I really wanted to stop by his grave as it had been two days since I had been there. Normally, I go alone as it is easier to cry like I need to, talk to him like I need to, or curse God like I need to for taking him. Since she was already talking about him I thought it would be ok to stop at his grave. I was worried that they had mowed and maybe discarded of all of his decorations and I couldn't fathom that my baby's grave could be bare. We were going to the store and if I needed to pick anything up I would. Trinity has only been to Peyton's grave two times, one of those times being the day of his funeral. We pulled into the cemetery and she stated that,

"We're going to see Peyton James? Where is he? Where is he? I can't see him. Mom, where is he at? Why is he here?"

I was trying to figure out exactly how to explain why we were coming here. I said, "People come to cemeteries to remember the people in their lives that have died. And since...."

As Jeremiah is driving Trinity yells, "Dad, turn this way, this way to Peyton."

This struck me as odd as she has only been to his grave two times and neither for any length of time. I started to think about all of these "special things" that have happened since the passing of Peyton...

04-7-2012

There have been some really strange and "God like" things that have happened. Let me start from the beginning....

Sometime in October of 2011, during Jeremiah's volleyball season, he had made the statement that he wanted to go and get "snipped". We had always talked about having two children so to him our family was complete. And really, I felt it was complete also but in the back of my mind I was so afraid of Jeremiah making this permanent decision, which is the reason I never got my tubes tied. I didn't like the idea of permanency for us. It's weird because I felt we were done adding to our family but in the back of my mind I had this nagging urge to convince Jeremiah not to do it. I didn't know why and I felt silly convincing him when I really didn't have a clue as to why I was so adamant about this. I remember standing in Peyton's room and talking to Jeremiah so logically that I really didn't want him to do this now and that I would get an IUD. And then I said, "We are so young, we're only 30. God forbid, what if something happened to one of our children? You just never know. Let's wait five years and if by 35 years of age if we are still sure then you can get snipped." I remember stating this so logically. *I said it but oh God, I didn't really mean it.* I mean, I never thought that I would ever have to go through this. But for some reason I was so passionately logical, *why? Was God speaking through me to our family because he knew that our family would become broken?*

While I was on maternity leave with Peyton I had received an email from my sister Jenny. She had forwarded me this message about how she had been reading and following this blog and how it had seriously changed her life. She had forwarded me the web address and was so adamant that I read this blog. It was about this couple, probably our age who had just lost a son. The little baby was only nine months old and he had succumbed to a brain tumor. The couple started this blog either before or around the time that their son was diagnosed and they wrote every day about what they were going through. While they were in the hospital they wrote, while at home they wrote, they wrote all of the time. I had spent two nights in a row reading through their entire blog and especially reading through their hospital experiences. I wept and cried while I read it and felt so lucky when I was able to close my computer screen and hold my little boy.

When Jeremiah and I were at Children's Hospital in Omaha I remember lying on the seat in Peyton's room and all of a sudden it hit me. Everything I was going through, everything I was watching the doctors do all seemed vaguely familiar. And then it hit me. I had read this blog a couple of months earlier, in fact, invested many hours reading it. Even though our experiences were different there was so much that was the same. There was so much raw emotion that was the same. I had read this blog having no idea that it was preparing me for my life to come. *Why was my sister so adamant that I read this when she was? Was this God's way of preparing me for what was to come?*

I do believe that God works through people to influence us.

During our initial visit to the cemetery Jeremiah and I were again left speechless. We decided to have Peyton buried at a cemetery that was located on our way home from work each day. We liked the idea of driving by Peyton as often as we could. We were familiar with this cemetery as well, as my mom would often take Trinity there as it had a beautiful pond area that had swans and ducks. We thought that this would be an appropriate place as Trinity might be somewhat familiar with it. Because of this we thought it would be neat if we could find a couple of plots down by the ponds. The pond area is such a beautiful and most surely a "sought after" area. We figured it would be impossible to find plots in this area but thought it was worth a try. The lady helping us looked around the map of the cemetery for open plots; three to be exact. I told Jeremiah that I needed my baby boy buried next to me. I never thought I would be 30 years old buying my burial plots, let alone buying my son's. The lady was looking intently at the map and then said, "Kids, I just don't see anything open in the pond area. That is such a beautiful and wanted area." Jeremiah and I looked at each other like 'at least we tried'. And then she said, "Well, just a minute kids, let me go check on something." She came back two minutes later, "Kids, I don't know how I missed this but there are six open plots down by the pond. There are two sets of three plots. I'll have the guys put a marker on it and we'll go look at it to see if those are ones you like. I also found three others right next to each other down by the area of the pond but up farther on the hill." This sounded pretty good, just maybe we did "luck out".

We jumped in my in-law's vehicle and followed the woman's car into the cemetery. She was going to take us by the plots nearest to the pond first. As we entered the cemetery we noticed that each section of the park was marked with a name that identified that location on a nice metal sign. As we drove closer to the orange cones that were representing the open plots, I noticed that the 'name' of this section of the park was called **'MEDITATION'**. I just froze. I couldn't believe it. I always called Peyton my meditation. Peyton is what calmed me. After a tiring day at work I would leave and feel so relaxed knowing I was going to go pick up the kids. I couldn't wait to interact with them. There was this magically calming feeling that Peyton brought me. We pulled up to the three plots right off of the road, directly across from the pond. These spaces were perfect and side by side. We figured it would be Peyton, me, and then Jeremiah. I didn't even want to look at the other plots because we found the perfect ones. *It was like they were meant for us to find, and in this surreal way I believe they really were waiting for us.* A bitter surreal way....

Last week while I was at work I had a guardian call me and ask me if I would be able to register her child for school. Later that day the boy and his family member showed up. I introduced myself and let him know that the kids call me Mrs. P. I asked him what his name is and he said, "Peyton". *What?* I just froze, I couldn't move. What did he say his name is? I must have heard him wrong. And then again, he said, "My name is Peyton." I couldn't believe this. *Dear God, why are you doing this? Are you testing me? Are you trying to give me a sign?* My face got very hot and my eyes welled up. I have to keep myself together. *Don't break down.. Don't break down...*

In my almost seven years of working as a counselor I have never worked with a student named Peyton. Never, Ever. *What are the chances of working with one so closely after losing my precious Peyton?* Later this day one of my counselor friends so confidently stated that this was God's way of sending me a sign that Peyton is o.k.

A couple of days later I was on the phone with my little sister and re-telling her about this recent situation. In the background the TV in the living room was on and it was covering some of the basketball games from March Madness. I don't know what teams were playing as I wasn't watching it. Jeremiah had left it on earlier. I was telling my sister the story and then I looked over at the TV screen and they were showing a basketball player and his name "Peyton...." came across the screen. *Good lord, really? You are really trying to give me signs. I believe you are speaking to me. I just don't know that my ears are open enough to hear you.* I still can't believe my Peyton is o.k. If he were o.k. he would be in my arms laughing and smiling. By now, he would be about 8.5 months old. He would likely be scooting, crawling, and rolling effortlessly. I will never know. I can only speculate and imagine what it would be like if Peyton were still here. I was thinking the other day that Peyton lived inside of my womb longer than he graced us on this earth.

I think about all of these "signs" and just wonder, are they really that? Or are they just small coincidences and thinking that they are some magical sign from God makes "this" that much more bearable? *I want to be faithful. I want to believe.*

04-08-2012

This weekend I called my sisters to touch base. As they were talking I realized that much of what they were talking about was foreign to me. They talked to me as if I should know or that they have talked to me about these things. But then I realized; it has been 2.5 months and I have been completely devoured by my own life. It hadn't even occurred to me that while I was 'frozen' the rest of the world truly did go on. My sisters' lives had continued on. They had talked to me about all of the changes that were happening in their lives. But I hadn't heard them. For 2.5 months I have been deaf to any other words hinting that life has continued on. I sat there on the phone and listened as my sister continued to talk about things I should already know, but I was hearing it all for the first time. A part of me felt very sad and guilty that I have been so wrapped up in myself that I haven't been 'present' for anyone else. It was also this true sense of reality that even those closest to me still had their own lives to live and that really, Jeremiah and I were truly alone in our suffering.

The other night while laying with Trinity in her bed she rolled over and said, "Mom I miss Peyton James. I want to hold him, I want to hold him now. Mom, I want to do rock-a-bye with Peyton James."

Trinity's tantrums are escalating. She is a very angry little girl. She cries all of the time. She is hypersensitive to anything. Her emotions are all over the place. She can't handle normal small life trials. She is struggling every day. She is exhausted emotionally and physically. She is sleeping very poorly at night and is having many nightmares. Sometimes she says she is having nightmares of monsters and others times of her Peyton James being hit by Anna. This woman has permeated every level of our lives. We can't even sleep peacefully. I never knew I could feel hatred this deep. Trinity's therapist this last week said that she believes Trinity is starting to shut down. She thinks that Trinity is so emotionally overwhelmed and in order to cope she is just shutting down. This makes me feel desperate. I lost my son, my daughter is struggling to function every day, and Jeremiah and I just sit here staring at each other wondering what we ever did to deserve this.

I was talking to my sister the other night and I was trying to explain the many facets of destruction that we have encountered. There are so many layers that I would never have even thought about. We lost our son and our future with him. Trinity lost a sibling and now believes that babies die. She also doesn't understand why some of her friends have baby siblings that are alive but that her baby brother is dead. She is so lonely. I have changed and the old me is gone as well. I now base everything on, "before Peyton" or "after Peyton". The old me, the before me was somebody that I was proud of. I really admired me before. I liked my personality, I liked my sensitivity, and I liked my genuinely positive outlook on life. That person is gone. I don't think I can ever get her back. I am very uncomfortable with the new me. I don't know this person. I don't really 'care for' this person. I don't know how to accept the new me, how to be the new me, how to be comfortable in my new skin. Jeremiah is different than he was before. As a result of both of us individually changing, we have changed as a couple. The relationship we have been comfortable with for 12 years is now different. Not necessarily for the worse, or the better. The hard part is that we have been so used to each other for so long but now those people that we knew so long have changed individually, which has caused our relationship to change. I just never knew so much could change. It feels as if our lives have been taken from us. We're trying to make a new normal but that entails making a new everything.

04-09-2012

"Hi my dear Peyton. I am sitting at your grave today, wishing so deeply that I was holding you close to me. Daddy and I were here yesterday and we weed eated the grass around your grave and placed the decorations neatly at the head of your grave. Your marker should be in soon, hopefully before Memorial Day. Today was an o.k. day at work. I thought about you a lot today. I am very lonely for you today. I thought this would get easier as time went by. How could it? I am trying to fight for you. I want you to look down on me and be proud that I am your mommy. I am trying to speak for you; I'm just having a hard time getting anyone to listen. I will find justice for you my baby, some day, some way. I pray every day that Anna is suffering so deeply. Peyton, you were my perfect baby. I was so happy to be blessed by you. I would do anything to have you back. In this surreal sort of way I am no longer afraid of death; I have you to look forward to. Trinity is aching very desperately for you. I am trying to comfort her, I am trying to let her know that you are ok. Peyton, I hope God is tending to you like I would have. I hope you are smiling and laughing. Daddy had surgery this week on his knee. He was so calm this time. He usually gets nervous as he's always afraid he won't wake up from the anesthesia. But,

this time he was calm. He told me later that he wasn't afraid anymore. If he didn't wake up he would get to see you sooner. He was hoping that if he would wake up that he would still have some out of body experience that would allow him to see you. Please know you are so dearly missed and loved. I know that God took your pain away and I am trying not to become vengeful, for your sake. But, it is very hard for me. It is hard for me not to want justice for you. I so desperately want to bring peace to your death. I want all of the questions to be answered, all of the pieces to fit together. I want to know that you are laid to rest with everything on earth 'just' and 'right'. Every part of me trembles for you. Baby boy, if the right amount of love could bring you back you would be here now with me. I have loved you so much, prayed for you so much, and ached for you so much. I know that you are now the one looking out for me. Please know I am fighting for you. I love you so much baby boy."

Another Hoop

04-11-2012

Last Thursday Jeremiah and I had our polygraph tests. I went at 9:00 a.m. and Jeremiah had his at 12:30 p.m. The night before our test I was so nervous. It's this feeling of being so scared. We know we didn't harm our dear Peyton but we have felt like we were already "falsely" questioned by the police when we had to go through the interrogation. I kept trying to calm myself. I didn't do anything wrong. But, I was still nervous, and then I became more nervous because I was already nervous and so the cycle continued. I don't really have a "shut off" switch. I know my mind runs a hundred miles a minute all of the time, it's what I do. I think all of the time. I prayed that God would help to settle my busy mind. *Dear God, please help me today. Please help calm my nerves so that our truth can be spoken. I am trying to speak for our son but I need your help in order to do it.*

I showed up in the morning desperately needing caffeine. I don't usually eat breakfast but I always have caffeine. I didn't drink any on my way for fear that it would make me more jumpy than I already was. Lord knows I didn't need that. My lawyer introduced me to the polygraph examiner. He was a professional looking man who you could tell took his job seriously. The examiner was dressed sharply in a suit and his demeanor and personality seemed calm and straightforward. He also had a little humor which helped to take the edge off. I suppose he is used to people being nervous. He started to get to know me and ask me questions about my past and who I was. He explained that he needed to start to learn about me. Oh gosh, here we go. We spent a lot of time talking about my past. I remember him asking me on a scale of 1-10 how honest I felt I was. My reply was, "10.5". I said this because I am often the person that is told "too much information". I tell everyone, everything. Good, bad, or indifferent I am an open book. I have lied, I have fibbed, and I have exaggerated the truth. I have even lied by omission but I could never lie about intentionally harming anyone or anything. My conscience would swallow me alive. Many times throughout the testing I found myself sweating and trembling. I never really understood how polygraphs work. Now I know more than I want to know. Once I was hooked up and ready to test the examiner asked me a mix of questions. Some of the questions pertained to Peyton (Did you strike Peyton? Did you cause the injuries to Peyton? Etc.) Some of the questions were "ever" in your lifetime questions (Have you ever intentionally harmed someone? Have you ever lied about something knowing you would get away with it?) Since taking the polygraph I have learned the reason for these types of questions. They ask you relative questions which are questions pertaining to the event and then they ask you control questions which are the "have you ever". Based on my research I learned that the "innocent" person will show more physiological response to the control questions versus the relative question. The theory is that an innocent person knows that they didn't "do this" or "do that" but that the "have you ever in your lifetime" questions are more intimidating because well, what if I did something but don't really remember it? The time with the examiner actually went pretty fast but I wouldn't want to take one again. Next it was Jeremiah's turn.

The following morning my lawyer called and informed me that Jeremiah and I both passed our polygraphs. It's interesting because there was this relief that came over me. Obviously, not because we feared we wouldn't pass but because it was one more step completed, one more hoop to jump through. That's the sad part, we shouldn't have to jump through any hoops. We shouldn't have had to do this. We shouldn't have had to go through any of this. But we have, and we are. And again, we fight to get through one more step, one more day.

I talked to my lawyer this week on the phone and he said he was ready to forward on my test results to the county attorney. After doing this the county attorney responded that I should have gotten a copy of the autopsy and that the medical examiner wasn't able to determine a manner of death due to a lack of evidence.

I talked to my mother tonight who asked if she could call the county attorney next week. My father also called and explained that he is going to call the county attorney next week, as well as the police investigators. What would we do without all of our family?

Jeremiah and I are going to demand for a face to face meeting next. I just have this feeling that they don't want to meet with us. Why would they? How could they face us knowing that our son was murdered and they aren't going to pursue his case? Deep down I feel like they know that Anna did this. I believe they don't want to prosecute without a slam dunk. If they won't meet with us or if the meeting is insufficient, could we go to the media? We are trying to give them so many opportunities to do the right and just thing. What are they afraid of?

After work yesterday I followed my normal routine of stopping at the cemetery on my way to get Trinity. As I pulled up to Peyton's plot I noticed that something looked different. I saw something gleaming. I got out of my car and as I walked closer I saw it, his marker was in and it looked amazing! I mean, as amazing as my dead son's marker could look. I was hysterical. *Dear God, this makes it so real. I can no longer pretend that I am just sitting on this bare earth every day relaxing in this beautiful cemetery. I have to admit now that this marker sits atop my buried beautiful, innocent, precious baby boy. I am weary, I am weak, and I am so desperately lonely for my son. Will this pain ever go away? Will my longing ever cease? Will I ever understand why?*

I sat next to Peyton's new marker and just bawled. This was one of the hardest cries I have had in some time. I am so broken, so weak, and so terribly devastated. Time is not healing my wounds nor fixing my family. *Please God, provide us with some sort of answers. I am trying to be faithful, I am trying to "carry this", but my shoulders are getting very tired.*

Since Peyton's birth I get night sweats during my sleep because my hormones are still all over the place. This is so hard for me to endure. This minor annoyance used to make me smile as it meant that I was so lucky to have a beautiful baby. I continue to have night sweats but my baby no longer lives. Every night I am reminded of my tragic loss.

When Peyton was born I decided that I would take some extra days on maternity leave that I would have to pay for. I was given 8 weeks of paid time off as I had accumulated enough sick days. I decided to take two and a half additional weeks unpaid. I am so grateful that I decided to take that extra time to be with my son. My checks have been debited $471 every month since Peyton was born to pay for the extra time I took off. This month was my last month to be debited. It has been hard to continue to pay for a baby that is no longer here. Jeremiah and I are still paying off his medical bills from being born. Now, we are simultaneously paying on his medical bills from his death.

"Peyton James, I am so lonely for you tonight. My heart weighs heavy for you. I miss your chubby cheeks and your happy smile. I miss smothering you in kisses. I miss rocking with you. I miss changing you. I miss feeding you. I miss bathing with you. I miss interacting with you. I miss watching Trinity interact with you. Baby boy, I miss everything about you. I'll love you for a lifetime."

04-15-2012

Over the weekend Jeremiah and I came to this new realization. We are sick and tired of being 'sick and tired'. We are tired of not talking. We are tired of watching what we say and how we say it. We are tired of all of this 'hush-hush' bullshit. We are tired of remaining silent so that "they" can sit on their asses and do nothing. All of the grandparents are at this point where they are sick of doing nothing as well. Everybody is coming to this same destination and realization. Nobody wants to call any shots. Nobody wants to step up and take charge. Nobody wants to stand up and say 'this is what happened' and this is 'what needs to be done.' I feel like the medical professionals, the lawyers, and the police officers are all not willing to stand apart from each other and say what they know to be true. It's like everybody is 'afraid' to put themselves on the line for fear of it coming back on them. It again, if true, is another reality of the politics that rule our world. This is so saddening to me. What happened to being able to tell the difference between right and wrong? What are people so afraid of?

Our family representative called and talked to Dr. March the medical examiner. She was very cautious in what she said to him. She wouldn't give any opinions or offer much information at all. I had some questions written out for him to ask her. She didn't really answer any of them. She didn't want to say anything that could be traced back to her. Why won't anyone talk? God Dammit, we are the victim's family, this is my child, WHY won't anyone talk to us? I deserve to know what happened to my son. If they lost one of their children wouldn't they want to know why and how they passed? *Someone please tell me what happened to my baby boy? Someone out there please help me, please help this family, please offer me some type of explanation.*

When our family member was talking to the medical examiner she mentioned that it would take a considerable force to fracture the occipital bone. She made a point of mentioning that dropping a child could cause this. When our family rep made the comment that Dr. Sutherland said this was one of the most severe cases of retinal hemorrhaging she had ever seen, Dr. March's response was, "I wouldn't have said that". What does that mean? Why won't she give her gut reaction? Isn't her job to speak for those left unspoken? Isn't she supposed to want to bring peace to a death? She just isn't willing to do that. She won't offer anything. Her comment about dropping a child that made me question if that is what she believes happened. Does she think based on her findings that Peyton was dropped? I am so confused. In her autopsy, it states that Peyton had severe traumatic brain injury, most likely non-accidental. What??? How could she even state this but then consider dropping? Or is she just throwing that out there as to be completely neutral and show just what kinds of injuries could cause a fractured skull? Deep down I would feel so much better if Anna did accidentally drop Peyton. It's easier to swallow an accident than to fathom an intentional act. But that's the thing, why won't Anna just say what happened? She leaves us here with nothing. Nobody is talking to us and so we are left to try and interpret the little amount of medical information we do have. We don't know what this stuff is so we research on the internet and try to make sense of it the best we can. News Flash: We're not medical professionals. We don't even know how to interpret the information we do find.

04-18-2012

"Baby boy it has been almost three months since you passed. I can't believe that it has already been that long. It does feel like eons since I last held you. You have now been gone half the time you were alive here on this earth. Every day when I come to visit you I walk up to your marker and just break when I see your picture. Even though it has been three months and feels like so long since I last held you, I can feel your baby soft skin, smell your baby fine scent, and hear your happy, giggly, laugh. These senses are so real for me. I wish so badly that you were here and these "senses" weren't just memories. Baby boy I miss you so much. Part of me died when you died. This idea does give me some peace that a part of me is with you. I am doing everything I can to advocate for you. I just really didn't know.

I didn't know how hard it would be to try and live without you. Every tissue of my body is starving for you. My mind is starving for answers. I need to know what happened to you. Every day I wish that I would have kept you home with me where you would have been safe. If I had only kept you home with me you would still be here. This wouldn't have happened. I miss you Peyton. You were my perfect baby, you brought me so much peace. If you were here now you would be cruising around our floors and laughing at the dogs. I love you so very deeply baby boy. You were my perfect angel."

Dear God, will you ever tell me why this has happened? Will I ever know why I had to bury my baby boy? Please give me some sign.

This week my lawyer emailed the county attorney and asked if we could meet face to face with them. He emailed back that he felt this wasn't an appropriate time to meet with us as all they would be able to state is that "they are still investigating". What can they possibly still need that they don't have? What are they waiting for? I just don't get it. How can this take so long, how? How can Anna continue to remain silent? Doesn't she feel guilty? I just want to know. What happened to my son? How did he get a fractured skull? How did he get retinal hemorrhaging?

I had heard a rumor last week that Anna had contacted DHS and asked to do daycare again. WHAT?! Are you kidding me? Clearly something happened to my Peyton in her care, either intentionally or unintentionally. Why won't she tell me why I had to bury my son? How can she pretend this didn't happen?

04-19-2012

Today is a Thursday and it is exactly three months from the date that Peyton sustained life threatening injuries while at daycare. I can't believe it has been three whole months. I can't believe I have made it through these terribly long three months. I can't believe I still hurt like I do three months out.

I was talking to my sister this afternoon and explaining anything that is or mostly, isn't happening with Peyton's case. I have this feeling that his case will go unfounded and that Anna won't be charged with anything. I also feel like everyone in the community knows that Anna hurt my baby badly, intentionally or unintentionally. I think there may be two important doctors that have two different viewpoints as to what happened to Peyton. I know that the police investigators are waiting on opinions from Dr. Sutherland, in Omaha, and Dr. March, the Medical Examiner. I think that Dr. Sutherland will stick by what she originally said about how Peyton acquired his injuries and I think that Dr. March will have a broader spectrum of ideas. Dr. March made the comment to my father when asked what kind of force it takes to cause a fracture in the occipital bone, she said "considerable force". She made a point in mentioning that even dropping a child could cause this type of injury. For me, that takes on a whole new meaning. Was this truly intentional and "Shaken Baby" or was this some terrible accident that Anna has covered up? I have been so sure for so long that it must have been intentional and malicious. But now, after hearing Dr. March's statements, it makes me wonder if it was really an accident?

For me it is easier to believe that this was a terrible accident than to believe that a friend of mine killed my child. The bottom line to any of it is that she lied. Even if it were an accident she lied by omission. If the doctors knew there was head trauma a craniotomy could have been performed at 9:30 a.m. instead of at 5:30 p.m. I don't know if that could have made his prognosis better but at least he might have had a chance. Anna took that away.

Through all of this tragedy all I have really wanted is answers. No amount of time she would spend in jail, or fines she would have to pay could ever bring peace to my son's death. But the answers maybe could bring peace to my mind. I wouldn't have to search for the answers because I would finally have them. Even if those answers are terrifying I would still have them. I wouldn't have to keep searching.

I was very angry today. I was so angry and terribly devastated all in one small package. I talked to my co-workers who stated that, "Courtney, don't let the anger take over. Please don't allow it to consume and take your life. Focus on the living. It doesn't matter what the facts are you have to accept that intentionally/unintentionally she killed your child. Accept it, feel it, and focus on what you need to do next for your family. Anna's life is a hundred times more miserable than yours now. She has to live with the guilt that she killed this small child. It will affect every part of her being. You and Jeremiah are free. You don't have that guilt because you never caused this to happen."

When I was talking to my sister and trying to update her on small changes I explained to her that I really wanted her to write a letter and send it to the detectives and the county attorney. This week in our family representative's conversations with them they seem to make statements that are so "neutral" for a lack of words. They won't acknowledge that Jeremiah and I are not suspects. It's like their way of saying that 'they still don't know who harmed Peyton'. In the back of my mind I am so offended and angry and bitter. I pray to God that in the back of their minds they know it is Anna but that they have to appear neutral because of their professional roles. I want my family to write letters so that these professionals know who we are and what kind of people we are.

I was talking to my sister about all of this journaling I have been doing. I have every intention of turning it into a book. Nobody may ever buy it but if one, just one family bought this, it would be worth it. I wish so badly now I could go out and buy a truthful book about someone else living our nightmare. Right now Jeremiah and I feel so alone. No matter what anybody says or doesn't say, nothing really helps. But I want to publish this, as raw and truthful as it is. I want the public to understand our devastation, the investigators and county attorney to focus on the right person, and Anna to know that 'we know' what she did to our son. I don't know if those are the right reasons, but they're my reasons, or at least some of them. This really, has been my therapy. I don't have to worry about anything. I can just write. Right, wrong, or indifferent this is our tragic experience. I was trying to piece together what my purpose of the book would be. I'm still not really sure. One thing I do know is that really, this has been my "Faith Journey".

And really, this has been my faith journey of everything. This tragedy is testing my faith in God. There have been moments where it is hard for me to believe that he exists. I am struggling to understand his 'role' in our world and life. But I am holding on and I'm trying to learn.

This is testing my faith in myself. Can I really get through this tragedy? My shoulders are getting weak and I don't know how much more I can handle. I am trying to remain strong and prevail, but I am getting very battle weary.

This is testing my faith in people and trust. Are there really good people out there? Do we really truly know anyone like we think we do? Are people generally more concerned about themselves more than others? I am trying to be hopeful that there are trustful people, truthful people, and caring individuals out there.

This tragedy is testing my faith in loving. I have never felt hatred like I feel now. I never knew I could feel so bitter and revengeful. I am trying to understand that hate will not heal me. I am trying to love when all I know how to do is hate.

This is testing my faith in marriage. Jeremiah and I would fight sometimes, we would bicker, and sometimes we would engage in hurtful words or actions. A lot of times we would knit-pick about the small things. But now, after going through all of this, all of that small stuff is so petty, so unimportant. I could care less if Jeremiah helped with the laundry, or if he mowed the lawn, or if he left his dirty clothes on the ground. None of that matters anymore. It is so insignificant. It just sucks that in order for me to "learn" that, I had to lose my son.

This is testing my faith in our justice system. Are people really held accountable? How are innocent people charged with crimes they didn't commit, yet people who commit crimes are not charged? Is it really about doing what is right, or is it doing what one can get away with? I am trying to believe that we live in a society that ultimately wants what is 'just' and 'right'.

This is testing my faith in politics. Do people in high positions really want to do what is of dignity? Or are they so infatuated with what people think about them and how they appear to the public? Are elected officials more concerned with keeping their communities safe or are they more concerned with ratings and winning records? I am trying to believe that individuals that go into these positions have a true longing for positive change.

04-20-2012

Today I heard the news that Brett, Anna's husband, has made comments about "This will never go away and that people won't forget." He said that, "My wife will always be labeled as the person who caused this." WHAT? Well no shit she will! In my opinion she should be glad that is all that she will endure. I was so disappointed when I heard this from my friend. In this revengeful way I wanted to hear that Brett looks miserable and that they were having marriage problems. I don't wish any ill will against Brett, I really don't. I genuinely believe he has no idea what happened in his home. I believe Anna will take "this" to the grave. Brett is sensitive and there is no way that he could know about this and keep it bottled up. So really, I don't want him to hurt but I so desperately want her to hurt as badly as I do. I guess I just want some indication that she is feeling horrible and falling apart.

Through all of this I keep thinking, could it really be that Anna doesn't know what happened to Peyton? I mean, could one of the kids have done something to Peyton while Anna was getting breakfast ready? I know I asked the doctors in Omaha this and they stated that 'no this wasn't possible' but I just can't understand how Anna can pretend that nothing happened. Could one of the kids picked him up and dropped him or hit his head on the coffee table or drop him by the fireplace? I feel crazy thinking this but I am getting desperate for answers. I just want to know what happened to my son....

04-23-2012

I have spoken to so many people about what is "not" happening with Peyton's case. So many people are just shocked to hear that nothing is happening and that this will most likely go unfounded. My sister stated it best when she said, "I think people generally believe that when someone does something wrong they will be punished or held accountable. I think a case like Peyton's could generate so much media because nobody would want to hear that something like this could happen to a child and yet no one is held accountable."

I think about Brett and Anna a lot. How can Brett truly believe that his wife had nothing to do with Peyton's injuries? How? This is so hard for me to understand. I suppose when you love someone you genuinely believe in their innocence. Again, I suppose it is hard to realize that you don't know someone like you thought you did. I understand that feeling.

For my mind, my healing, I just wish I knew how he acquired a fractured skull. How? It's like I am frozen in this place where I can't move on further without knowing how he acquired this injury? I am at this point mentally where I want to know, even if that meant no one was held accountable. I wish they would put me in a room with her and mother to mother, I could beg her to tell me what happened to Peyton. If officials went to her and stated that there would be no consequence, would she tell what happened? No matter what consequence there would be, it would never be enough, I know that much. So maybe, that part doesn't matter. I just want to know what happened.

I can understand an accident. I can understand being scared. *But*, I cannot understand the omission that likely contributed to Peyton's death. Could it be that she truly doesn't know what happened to him? Could one of the kids have picked him up or dropped him? But, what about what Trinity is saying? Trinity's story has been the same for three months. How can it not be correct?

Originally, while in the hospital with Peyton my mother made the comment that even if this was an accident and instead information was withheld, that is a true indication of character. Being afraid, being scared is no excuse to not do the right thing.

I find myself running through my mind replaying the night before Peyton's injuries. I keep searching if something could have happened on our watch. I so desperately want answers. This also angers me. I so desperately want answers that I am willing to look in our direction. But, there is nothing. Nothing happened to Peyton on our watch. He was happy, healthy, and never injured in our home.

Today at work I was talking to a friend about babies. This conversation was uncomfortable at first because everyone has a different opinion about when we will truly be ready to have another baby. I know that Jeremiah and I are not done with our family. We have a wonderful family and Jeremiah and I are good parents. I want so badly for Trinity to have a sibling, she gets so lonely. She was such a perfect big sister. I just thought I was done being pregnant. I thought my life was "planned out". I wish it didn't have to take me losing my son to realize that really, I am not in control of what happens.

Dr. Sutherland sent me an email this morning. As soon as her name appeared in my inbox I just froze. *Dear God, my stomach is hollow. This is who I have been waiting for. Can she tell me anything? Please allow her to give me some information that nobody else will.* She expressed that she would be happy to talk to me on the phone. We emailed back and forth and we set a time for Wednesday to talk. I am going to make a list of questions to ask her. Based on her short email I was given the impression that a "decision" was made by the county attorneys and unfortunately, I just have this feeling that it will be labeled as "unfounded" or "open". I hope I am wrong, I just don't think I am.

I wonder if there will be a day when I am no longer consumed by my grief. I am so lucky to have amazing friends and family. I don't know what I would do without them. Thank you to the people that still acknowledge that Peyton is still living inside of me, even though he no longer graces this earth. He is very much alive in my mind.

"Dear Peyton,

I came to visit you two days ago on the 21st but I couldn't journal that day; that was exactly three months since you died. I just couldn't write. I thought of you every second, of every minute, of that entire day. I hope you hear my prayers to you. I wish you were scooting around our floors and laughing at your sister. In my mind, you are. I hope you are playing with your other sibling and telling them all about mom and dad and your wild sister Trinity. She misses you baby boy. Thank you for being my perfect baby. Some days I am so terribly angry for what has happened to you. Other days I try to be thankful for the six months that I was blessed to spend with you. I am doing my best to speak for you. Please don't be disappointed in me if I can't get anyone to listen. I love you so much Peyton James."

Later this evening I was on social media and I found a picture on my aunt's page of Peyton and I. It is actually the only picture of Peyton and I. As a mom I'm always the one taking the picture and forget that maybe I should be in them. I changed it to my profile picture and then I just lost it. I started bawling and bawling. He was so beautiful and perfect. I just don't understand how and why this has happened. I just miss him so much. How will I ever get through this? I don't know that I am strong enough to do this. Will I ever find peace in my son's death? *Dear God, please pick me up and carry me through this. I regret to inform you that I am not as strong as you think I am.* I feel I am at this point that there is nothing I can say that I haven't already said. I just keep writing the same things hoping that the next time I write it won't hurt quite as much. Unfortunately, I am wrong. The hurting just never stops.

04-25-2012

Today I was supposed to have a phone conversation with Dr. Sutherland. Unfortunately she was at one of the hospitals and wasn't able to make it back to the office. I can't imagine how busy she truly is so the idea that she is even willing to give me precious moments is nothing short of admirable. Last night I stayed awake writing out questions that I wanted to ask her. She emailed me this evening saying she was sorry about not being available and that she would be willing to reschedule for Monday.

This morning it's as if I woke up with this fire burning inside, an anger that is tired of being caged up. So I called the Victims Compensation program, which is located at the State Attorney General's Office. I talked to a lady there and explained Peyton's case and who I was. At first she seemed very skeptical and guarded. Finally, after telling her our story she opened up and seemed like she wanted to help us. I suppose there are people out there who try to take advantage of the system but, I am not one of those people. I have worked hard for everything I have. This time though, I believe I deserve help or compensation. The lady expressed that she was still waiting on the investigators and that if I would fax her a copy of the autopsy she would also request medical records from the hospital. She stated that she would try to go at it that way, whatever that means. I think she has to build her own case to support that we are really victims.

My father had given me the phone number of a lady in town who is an advocate for victims of homicide. I met with her this afternoon and we talked about everything thus far. I talked about my devastation and this instinctual drive to find answers. I explained to her that I am so compelled to search for answers as I feel it is my responsibility to fight for Peyton. I want to find the answers that nobody can give me, maybe the answers that nobody else has. I don't want to let Peyton down. She explained to me that I need to take time for myself. I agree with this, the problem is I don't really know how. I mean I do but, where do you start?

I am a caretaker by nature, which might explain why I went into counseling. I want to help people and I get satisfaction from doing so. I guess it gives me purpose and drive and it makes me feel like what I am doing is worthwhile. I genuinely care how people are feeling and I genuinely want to help. So, to be in the opposite position, to be the one that now needs the "helping", that is tough. I know that in order to take care of others you have to take care of yourself. That is like the counseling motto. It is true but also hard to do.

I long to make sense out of this tragedy. Some way I have to do something with this experience. What have I learned that I could share with others? Really, not much, or at least what I have learned, sucks. If anything, I could share my experience and harsh realities. I could share this journal.

"Dear Peyton James,

Mommy has been very tired this week. Emotionally my grief has consumed me. There have been nights where I've struggled to function. I thank God that your daddy is such a good husband. He stepped up and took care of Trinity trying to allow me the ability to take care of myself. I am still fighting for you but I think I might need a small break. Please don't think I have stopped fighting for you. I just need a couple nights of good sleep and a few peaceful moments. I need to gather back some of my strength. I'll see you in my dreams sweet baby."

04-26-2012

Jeremiah talked to one of our lawyer friends yesterday about pursuing a wrongful death suit. Is there any chance this was an accident? Maybe this was an accident and she became scared and therefore didn't reveal the truth. The problem is that Peyton didn't get the care he needed or when he needed it because she chose to hide the truth. We make choices every day and then have to live with those "choices".

04-27-2012

This week, today, lately, I am so in between being so angry and yet so battle weary and exhausted. Today, I am very tired, very weak, and very much on auto-pilot. I will hopefully get to talk to Dr. Sutherland and maybe get at least a few answers.

The lack of communication that we have received is quite frankly, traumatizing in itself. The being left alone is almost as bad is being hounded about what we don't know or have already said. Or maybe it wouldn't matter what they did or didn't do. My son is dead and nobody is paying for it.

Trinity had therapy today. This morning at home she was challenging. She was very angry this morning and tends to take her anger out on me. I am the one she cuddles with and shows affection to but, I am also the one that is the target for her anger. I think the therapy is helping. If anything, her therapist has given me ideas of things to work on at home. She told Ms. Erin that mom and dad are mad. She is right, but I thought we were doing such a good job of hiding it. She is so smart and very perceptive. I guess I wasn't hiding it as well as originally thought.

While Trinity was in counseling I used that time to write some important thank you notes. Part of my "getting through this tragedy" is trying to acknowledge all of the people that aided in rescuing us. Doing this allows me to feel a sense of gratefulness and keeps some of the hate from taking over. Jeremiah and I had received so many cards from so many people. I spent the most dreadful weeks after Peyton's passing consumed in writing the thank you's. I had family volunteer to help but really, I needed to do those in order to function.

Tonight I am tired, weak, and weary. I am so tired that I cannot even write.

04-29-2012

My amazing brother wrote this letter to send to the investigators and the county attorneys' office on behalf of our family. Here it is below:

Gentlemen,

My name is James Jergens and my sister is Courtney Pottebaum. I am writing this letter to voice some of my concerns into the investigation of my nephew, Peyton Pottebaum and to possibly get some information that will help ease the family.

Let me first start off by thanking you both for the time you and your teams have put into this case. I'm sure you will agree the number one goal is to find justice for Peyton. I live in Northern California, so I only see my niece and nephews a couple times a year. When I do have the pleasure of visiting, I have the benefit of playing, giving them my undivided attention and spoiling them as every uncle enjoys. I was fortunate to meet and interact with Peyton this past Christmas.

We have been positive, patient and cooperative through this investigation, but that patience is starting to run out. They are running out because we feel little is being done. We have reviewed the same autopsy and DHS report that you have received. My only question after reviewing those, doing research and talking with other legal and medical professionals is, why aren't there any charges being filed? After talking to a couple of legal professionals it seems the general consensus is that there is enough to charge the daycare provider. My only concern is if she hasn't been charged by now then she won't be charged for anything. Someone needs to be held accountable. The family wants to know if this was an accident that went wrong or if this was intentional. We want to know how Peyton passed. We know the injuries he sustained, but we don't know how it happened.

We know a few facts...Peyton was acting normal the morning he was dropped off at the daycare provider's home and was happy and smiling according to the daycare provider and her husband, which they stated in the DHS report. Peyton ate well the night before and the daycare provider fed him the morning of January 19th. We know the injuries Peyton sustained as well as the opinion of medical professionals that his symptoms would've been immediate. The one fact that stands out is there were four people that took polygraph tests. Three people have passed and one has failed. The person who failed just happened to be with Peyton the moment he quit breathing. Trinity, Courtney and Jeremiah's daughter, has also explained countless times in detail what she saw the daycare provider do to Peyton.

I understand that other family members have contacted you and have expressed concerns. I also understand they've been told very little and that the case is still being investigated. We are praying the

Woodbury County Attorney's Office and The City of Sioux City does what the Woodbury County Attorney's website states. Among other things it says "...fighting for the protection of abused and neglected children". We have been instructed not to discuss anything with friends or the media while the investigation is ongoing. So far we have respected those requests. We are aware and ready to accept that there might not be any charges filed against the daycare provider. If this is the case, please let us know. This will allow the family to move onto the next step. I have two other sisters and we all live in major cities that stretch from the West Coast to the East Coast. There are organizations, representatives and child advocates that would help bring justice for Peyton and to bring closure to Courtney, Jeremiah, Trinity and the rest of the family. By no means is it our intention to interfere with your case or investigation, but something needs to be done in the near future and questions need to be answered. I can promise you that we will not fade away from this.

I appreciate your time

Regards, James Jergens

Isn't my brother awesome and great? Everything he states is honest and direct which, quite frankly, is what we need. How many other babies have died like Peyton died? How many families have been affected by tragedies like ours? How many other families never get closure or justice for their children? How do they cope? How do they move onward? When are they told that nothing is going to happen?

The lack of communication towards our family has been one of the most surreal issues of them all. I know that we have lawyers but the authorities could talk to our lawyers. Of course, they're not. I really wish I knew what these people thought.

Tomorrow I am supposed to be able to talk with Dr. Sutherland. These are the questions that I want to ask her:

*Does she still feel that this tragedy is "Shaken-Impact Baby Syndrome"/ Abusive Head Trauma?

*What is her understanding of the county attorneys' office opinion?

*Did the medical examiner's findings point to an accidental/intentional injury?

*What has been her experience in these types of cases?

*Anything else we can do or anyone else we can contact to help us advocate for Peyton?

*Can accidental injury cause retinal hemorrhaging?

*In cases like these is there usually a pattern of prior abuse or do they seem to be isolated?

*If there was indication of head trauma and a craniotomy performed earlier, could Peyton's prognosis been different?

Hopefully, Dr. Sutherland can give me insight. Good, bad, or indifferent, some information is better than no information. I have often thought about hiring a forensic pathologist who could look over all of the information collected thus far just to see if a different set of eyes could pick anything else out. It's just so sad to me that someone in our position has to do this. We shouldn't have to fight for our son. We should be able to rely on our justice system to do that for us. We are strong-willed and determined and somehow, someway, in some foreign time, we will "get through" this. But, we will never "get over" this tragedy. I will never "get over" my son...

04-30-2012

Today I spoke with Dr. Sutherland. There isn't a lot she could tell me. But just talking to her brought me some sense of peace. I asked her if after viewing the autopsy if she believed this could have been accidental. Sadly, her response was no. She still felt very strongly that Peyton was a victim of abusive head trauma. She said that one of the key markers was his retinal folds. She said she has seen a lot of accidental trauma and she believed this was not that.

Dear God, I had hoped that today could bring me some answers, answers that I want. Unfortunately, they are not the answers I want. It is so hard for me to accept that someone intentionally harmed my child and then let him die. My anger seeps out of my pores and controls my soul. I desperately want peace but, really, will I have that? How can this woman live with herself? How does she sleep at night? I hope my son haunts her at night for the rest of her life.

Dear Peyton,

I am sitting next to you today and it is so beautiful in this cemetery. I look at your picture not really yet accepting that you are no longer here. Last night I was going through pictures to put in frames and Trinity picked one up of you and hugged it and kissed it. She started crying and said, "Mommy I miss my Peyton. I so sorry he have to go to Anna's house. I sorry Anna hurt my baby brother." I hugged her, cried with her, and kissed your picture with her. Trinity wishes she could have saved you and I wish I could have rescued you both. I am so sorry that I took you to her house. I am so sorry that I took you to a person like that. I didn't know. I didn't know she was capable of that. I thought I was taking you to a safe and nurturing place. My Peyton, did she ever hurt you before? Did she ever hit you or shake you before the day of your demise? Were there signs that I should have seen? I would have done anything to protect you. I just didn't know. It will haunt me for the rest of my life that I had someone like that watch my babies. I am so sorry....

I miss you so much. I long to kiss your chubby, full cheeks. I would give anything to spend one more day with you. When you look down on our family do you miss us? There are days that are so unbearable, and there have been some days where I smile because I want you to know that before you died I was happy. I want you to know the real me, not this me. I was happy, content, blessed, gracious, appreciative, genuine, and loving. I was so happy with you. I never knew I could be that happy. Baby boy I won't give up on you. I won't give up on us. I am still looking for some sign of hope.

I love you my sweet, innocent, Peyton.

What do other families out there do? How do they go on? Have other families ever gotten justice? I feel like we are being told, "There's nothing we can do to help you. Tough, deal with it?" How do these other families advocate for their beloved child? I will never understand how this can happen in the world we live in. How?

I am angry, devastated, hurt, miserably functional, isolated, hollow, and terribly consumed by my son's death. Someone, anyone, please help me. Please help my son. I am surrounded by people but so lonely inside.

Please God, help mend this family. We are "worth" it...

05-01-2012

Here I sit tonight so angry and hurt. It's May. I thought I would be in a better place. But I'm not. I had a meeting today with one of the families I work with at another building. All night I couldn't sleep and dreaded the morning meeting for fear that I would run into Brett, Anna's husband. I genuinely believe that he doesn't know what his wife did to my son. He believes her. I guess I thought that maybe he would put all of the pieces together and realize that something very bad happened in their home and Anna was the only adult there. But he doesn't know all of what we know, which makes it even more traumatizing. If he knew what we know would he still be in denial?

Later in the day I found out from a trusted friend that Anna is babysitting again. WHAT?! I couldn't believe it. I can't believe it. How can they allow her to do this? It was my understanding that she couldn't babysit as long as the case was open. Her not being allowed to watch children gave me the only small victory I have had. At least in some small way something was being taken from her.

Tonight, I have realized that there is no thing as justice and that something is so terribly wrong with our system or lack of it. How can so many people who are truly innocent be treated so badly by our "system" yet, people that are untruthful, selfish, destructive, and guilty get away with horrible crimes? A friend made the comment to me tonight that "we're punished for being too honest". She is right. We have been honest, straightforward, and cooperative and we have received no help, no sympathies, no justice, yet, Anna can outwardly lie, change her stories and refuse to talk. She gets to continue her life as if my son never died. She gets to pretend that she doesn't know what happened to him. She gets to pretend that she never caused his death. I hope that my son visits her every night. I hope that he reminds her of all the lives she took away that morning.

I so badly want her to have some mental breakdown and confess to everything. Will that ever happen? Will she be able to bury this deep within her and act like it never happened? Will Brett ever learn the truth about his wife? I have prayed for him; that he will realize what she did.

What does our family need to do for these authority figures to advocate for our son?

The Clock Keeps Ticking

05-07-2012

I can't believe it is May already. Time keeps going by, but my mind and heart are so deeply stuck back at the days of my son's death. I try to move forward and some days I do but then, unexpectedly I am thrown back into this whirlpool of emotions. *God, I miss him so much. Will my aching ever cease?* I have been doing some individual counseling for the past couple of weeks. When I met with this counselor last week, she explained to me that she felt as if I was re-traumatizing myself. She said that in her whole career I am only the second person she has said that to. What should I be doing differently? How do I keep that from happening? I feel like I must be strong everywhere. When I am at work, I hold it together. When I'm at home in the evenings, I hold it together. When can I just break down? That is why I go to the cemetery. I go there every day because I know I am safe with my baby. I can cry to him and tell him how much I miss him. I had a friend make a comment to me: "He's in Heaven, he wouldn't want to come back here." Maybe she is right but to me, this will always be the only place that he should be.

Every day I try to "make sense" of Peyton's death but still, 3.5 months out I am still clueless about my lesson. I found out last week that the county attorney is getting the state involved to try and help with the case. I was happy to hear this. At least I can try to make sense that everything that could be done is being done.

I wish the investigators would stick me in a room with Anna. I wish they would let me question her and beg her to tell me how and why my son died. Could she face me mom to mom? Was this true 'shaken baby' or could she have accidentally dropped him causing some unconsciousness and then shakes him in panic? I fear that really, I will never know. How can she live with herself? How can she lie to herself? How is it that her friends and family can't see through her?

Jeremiah and I live with skepticism every day. I see people look at me different, act different around me, and sometimes straight up avoid me. Maybe because nobody really knows what to say. Maybe because nobody knows what happened. Maybe because everyone is afraid that this will be contagious; that they will get 'this death'. What I do know is that somehow and someway I have to find a way to bring justice to my son. How can I do that? I believe first, I must bring peace to myself. I am full of anger and rage, and hate. There are days when I wish I could cause pain to her. But that is not who I am. But, how do I find peace? How could I ever be at peace when my son has died? I think I have to believe that I am not in control. I must have true faith that God will take care of all parties involved; that God will hold her accountable later. I had a friend say to me, "This will all come out some day, some way. It just may not be on your timetable." I hope he is right. It is having faith in something that isn't tangible.

I know that deep down I need to get healthy; whatever that really means. I don't think I'll ever really be 'healthy' again. I received a letter from another mother who has lost a child. I met her at the Compassionate Friends group. In her letter she stated that even most bereaved parents can't relate to the idea of a child being taken by the hand of another.

But I need to start healing. I just don't know how to do that. How do I bring peace to my mind? *God, I keep looking up, please don't give up on us. Please help me to get through this. Please help me to begin to heal. Please take away my hate, my anger, my depression. Please allow me to trust that you will take care of this. I need to be a good, healthy mom for Trinity. A good wife to Jeremiah. I have been so checked out these last three months. I need to be healthy for my family. I know that the hate for this woman will not heal me.*

The sad reality is that people don't know. They don't know what we know. They don't know what she did to our son. They don't know what we didn't do. They don't know the story. They don't know the truth. They don't know that this woman is getting to walk away. They don't know that my baby was killed.

Endless

*"The wheels keep on turning,
All hours of the day.
I keep hoping and praying,
That God will find a way.*

*I keep hoping that the days will bring,
A sense of answers yet untold.
To clear the minds of all alike,
And not let this case turn cold.*

*Please let this mother know,
How her infant's death came to be.
She grieves all night and day,
For answers that no one can see.*

*Please bring peace to my sorrow,
And hope to my hopeless mind.
That one day the truth will come out,
And the resolution we will find."*

Author: Courtney Pottebaum

05-11-2012

This week has been going by and I feel like I really can't recall it. I have been in this weird hazy cloud where I can "go through the motions". I feel so removed from my life, this world. I can't say that I am overly depressed; then again, I don't know what a "normal" depression would feel like in these circumstances. But I am not happy or content either. I guess I am hopeless and really, I am helpless. I am removed and the reality is that no matter what I say, what I do, my fighting may not bring justice for Peyton or my family. I feel bad for Jeremiah. My distance has probably most affected him. When he is hurting, he so badly yearns for touch. I, on the other hand, close up and try to fight for myself. I explained to Jeremiah that I'm sorry I have been so detached. I guess, it's my way of trying to deal with my own emotions. I am just lost. I don't know how to feel, or what to feel. I'm not completely depressed, but I'm not "happy" either. I'm just there and there, and anywhere but "here".

This next week I have an appointment with my doctor about possibly getting my IUD taken out. I talked to my counselor about this. I don't know what to do. Should I have it taken out or not? Jeremiah and I have talked that when I get it taken out, we aren't going to "plan" any more babies. *Did you hear that God? I won't plan anymore; at least I'll try not to. I do have faith that you will decide when it is or isn't time, as hard as that is for me to say. The last two babies that we "planned" didn't work out too well. I hope Peyton's passing wasn't your way of trying to help me to understand that I'm not in control of my life like I thought I was. I don't believe you would be that cruel as to cause this to happen. But I do wonder why you allowed this to happen? Why didn't you intervene? Why didn't you stop it? I understand there is evil, and this was evil. I also believe that you have a much greater plan than I can see or understand. I am faithful that you will use this for your work, that you will use this for good. That's what I want you to do. Please use this tragedy to instill goodness in something, someone.*

I think about all the authorities in Peyton's case. What do they think? I do believe they want justice for Peyton as well. Please help to guide these professionals to use their talents to find the evidence they need to bring the truth forward. I believe that someday the truth will come out. I also understand that it may not be on my timetable.

This last weekend we went out of town to see Jeremiah's sister's twin baby girls. They have been in the NICU for about a month and were finally released to come home. Jeremiah and I really wanted to go see our new nieces but in the back of our minds there was this overwhelming sense of loss. We wanted so badly to see the girls and the visit be truly about congratulating their family. But that was easier said than done. Jeremiah and I wanted this visit to be about them, not about us. All week we fussed over the trip with this anxiety in the back of our minds. I was worried about what my reaction would be. Could I hold another precious baby and not curse God for taking mine? I know that his sister was nervous too. I think she felt guilty that she was blessed with two and we couldn't even have one. I was worried about Trinity as well. How would she handle the girls? Would this make her miss her Peyton even more?

When we arrived at their house Trinity was the first one to run in. She couldn't wait to see the baby girls. She made her way into the bedroom with Jeremiah's sister and stared at one of the girls asleep in the pack in play. She asked her aunt, "What's wrong with it?" Her aunt explained that nothing was wrong and that the baby was just sleeping. The last time she saw a baby sleeping was Peyton in the casket.

Next, Trinity looked at her aunt and matter-of-factly stated that, "I have a baby too. Peyton James is at home. You know what happened? Anna, she hit Peyton in the head like this, and then she shake him, then she throw him on the carpet. He lost his breath, the doctors try to fix him, but he died. So that's what happened."

Jeremiah's sister just started sobbing. I came into the room at the tail end of Trinity's statement and asked what was wrong. His sister said, "She just told me. She told me the whole story, everything that happened."

My unsurprised response was, "Imagine hearing that all of the time. Can you see why Jeremiah and I get so angry? A 3 and ½ year-old can't make that up."

Last week my co-worker wrote a nasty letter to the county attorney stating her feelings about the public seeing no movement on Peyton's case. She didn't tell me she wrote it until she already sent it. Tonight, she texted me letting me know that the county attorney did write her back and that she thinks she pissed him off. I don't know if that's good or bad. Jeremiah and I are not responsible for what other people do. I believe people are more interested or obliged to get involved when an injustice is happening to a defenseless child.

I have been reading the book, "The Shack". So far, it has been a good read. In the book a father takes his three youngest kids on a camping trip. While on the trip his youngest gets abducted and murdered. The book is his journey through tragedy. Towards the end of the book the main character has an experience with God. God asks the main character to "forgive" his daughter's murderer so that God can "redeem" the murderer. This part of the reading is very difficult for me to understand. I know that forgiveness is something that opens up the heart and mind for true healing but how does one 'forgive' the murderer of their child? To me, I would want to know that God will judge the person in charge of killing my child. Do people need the threat of punishment to behave humanely?

05-13-2012

Happy Mother's Day

"Dear Peyton,

Today would have been our first Mother's Day together. I imagine you would be smiling, giggling, and crawling around. You might have even been able to pull yourself up by now. I picture myself holding you and kissing your chubby cheeks. I was always kissing you. You were so intoxicating. My perfect, precious boy. Lately, I have been asked on numerous occasions if I have any children. I say yes, I have a 3.5-year-old little girl and a 10-month-old little boy who lives in heaven. People just stare at me not knowing how to respond or what to say. I am trying to come to this place of peace, to the center of my core peace. I will always fight for you, Peyton. But I need to get to a place where the anger doesn't consume me, where it doesn't define who I am. I think about you every second, of every minute, of every hour, of every day. I was so lucky to be blessed with you. You were such a delight, a gift, a blessing. I was the happiest I have ever been with you. You made me feel whole. At night I dream about you. I think you visit me in my sleep. I can't wait to hold you again. I yearn to rock you again and kiss you and smother you with love. God, the longing is so deep. The hollow core of my being holds a void that only you can fill. Peyton James I am so in love with you. Thank you for blessing our family. I am kissing you over and over again. Please feel my love wrapped around your little body. You were the best mommy's day gift I could ever have wished for. I love you so much Peyton James."

05-14-2012

I made it through my first Mother's Day without him. Somehow, in some way, it didn't quite kill me. This year of "firsts" I think will be hard but really, the rest of my life will be hard. I will always imagine that if he were here now, he would be doing this or doing that.

I am trying to find this balance of inner peace. Trying to balance hopeless with the hopeful, no easy feat. I found out last Friday when I picked Trinity up from daycare that one of the detectives had stopped by her school and visited with the director and requested the documentation that the school has been keeping relating to what Trinity has told them. This made me feel joyous inside. I don't know exactly what Trinity has told them, but I know it is probably the same "story" that she always tells everyone. It made me feel good to know that they are at least willing to look at what she is saying. At least I know that in some way they are listening to her. Much of my frustration has been consumed with the idea that I have a 3.5-year-old little girl tell me and anyone else who is willing to listen to what happened to her baby brother. Trinity is their star witness; whether they understand that, I don't know. But at least they got the documentation from the school and can read it and make their own sense of it. At least I can say that someone has heard her.

In trying to make peace with myself, this situation, I guess, I must make peace with God. I have to surrender and accept that I am not in control of my life. I have to believe that there must be some greater plan that I can't see. I must have faith that my child's death is somehow going to affect the greater good of this plan. I must have faith in all the things I don't see or understand. I must learn how to surrender everything for the sake of my soul. If I continue to hate her, she will consume my life. I cannot forgive her, but I must have faith that God will settle the score on his timetable. I have to believe in karma. I must find a way to live even though my life has been taken.

Some Day

"I miss my dear Peyton,
so precious, so sweet.
I long for the days,
again we will meet.

I will hold you and love you,
and snuggle so tight.
I will rock you and kiss you,
and hold on with all might.

We will sing, we will dance,
we'll read and we'll play.
We'll make up the time,
and define a new day.

I envision these moments,
I beg and I plead
Why did God take you?
I can't fathom this deed.

I hold faithful and firm,
that indeed there's a plan.
Through God's will and his way,
That he'll hold out his hand.

In the future, the moment,
where I long to be.
Holding my dear Peyton,
my precious, perfect baby is he."

Author: Courtney Pottebaum

05-21-2012

I can't believe it has been a week since I have journaled. Maybe that is an indication of my healing, or maybe not. It has been exactly four months since you died. Tonight at 8:30 p.m. it will be four months from the time I last kissed you and begged that God would fix you. Nothing new has transpired. There have been no changes, no charges. Four months out and my heart still aches for my baby. *God, I miss my Peyton so deeply. I long to make sense out of this tragedy.*

Last Tuesday I had a doctor appointment with my doctor to talk about getting my IUD out. The decision was made to get it taken out. Not that I am ready or not ready to get pregnant again. Really, I don't think I'll ever be ready. Deep down I just don't want to plan anymore. My plans haven't really prevailed. I have learned the hard way that God is in control. I guess I feel like when he wants it to happen it will, and if he doesn't want it to happen, it won't. I also realize that I will never understand his plan or my role in it. I just wish that he didn't have such confidence in me to deal with Peyton's death. Some days I am so terribly devastated, other days so hateful and revengeful. But most days I am dealing with this the best I can. Most days I am trying to keep the hopeful from becoming the helpless.

I really want the answers to Peyton's death. More than anything else I want justice for my baby. But, just maybe this isn't my fight. Maybe, this plan, his plan, serves some higher purpose for good. Again, I guess I won't know. All I can do is wish and do the 'what if'.

Trinity told me yesterday that she misses Peyton James. She said, "She is tired of waiting and is ready for him to come home."

05-29-2012

The end of May already. I really haven't written much this month. I needed a break, a break to concentrate on the "living". Deep down there were moments where everything seemed somewhat normal. We have had moments of laughter and fun and there have been moments where I enjoyed myself. I have gone to his grave and not wept. I have taken time to focus and interact with Trinity. True, "in the moment" interaction with my daughter. I put my "IPad" away and turned my phone off and just focused my energy into my family. It was refreshing to laugh and to find joy in doing some small task. I guess, while not journaling and "taking my break" it was also easy for me to 'forget' the horrible trauma that our family has endured for the last four months. The reality is that I can 'take breaks' and momentarily be "normal" but soon I start to regress and admit that deep within my being there is a hole that cannot be masked.

My longing for Peyton peeks out. I have visited Peyton a lot lately and taken Trinity with me.

Yesterday was Memorial Day and of course, I was reluctant about the day as again, I would have to admit that my son was dead. But the day wasn't as bad as I pictured it would be. Trinity and I bought flowers and decorated his marker beautifully.

Yesterday morning when we awoke Trinity looked at me and said, "Mom I want to see Peyton's grave. I want to see Peyton. You take me there?"

So, I did. On the way in the car she said, "Mom I am ready to see Peyton James."

I say, "Honey I'm driving to Peyton's grave now."

"No mom, not his grave. I want to see Peyton. You take me there?"

"Honey, I am driving right now to go to Peyton's grave."

"MOM, NO not the grave. I want to see Peyton."

Sadly, I state, "Trinity, Peyton isn't alive anymore. Peyton is dead. We can only go to his grave. We just have to remember him in our hearts."

Trinity cries, "Mom stop, yes he is alive. I want to see him now. Please take me there."

Tears just streamed down my face. There was nothing I could say that could help her understand. It's as if she believed that if she begged hard enough her dream might come true.

Later in the morning my friend texted me and asked if me and Trinity wanted to meet her kids at one of the parks to play. Amy and Brayden are two of our good friends and their two little ones have become good friends of Trinity's. They have walked this journey with us.

When we got to the park Trinity was running around having a blast with the other kids. Towards the end of our time there she sat down at the top of a slide with her hands under her bowed head. She sadly stated to Amy's son, the other 3-year-old that she, "Missed her Peyton James and wishes he would come home."

I heard Amy's son ask, "Where is he?" Trinity just shook her head as if she was still trying to figure that out.

Trinity's behaviors have improved, and she has more good days than bad. I am sure that helps me to cope with our new life. There was a night last week where I became emotional for Peyton. Trinity looked up at me, rushed over and cupped my chin. She asked, "Mom, you miss Peyton? Mom it's ok, we remember Peyton." My little girl talked to me like she was 16 years old. She knows things she shouldn't know.

Last Thursday was our last week of school. It was my last day to work with the kids that I have worked with for three years. It made me sad to know I won't be serving them any longer. Deep down it felt like another heavy loss. Whether they knew it or not these kids helped to save me. They gave me something to try and focus on and look forward to during my weakest weeks after Peyton's passing. I am forever indebted to these amazing and wonderful kids.

At the beginning of last week there was a student that I work with who was having a bad day. She was sent to the office, so I asked to talk to her to see what she was upset about. She came to my room and explained her frustrations. Suddenly she looked up and stated, "I went to see Peyton. I was at home and I just felt like I needed to go pay my respects to him. I asked my mom if we could go get some flowers and take them to Peyton's grave. How do you do it Mrs. Pottebaum? It's so sad."

I tried not to show a reaction but tears ran down my cheeks. She got up from her chair and came over and hugged me. I told her, "Thank you for checking on him. That means a lot to me."

05-30-2012

I met with my counselor this afternoon for my counseling session. I was more emotional than I have been the last two weeks. I also think that when I meet with her, I give myself permission to let it all out. I don't know where I would be if I hadn't picked up the phone, called and asked for her help. She is helping me so much. She listens and challenges things I say. She gives me things to work on and has me think about perspectives that are not mine. Really, she is saving my life. She gives me hope that I am dealing with this and trying to steer me in the direction of positive healing.

Jeremiah's older sister and her family came to visit us this weekend. Her son and Trinity played all day Saturday outside while we adults talked. It was nice to see her with someone her own age that she could "just be a kid with." It was so thoughtful of his sister to come see us, especially on this weekend. It was a good distraction for us and kept us thinking about the holiday approaching. In the beginning when we were in Omaha his sister had dropped everything and met us there to be with us. She took care of us in our most desperate hours. She paid for our hotel room, talked to the doctors and nurses, she bought us food and drinks, and she communicated with other family members. For those first twenty-four hours she was our lifeline. Jeremiah and I will be forever indebted to her. Somehow, she knew what to do and how to do it. She graciously picked us up and walked us through the initial storm. She was a true Earth Angel.

Trinity is talking about Peyton a lot this last week. It's weird because really for the two weeks before she wasn't really saying much about him. I don't know what triggered it this week, but something has. Yesterday after nap time Jeremiah and I took Trinity to the park to play. When I asked her what was wrong she started crying and said that "She missed her baby brother." Jeremiah picked her up and held her while she cried. I sat along the side of the play equipment and cried as well.

I do believe we are moving in some positive directions. I do feel we have had more good days than bad.

05-31-2012

Tonight, I was lying in bed with Trinity reciting the phrase, "Tonight I am going to dream of lollipops and ice cream cones, my mom and dad, and my big safe home." This is something we say with her at night before bed as a suggestion from her therapist to try and help alleviate the nightmares she has been having. She rolled over on her side and just when I thought she was sleeping she turned on her back and started crying. She said, "Mommy I miss my brother Peyton James. I don't want to go to Anna's house anymore. I don't want her to hurt my brother anymore."

I just sat there and was initially so saddened. My baby girl still visualizes what she saw happen to her baby brother. She misses Peyton so much. It's as if what she witnessed Anna do to her brother is permanently etched in her mind. Then, I became so angry. We are four and half months out from Peyton's passing and my baby girl is still so terribly scared about what she saw happen to her baby brother. This woman has scarred my daughter and inflicted such intense fear into her little mind.

I put my arms around Trinity and said, "Honey, you will never go back to Anna's house again. You are safe with mommy and daddy."

When I have talked about Trinity's recounts of what she saw happen to her baby brother some people just look at me as if they are analyzing what I am telling them. A few have made the comment that, "Kids often repeat what they hear", I think trying to help relieve me that maybe she is just repeating what she is hearing from the adults. That's the thing. She has always had her own story, her own version of what she saw. When I listen to her week after week tell her story and I see the fear that is etched into her face, I know that what my daughter saw is what happened to my son. There were months that I was grateful for Trinity's expressions as it gave insight and information into what happened to Peyton. But now, four and a half months out I so badly wish that she will soon forget about the details of what she witnessed. Now, I yearn for the days when she doesn't remember so vividly what happened to her brother. At this point, those memories haunt her. She can't even escape them in her sleep.

I do feel that emotionally I am in a better place. I started to break my Zoloft pill in half. I can tell I have been more emotional the last couple of days and I'm sure it is in part because of the lessening of medication. But I am at this point where I don't want to be on medication to the point where I am comatose from feelings and emotions. I don't want to just 'escape' these feelings and hope that someday when I do go back down on my medication that everything will all be dealt with. I guess I just don't want to mask my pain, just help alleviate it. I thought that being it is summer maybe I can try to go down and see how I feel. If I turn into a complete basketcase I will increase it.

Jeremiah's aunt called tonight and wanted to know if there has been an update on Peyton's case. Unfortunately, we had to tell her no. She said that she and a group of women at work are not willing to let this 'die'. *God bless all of them. Please stand up for us, our son, and let the important people know that Peyton matters.*

06-06-2012

My dad came into town Monday night and is going to be staying with us for a while. He made the comment to me that "there is something unnatural about coming back to see your grandson's grave". He went with me last night as we took Trinity to her first night of gymnastics. She did great and was really happy to be there. She was jumping around and smiling, and it was exciting to see!

Lately, Trinity has been expressing how much she misses Peyton. Almost every day she talks about missing him and wanting him to come back. In the bath last night, she wanted me to play Barbies with her. She wanted the Barbie I had to be her dead brother and her Barbie would be her. She told the dead brother Barbie that she missed him so much and that she is so sad. She told the brother that she wishes he would come back and that she doesn't know why this happened. I just sat there and listened to her talk through her feelings. I felt like she was a 16-year-old and asked the same questions that I have. She went on to state that "she was watching cartoons when Anna hurt Peyton Brother James."

Overnight I heard Trinity crying and she yelled my name. I went into her room and she was awake and crying and saying that she missed her Peyton James and she wants him to come home. It was 4:00 a.m. in the morning. My poor girl can't even escape her sadness in her sleep.

I understand this is a process, a very long process.

06-07-2012

I was talking to my father tonight and I told him that I have tried to search for stories of other families affected by Abusive Head Trauma (ABT) and I really haven't found much information. I have this theory and I may be completely way off base but, I believe that because of the nature of the trauma and the timing of the trauma many parents are in a position as being a 'suspect'. And, yes, I understand that some of these parents legitimately are responsible for the abuse of their child. But I also believe in the parents who never harmed their child and the abuse happened by someone else caring for their child. And once someone is innocently labeled a suspect it changes all 'fight' within them. In these cases, as in ours, these families I believe, are so terrified to be labeled a suspect and fear the idea of being wrongly and falsely accused. I believe these families then fear to fight for their child's justice because they are so afraid for the light to be falsely shone upon them. Maybe I am wrong. I just don't think so.

My father talked to the county attorney today who stated that the state is reviewing Peyton's case. They haven't accepted it nor rejected it. My counselor and victim advocate also questioned the county attorney today about the status of the case and was given the same answer. And then, my friend, Amy wrote a letter stating her opinions about the investigations. I am sure the officials are very annoyed after today's mass contact but again, we cannot control other people's actions. We cannot keep friends, acquaintances, or even strangers from making contact to express their concerns about Peyton's case. Jeremiah and I have been very professional about what we have or haven't said to friends. But I know that there are so many in the community that want to know the status of the investigation. They want to know that a defenseless baby is being defended.

I suppose part of our healing is the attitude change that must accompany it. I must find a way to accommodate Peyton's loss into my life or vice versa, depending on the day. I have to find a way to accept his death and continue to live. That is my goal. I want to have a happy life. I am only 30 years old and way too young to feel this desolate and this bitter. The attitude that I have 'most' days will only ensure that I have a lifetime of miserableness ahead of me. I cannot live that way for my daughter. But I know too much and feel too much that a 30-year-old shouldn't feel. And I have the bitter firsthand knowledge of knowing that when my parents told me as a child that 'life isn't fair', they were right. And, sometimes it doesn't matter how good of a person you are. Sometimes, it really isn't about what is 'right'. And, sadly guilty people aren't always brought justice. It's such a sad reality and maybe as parents, our job is to shield our children from these realities. Maybe our goal is to raise our children into the society members that our society 'should' be made up of and hope that our kids never find out 'the way it really is.' Or maybe, it's all just a crap shoot and it doesn't matter how much good there is, there are always these evil beings that prey upon easy targets. But, then again, I've never thought of myself as an easy target.

Really, I don't know much of anything and what I do know, I shouldn't know. I guess it boils down to the quality of life that I am willing to live for the next fifty or so years of my life. *God, please don't strike me down for planning. I am only making a hypothetical guess as to how long you may allow me to grace this earth. And yes, I will work on my attitude.* I want a happy life, a joyous life. I just need to decide how to make that happen with the hand of cards that I have been dealt. I know it can be done. I see these amazing people that have been dealt such horrible circumstances do amazing things with their lives. But I am not these extraordinary people. I am the girl next door, who generally believed in the best of people, who clearly was over-trusting and too optimistic about this life on earth. So somehow, I must find 'a balance'.

Trinity cried a lot tonight and said that she "missed her Peyton Brother James." Every time I hear those words escape her mouth daggers are twisted in my soul.

06-15-2012

Tonight I am a mess. My dad has been staying with us for almost two whole weeks. He left this morning to go back to Arizona. While he was here, I wasn't overly emotional, nor did I seem to brew too much about the issues with Peyton. But tonight, I have just fallen apart. Maybe this is what they mean when they talk about the groves and valleys, the ups and the downs. I don't know. I think while my dad was here, I was distracted, and I felt "safe", like maybe, he could protect me from my pain. But, knowing he is gone now, I am forced to admit that I have to be strong again.

Trinity has been emotional the last two weeks but sadder than anything else. The sadness she feels in those moments feels so horribly defeating because as her mom there's nothing I can do to soothe her pain.

Trinity went to Nana and Papa's tonight to play and spend the night. I think all day Jeremiah was looking forward to being alone together. I did some errands in town and stopped by Peyton's grave before I went home to give my undivided attention to the man that deserved it.

So here I am, staring down at his beautiful marker and the pain still radiating through my pores. I will never forgive Anna. I just can't. She took my son, a part of my family, and a part of me. I am so "closed up" now, even from Jeremiah. I don't like to be touched or held and I prefer distance than anything else. I know this hurts him. But I am so hurt by the loss of my son. It's like the only way I can function, to be here, just not really emotionally "here". There are days when I wonder when someone will again get away with taking something or someone away from me? How can she live with herself? If she only knew the pain she causes every day. Is she remorseful for the death of my son? I wish that she could feel the loss and pain I feel right now, almost five months after losing my son.

We received a copy of a letter today that our civil lawyer mailed to Anna basically asking for someone on her behalf to contact him concerning the death of Peyton. When I read it, I felt a little sense of hope that maybe it will cause her stress when reading it. Again, even though I know I shouldn't 'hate' or be vengeful, deep down I want her to feel the pain and loss that I do. I want her to know what it feels to bear an unbearable loss. I want her to feel pain...

"Dear Peyton,

I sit tonight at your grave, which is decorated gorgeously. Anything for my beautiful baby. I worshipped you while you lived, and I will continue to worship you in death. It is beautiful here tonight in this cemetery. It's so peaceful. I think we picked a good place to bury you. Someday I would like to have a bench and plant a tree here. When I think about your death, I still can't believe that this has all happened, that you are now dead? It still seems very surreal. I have experienced some true 'in the moment' experiences where I am present for Daddy and sister Trinity. I know you would want me taking care of them the way I would. I just wish I was also taking care of you. In one month, you would have been one year old. I imagine you would have been chubby and wobbled along our house giggling your way around. I had all these hopes and visions for this summer, before your death. I am trying hard not to get caught up in them. I hope God is tending to you. I bet all the women in heaven fight over you to hold you. You were such a charmer. Your sister Trinity misses you so much. She still cries a lot for you. Baby boy, she still talks about what she saw happen to you. As my son I always imagined doting on you through elementary years, watching you play sports as you got older, and then wanting to protect you when girls started to catch your eye. I think there is a special bond between a mother and her son and some days I am overcome with sadness when I realize I will never have that with you. I would have done anything to protect you. I would never have taken you to her house if I thought you were in any danger. I didn't know what she was capable of. I love you so much. There is a perched spot in my heart that is only accessible to you. I would give anything to hold you one more time. I'll love you for forever my perfect baby boy.

It's time for me to go home. It's time for me to focus on your daddy."

06-21-2012

Today is exactly five months since my baby boy Peyton passed from this earth. I can't believe it has been five months, today. I went and visited Peyton. I bought a little angel statue that I put on his grave. I bought a matching one to put in my garden here at home. It says, "Love: He walks with me, he walks within me." I saw this and it just hit home. Everywhere I go and everything I do is still surrounded by the grief of my son. I am coping and I am trying to be as optimistic as I can. It's weird, but really, I don't want to or know how to feel optimistic about anything. I just feel realistic, like this, all of this is just what it is. I can't change it, I can't deny it, and I must live with it. I hate this woman, but I won't let the anger take my life over. She has to live with herself. She must live with the reality that God knows what she did, and she will pay at the end.

A week ago, I didn't get my period as I should have. I took a couple of pregnancy tests, which revealed light blue positive lines. I just had this feeling that I would miscarry. My last miscarriage started out this way. I didn't write as I didn't want to get excited nor dwell on what I felt might happen. Last night I started bleeding and today I had bad cramping and went to the bathroom and passed some tissue. It's weird but really, I knew this would happen. I didn't initially get excited as I would rather prepare for the worst that way if, and when, that happens I can cope with it. Sounds pessimistic, but to me it is very realistic. To be honest, this outlook really is what has gotten me through Peyton's passing. *Maybe this miscarriage is God's way of letting me know I'm not quite ready or maybe, Peyton isn't ready to share his mom. Or maybe, this is God's way of letting me know that it's time to let him take the wheel.*

I guess the good news is that at least we know we can get pregnant again. I do feel that Jeremiah and I are living and coping the best way we can, and I am proud of how we are dealing with all of "this". One of my counselor friends made the comment that maybe the best way to live is to discontinue having expectations of other people. Maybe that is the key, to stop having expectations of life. Like it will be, whatever it will be. I can either buck it at every turn or gracefully embrace it and follow along.

06-29-2012

For the last month and a half, I have tried to "distance" myself from the all-consuming pain and overtake of emotions that I have been filled with since Peyton's death. I have tried to live without him, feel without having him here, and concentrate on the family I have left. In order to do that I felt I had to give myself some "distance" from my journal and only write when I really felt compelled to do so. Obviously, I am still trying to figure out how to have a balance of my life and losing Peyton. Tonight, we were at Jeremiah's parent's house and his mom was telling me about an incident that had happened with his aunt at a restaurant and how our names were brought up and his aunt defended us. I do know that there are people out there who don't know the real story and who have made up their own minds about Jeremiah and me. But, deep down even though I know this, it doesn't mean that it still doesn't hurt when I hear this. It devastates me to hear that someone views Jeremiah and I responsible for our son's death. How can anyone think this? What information are they hearing that is making them believe this?

Throughout the last five months this is the part that Jeremiah and I have "ignored" for lack of a better word. We were so emotionally "spent" that other people's opinions didn't matter to us. Five months out, they still shouldn't matter to me, and most days they don't. But, some days, like today, it resonates an angry fire within me. God forbid, someone expresses to me what they thought about me; I know I'd take their head off.

What are Anna and Brett saying to people? What is their justification? Our civil lawyer is moving forward and trying to get the ball

PEYTON'S PASSING

rolling for a civil case. I really like him. He's professional and aggressive and most importantly, he knows us.

Two nights ago, I attended one of my "Compassionate Friends" groups and much to my surprise, I lost it and told everyone, everything about Peyton's case. They just looked on in horror and listened like the bereaved parents they all are. They, of course, knew what to say to comfort me and what not to say. I'm glad I found this group.

Five months out I still ask God what my role is in this life of mine. What am I supposed to gain from the torture that has been bestowed upon me? I want to publish this journal. I want people to know about this trauma. I want to be the voice for other innocent bereaved parents whose loved ones were victims of abusive head trauma. I want to beg parents to be so careful of who they take their children to for daycare. I thought I knew who this woman was, but I did not. I want other parents to question who they take their children to and be so open to any sign that I could have missed. And if this tragedy strikes other innocent families, I want to beg these families to fight for what they know is true. It is so easy to become emotionally exhausted and detach and just "give up". I want to do that every day. I'm still tired, I'm still emotionally exhausted but I must believe that I can still bring peace to my son's death. And as the doctor in Omaha said to me, "This is not a sprint, this is a marathon." That doctor would never know how true his words would ring in our lives.

07-08-2012

Jeremiah and I went out to eat two nights ago alone. This was the first date we have had since Peyton's passing. People have told me that we need to go out and get away and not talk about any of this trauma. That's the thing, there is no escaping it. We can't not talk about it as it is intertwined into every cell in our bodies. While out, it was this realization that for that last five months we have been isolating ourselves at home. I kept looking around wondering who was looking at us or talking about us. This whole trauma has created a paranoia deep within us because we know that there are people out there that believe that Jeremiah or I did something to our son. We've heard the stories, we've been given the looks, and people have treated us differently. It's not fair. Again, another level of the trauma that we have endured. I wish the county attorney for a second, could experience this trauma. I so desperately want him to know what nightmare we are living every single day. I want him to experience this and then tell me that this is "ok". He is the one person that could stop this, that could "try". But he isn't and some day when I am braver, I will send this journal to him and say, "Read all of this and when you're done pat yourself on the back for letting a murderer go free."

A Mother's Grief

*"You ask me how I'm feeling
but do you really want to know?
The moment I try telling you
You say you have to go.*

*How can I tell you
what it's been like for me,
I am haunted, I am broken
By things that you don't see.*

*You ask me how I'm holding up
but do you really care?
The second I try to speak my heart
You start squirming in your chair.*

*Because I am so lonely
you see, no one comes around,
I'll take the words I want to say
And quietly choke them down.*

*Everyone avoids me now
Because they don't know what to say,
They tell me I'll be there for you
then turn and walk away.*

*Call me if you need me
that's what everybody said,
But how can I call you and scream
into the phone,
My God, my child is dead?*

*No one will let me
say the words I need to say,
Why does a mother's grief
scare everyone away?*

*I am tired of pretending
as my heart pounds in my chest,
I say things to make you comfortable
but my soul finds no rest.*

*How can I tell you things
that are too sad to be told,
of the helplessness of holding a child
who in your arms grows cold?*

*Maybe you can tell me
How should one behave,
who's had to follow their child's casket
watched it perched above a grave?*

*You cannot imagine
what it was like for me that day,
to place a final kiss upon that box
and have to turn and walk away.*

*If you really love me
and I believe you do,
if you really want to help me
here is what I need from you.*

*Sit down beside me
reach out and take my hand,
Say 'My friend, I've come to listen
I want to understand.'*

PEYTON'S PASSING

*Just hold my hand and listen
that's all you need to do,
And if by chance I shed a tear
it's alright if you do too."*

Author unknown

07-13-2012

Happy 4th Birthday Trinity !!!!

Our baby girl is four years old today! I can't believe my baby girl isn't my baby anymore. She is such a big girl now. My big girl! We had a small get together for her birthday. We just had the grandparents, her aunt, and a few of our friends. We just grilled and had cake and ice cream. She had a fun time and it was bittersweet for me to see her turn four without any other siblings to join in her fun. She gets lonely a lot but she also is "starting to be my girl again". She doesn't talk as much about the trauma she witnessed. I am so proud of Trinity. She has overcome so much in her short four years of life. I think of when she was born and holding her and cuddling her. Daddy and I were so in love with our girl. Her personality was intoxicating. She will be starting pre-school in the fall. I know it will be a battle getting her back to school as she has been home with us all summer. To be honest, I think we all have needed that time to try and heal from the inside out. We have needed this time to redefine our family. Trinity looks so much like her daddy, and her personality is parts of both of us. Trinity is my strong little girl! I love you baby doll!

07-19-2012

Trinity is at Nana and Papa's house tonight. My siblings are coming to town this weekend to stay with us since Peyton's birthday is Monday. They will be here all week. Last night I was lying in bed and I couldn't get to sleep. I looked over at the clock and it was 10:00 p.m. I thought to myself that exactly six months ago Jeremiah and I were being driven to Omaha to see our baby boy. We were driving to Omaha not realizing that there was a chance we might not be bringing him home. In the midst of the trauma we had no idea how bad our son was injured.

07-23-2012

"Happy 1st Birthday to our precious Peyton James"! Today you would have turned one year old. I imagine that you would be a chubby little boy with strawberry blonde hair who would be now walking around our house. I imagine how you would be chasing your sister Trinity, taunting the dogs, and laughing your belly deep laugh. One year ago, you were born to our family and daddy and I felt so happy and proud that you were ours. You were our amazing and perfect baby boy. You were happy, content, and so very joyful to care for. We are still searching for the answers that nobody can give us concerning your death. Please know that I will forever fight for you and that I will never stop asking the questions that need to be asked. I told myself that I would try to be happy today and remember all the joy you brought us. I didn't know how difficult it would be to act normal today. I cry for you because I miss you, I cry for you because I so dearly love you, but most of all, I cry for you because you radiated a joyfulness within my soul. You made our family feel complete. We all so desperately miss you. Trinity still talks about you a lot. Thank you for being her perfect baby brother. Thank you for being our perfect baby boy. We'll love you for a lifetime sweet baby boy."

We had family over for a grill out to celebrate Peyton's birthday. All my siblings came back to stay with us. I can never repay them for all their support. They have carried me through so much of this trauma. We are so lucky to have such amazing siblings. They don't say too much, but somehow, they know what to do. We had a cake for Peyton and Trinity blew out the candle. A few weeks prior I talked with Trinity and asked her if it was ok if we had a birthday party for Peyton. I explained that even though he was dead I still wanted to celebrate his birthday. I told her that mommy and daddy might get sad but it's just because we miss Peyton. I said, "Trinity are you ok with this?" She thought for a moment and then said, "Umm, yeah mom, I ok with it. I blow out Peyton's candle."

After singing happy birthday and Trinity blowing out his candle, I wanted to get a picture of Jeremiah and I with a picture of Peyton in a frame. Jeremiah started sobbing and just shook his head and said, "I can't, I'm sorry but I can't." I just held him and tried to comfort him. Everyone around us just looked at each other not quite knowing what to do. This time I held Jeremiah up, I tried to console him.

After cake and ice cream we all made our way to the cemetery. I had written a letter to Peyton and my sister read it to him for me. Jeremiah's mom had gotten orange and navy-blue balloons, Bear's colors, for us to release after the letter. We told the kids that we were releasing the balloons up to Peyton. Some of the adults took the kids to the pond to feed the ducks while Jeremiah and I had a moment alone with Peyton. We cried and hugged each other and wished our baby boy Happy Birthday.

A couple of days after all our siblings had gone back to their homes, we received a package in the mail from my sister. She had necklaces made for each of us. How lucky are we to have such an amazing family? They just accept us, love us and try to carry us through this.

08-05-2012

We went out of town this weekend to see Jeremiah's sister and the kids. The weekend was really good. The girls have grown so much. They are four months old now and growing so fast. We went to Oceans of Fun yesterday. Jeremiah entertained Trinity and his sister entertained our nephew. I kept thinking that there was something I was supposed to do and indeed, there should have been. I should have been taking care of Peyton. I imagined taking him into the water and seeing him giggle as he splashed. We spent much of the day in the little kid parts of the park. I walked by a little baby boy who was sitting and splashing, and he so dearly resembled my Peyton. He giggled and splashed and laughed. I smiled and then felt my heart break as I acknowledged that should have been me sitting there with my little baby, now toddler. The day was fun but throughout the entire trip there were these brief moments of utter loss. It was nothing anybody said or did, but they were just these moments of 'what should have been.

Jeremiah and I received notification last week that we were approved by the State of Iowa's Crime Victims Compensation program. Specifically, we were approved for the homicide victim survivor's compensation program. It makes us question again, as always, how "they", whoever they really are, can let "her" go without any charges, any consequences, and any emotional restitution for our family. Please understand, I am so very grateful and appreciative for this monetary compensation for us and our immediate family. It will help to pay back our family for money spent on Peyton's funeral and burial, missed work due to services, and travel and lodging expenses. I will send the state a huge thank you letter expressing the thanks we feel. But, to us another part of the reality is that these people can tell that our son was killed and yet the 'somebodies' feel like they can't prove it. Often, as in our case, it is so sad that our justice system errors on the side of caution. I understand the fear of incarcerating innocent people, but the reality is that is still happening. Children like my son are killed every day and their murders never solved, their families never given answers. How can this happen? How does this happen? What in the hell is wrong with so many people that they could intentionally hurt a child?

I would really like to publish this journal as the longer I wait, the longer I may keep this rawness away from a family that needs 'realness' like we did. And, maybe, this would be too painful for another family like ours to read. But, for me, I needed this. I needed the rawness, the brazenness, the bruteness. I needed hope in any un-hopeable way if that makes sense. I needed to understand that my emptiness, anger, fear, isolation, longing, pain, and devastation was all terribly normal in such an abnormal time.

We will 'make it through this'. We will continue with our lives. We are still a family, an intact family. We will still fight for our son, but we will also live. This tragedy will still consume us but not in such an overt way. It will slowly intertwine into the fibers of our continued-on life. Our family is now 'our new family'. We are hopeful for happiness and a new journey. I don't know what will or won't happen in the justice for my son and maybe, we are at the end of that road. But, please trust me, with all the intricate fibers that make up my being, I will never 'get over' my son's death. I will never give up, become complacent, or accept that my son's murderer is walking free, watching other children and living her life unscathed.

"As you piggyback alongside me please notice all the care and dedication we will bring to your passing. I love you forever and you are always my perfect baby boy."

Part of me

"I thought of you with love today, but that is nothing new,
I thought about you yesterday and the day before that too.

I think of you in silence. I often say your name,
But all I have are memories and your **picture in a frame.**

Your memory is my keepsake, with which I'll never part,
God has you in His keeping. I have you in my heart.

I shed tears for what might have been. A million times I've cried,
If love alone could have saved you, you never would have died.

In life I loved you dearly. In death I love you still,
In my heart you hold a place no one can ever fill.

*It broke my heart to lose you but you didn't
go alone,
For part of me went with you,
the day God took you home."*

Author Unknown

08-06-2012

I worked today. Jeremiah and Trinity came to take me out to lunch and as I stepped into the truck Jeremiah said, "Remind me to tell you later what she said."

Jeremiah was driving on the highway towards my building. Trinity hasn't been on that side of town much since being at Anna's that morning. As they pulled closer to my work Trinity became anxious and said, "Daddy you no take me to Anna's house. Anna is bad, she hit my Peyton in the head like this, she shake him hard and then she throw him on the carpet. I hate her daddy."

08-07-2012

I took Trinity to gymnastics tonight and then got her an ice cream cone after. On the way home we stopped by the cemetery to see Peyton's grave and feed the birds.

Upon leaving Trinity asked, "Mom, what are all the flowers for?"

I explained that, "The flowers are where other people are buried."

She says, "Are they all babies?"

I responded, "No, they are graves of people who have died. Some of them are babies, or mommies, or daddies, or grandparents, or cousins. When someone dies, we come to the cemetery to remember them".

Suddenly she burst into tears and cried, "Peyton is dead? Peyton isn't alive anymore?"

I say, "Trinity, Peyton is dead."

She cries, "Why mom?"

I say, "Peyton got a bad boo-boo on his head. The doctors tried to fix him, but they couldn't honey, and Peyton died."

She says, "Anna hit Peyton on the head like this (demonstrating). She shake him like this (demonstrating). She threw him on the carpet mom. Anna really mad at Peyton. Anna didn't like Peyton James."

I said, "What were you doing when this happened?"

She says, "Me and Tyler watching cartoons. I try to save him mom."

Me, "Oh honey, you're just a little girl. Anna was really naughty, and I am so sorry I took you to her house. Did Anna ever hit you before?"

She, "Yeah a couple times like this (demonstrating)."

Me, "I wonder why Anna was so mad that day?"

She, "Peyton was crying. When she throw him on the ground he cried a lot; I cover my ears like this (demonstrating)."

Me, "Did Anna ever say anything to you after the ambulance left?"

She, "Yeah, she say I'm sorry I hit Peyton. It was an accident. I hate her mom. I miss Tyler. You take me to Anna's so I can give Tyler a hug and then you bring me back to my house?"

Me, "Honey, no I will never take you back to Anna's house again."

She, "You mad at Anna mom? Me too..."

A Thousand Words

"A Thousand Words Can't Bring You Back,

I Know Because I Tried,

And Neither Can a Million Tears

I Know Because I Cried."

Author Unknown

08-12-2012

We go back to work tomorrow! Our wonderful summer is officially over. This summer was very good for our family as it was a time for Jeremiah, I, and Trinity to regroup and redefine our family. We needed this time together to make a new normal. We enjoyed Trinity so much and both feel like we have fallen in love with her all over again. She was fun this summer and I finally feel like "we got our girl back"!

Somebody Knows Something

08-27-2012

It has already been a couple of weeks since I last journaled. Two full weeks of the new school year have gone by. Two weeks ago, I was in the bath with Trinity. Out of nowhere she turned around and said, "Momma you gonna have a baby?" I just looked at her not sure what to say. This question from her came out more like a statement, like she was telling me something I didn't know. I just looked at her and replied in shock, "Um, well, no Trinity not now but maybe God will give us a baby someday." She looked at me and then turned around as if we didn't just have this conversation. It was so weird. We haven't been around any babies recently nor have we talked about any babies. This was weird.

Throughout the night I thought of what Trinity asked me. My period was two days away from due but when I awoke in the morning, I decided to take a pregnancy test for the hell of it. I took it, still two days before my expected period, and it said positive. Oh my gosh, this is crazy. How did she know? *Dear God, how did Trinity know I was pregnant? I didn't even know. Were your angels talking to me through my daughter? Is Peyton trying to give me the message that it's ok to carry another baby? God, I am listening now.*

A week after this encounter with Trinity I was rocking with her in her chair watching cartoons. She was pushing off my lap for it was time to get into the bath and she looked back at me and said, "Mom, I hope you have a baby. I really like babies. I want you to have a baby." Again, I was shocked and was taken back by her words. We have not told her we are pregnant. We aren't even acknowledging it ourselves due to my history of miscarriages. *How does she know?*

Four days ago, when I was getting ready for work in the morning, I was standing in my closet wearing only my bra and underwear trying to decide on an outfit. Trinity was in the closet with me playing with my shoes and pointing out what she thought I should wear. Her taste was good! Out of nowhere she put her hand on my tummy and said, "Mom I want you to have a baby." I replied, "Trinity, why do you say that?" Trinity says, "Mom I really love babies. I hope you have *this* baby."

That night Trinity spent the night at her Nana and Papa's house, and she told them three different times how her mom was having a baby. Nana and Papa just listened to her, knowing that we hadn't told her or talked to her about the pregnancy.

Tonight, at Nana and Papa's house Trinity was playing in the living room and I was sitting on the couch. She came up to me and sat on my lap and said, "Momma I love you. You gonna have babies.." I replied, "We need to pray to God that maybe he will give us a baby someday in my tummy." My initial thought was "Oh goodness, she said babies, I don't have room for two!"

"Peyton,

Lately I feel your presence. I smile more when I think about you and cherish all the moments I had with you. There are still days when I long for you so dearly, well that is every day. But the dreadfully depressing days are getting fewer. I am still fighting for you. I promise you that I will never stop. Have you been talking to Trinity? Have your angels been keeping her company? Are you ok with sharing your mommy again? Baby boy, no matter what babies I am given in the future they will never replace my dear perfect Peyton James. I hope you are telling the other babies that I have lost about mommy and daddy. I imagine you are entertaining them and playing with them. I miss your happiness and the joyfulness you brought us. I can't wait to cuddle with you again. I love you so much. ~Mommy".

*"Death leaves a heartache
No one can heal,
Love leaves a memory
No one can steal."*

Author Unknown

09-07-2012

Here I sit today, many months from the day you died. I still have no answers for you my dear Peyton. Please know I am still searching. I applied for a scholarship through the National Center on Shaken Baby Syndrome to attend their annual conference in Boston, MA. The scholarship is not a large amount, but it is still a monetary amount to help us fund this conference. We will pay anything for you; we will pay anything to get answers or explanations. We are taking your autopsy, medical records, and DHS report in hopes of networking with medical professionals from around the world. Maybe they can give us the answers we need. Maybe they can, maybe they can't. But we won't know unless we go and try. I need to look up to you and shout that I am doing everything I can to bring you justice.

Trinity had her last counseling appointment today with Ms. Erin, as she is moving on to another adventure. This made me sad for Trinity as she has developed such a good relationship with her. I will forever be indebted to Erin for carrying Trinity through the trauma and allowing us to know that she would help us help our daughter. I don't know how Trinity would be doing had we not gotten her into Erin. She informed me that Crime Victims and the Sioux City Police Department have requested her records in working with Trinity. She said she sent off a packet of information to both parties and that she would call Detective Johnson today to do a phone conference. She also explained that she will give the detective her cell phone number so that she can be reached if it is needed in the future. She also gave me a recommendation for a therapist for Trinity if we should need one in the future. It feels good to know that some steps are being taken.

I am seven weeks pregnant as of yesterday! I have a doctor appointment on Tuesday so we will see if it is viable. For me, it is easier to prepare for the worst, anything besides that is a plus. I can tell I am pregnant. My jeans are tighter, my tummy more bloated, and I am so nauseous. Trinity told Ms. Erin today that she asks God to give mommy a baby.

I sit back and think of Trinity so often. She is such a strong little girl. She has witnessed such trauma and yet she has pulled herself up and continued on. She is such a special little girl. She has also forced us to deal and cope with the passing of her brother. She has forced us to realize that life must continue. My healing can largely be attributed to my daughter. She gave Jeremiah and I purpose when the world just seemed purposeless. She still talks about the trauma of what she saw happen to her brother and Jeremiah and I still have our bad days. But we are healing, a little bit at a time. We have always known that children are a blessing but now, we know that in more ways than one. We have realized how precious time and life are as we were only blessed with Peyton for 6 short months. But we also know that Trinity saved our lives, literally.

> *"If every tear we shed for you*
> *Became a star above;*
> *You'd stroll in Angel's garden,*
> *Lit by everlasting love."*
>
> Author Unknown

09-26-2012

I can't believe it has been eight months since my Peyton died. I hope there is a day when the utter loss of my son isn't still so shocking.

This weekend Jeremiah and I fly out to Boston for the Shaken Baby conference. We have mixed feelings about going. I know it will be hard to hear all the information, but I also realize that this may be our only opportunity for answers and networking. Please pray that this will bring us comfort. It will be hard to be away from Trinity for so long. I pray that she will do ok at Nana and Papa's house. We haven't been away from Trinity much since Petyon died.

On the plus side, I am still pregnant! Will we really be having another baby?!?

10-09-2012

Two weekends ago Jeremiah and I flew out to Boston to attend the 12th International Shaken Baby Syndrome conference. We spent four days and three nights attending this conference with the hopes of networking with other victim's families. We also hoped to have a better idea of what happened to our son. The conference was very overwhelming, but I am so glad we went. Session after session only reinforced what Jeremiah and I already knew. Peyton's injuries and story 'seemed textbook' of abusive head trauma cases and stories. We were able to network with the National Center on Shaken Baby Syndrome and most importantly, other families who have been through this. Of the families we met, there was a wide range of disability among the children affected. There was one other family whose baby was killed like Peyton was. We were able to have in depth conversations with these families, which helped more than anything else has. We exchanged contact information so that we can email or call. We were also invited to a private group that consists of all shaken baby victim families where we can have real in-depth conversations without worrying about what we are saying. Jeremiah and I were also able to do a little sight-seeing which helped to lighten the mood. If we had doubts before attending the conference all of those were wiped away after listening to these special doctors present. The aggravating part is also that most of the victim's perpetrators were prosecuted. Most were shocked when I explained that Peyton's case had not been.

A couple of days ago I had a doctor appointment and was able to hear the baby's heartbeat. It was in the 160's!!!! My tummy is getting big already. I started to tell people at work that we are expecting, as really, I wasn't going to be able to hide it anymore! I am still in shock that we are expecting. Trinity told me the other night that mommy is having a baby girl. If she is correct, I think I will faint! I haven't had a feeling yet whether it is a boy or a girl, but I know I will!

I think about Peyton a lot and what he thinks about sharing his mommy. I also hope he knows that even though I am now carrying another baby I will never stop thinking or fighting for him. I will always advocate for him. I wonder what he is doing in Heaven and who is taking care of him? I hope he is looking down at us and smiling. I hope he is happy and feels at peace. I hope he knows how deeply we love and miss him. We will love you forever sweet baby boy.

*"What we have once enjoyed
and deeply loved,*

*We can never lose.
For all that we love deeply*

Becomes a part of us."

Helen Keller

11-03-2012

Lately, as I wait, I am so torn as to where my energies should be spent. I want to fight for Peyton, louder than I have been able to. But, I can't. I have to wait for "them" to tell me what they are/are not going to do for my son. I want to tell the world Peyton's story. I want to advocate for abusive head trauma. I want to speak about the trauma we have endured. How can building a case take so long?

I haven't run into Anna or Brett yet, but I know that someday I will. I think it's a small miracle that I haven't yet. *Thank you God, for not allowing our paths to cross.* You have known that I wasn't strong enough to endure that. There were months that I didn't know what I would do around her.

Trinity has come such a long way. She is my healthy little girl again. She rarely talks about what she witnessed, and she rarely cries about missing her brother. Her nightmares have been less. She can talk about Peyton without hysterically crying. I am so proud of my daughter. She will never understand how she pulled Jeremiah and I through this. She forced us to "get through" this, to "deal", to "cope", and to "live". She forced us up this mountain. Without her I would still be at the bottom treading through my misery. Trinity saved my life; she gave me something to live for.

I am currently 15 weeks pregnant with our new addition. I have this feeling that it is a girl, but we'll see. I was right with Trinity and Peyton! I know that I need to feel joy for our new baby, and I do. But I am just trying to juggle this feeling of being stuck in the middle. I am at that fork in the middle of the road because I don't have an answer yet of which path I must take. I will either have to accept that nothing will be done in Peyton's case or I will have to prepare for the trial for justice for my son. I want this baby to feel the joy I have for it. But I also feel guilt that I am distracted from the pregnancy because of

Peyton. I don't want this baby to feel like they will always live in Peyton's shadow. I want her to feel loved and cradled by our love.

The hard part for me these days is staying quiet and professional. My natural instinct would be to climb to the rooftops and scream to the world everything that we believe happened to our son. But, of course I don't, and I can't.

I think about Jeremiah a lot. He doesn't talk a lot about the loss of Peyton. I know, what else is there to say? I just hope he isn't keeping it all bundled up inside. I don't want it coming out in some negative way twenty years down the road.

For months I was so afraid that Jeremiah and I would be interrogated again, and I was worried that I wouldn't be able to handle it again. But now that I am stronger and less vulnerable, I am not afraid of that. In fact, after Peyton's death I was numb and terribly weak. But now, I wouldn't hold back, and I know that the anger over this whole situation would come pouring out. I wouldn't let them walk all over me. I'd probably take their heads off.

I still think about Anna, not as often, but still occasionally. Has she just convinced herself that nothing happened to Peyton in her care? How does she go on living? Does she feel remorse or guilt? Does she know that she will pay some day, sooner or later? Does she have nightmares about what she did to my son? Will she ever confess? Would she ever meet with me face to face? It is still so hard for me to understand how she can just continue to live her life. How didn't I notice her mental instability?

With the holidays coming up I feel a sense of anxiousness as this will be our first Thanksgiving and Christmas without our boy. And then, right after that our year mark of losing our beautiful son. I would never wish this pain on anyone. The agony never leaves. It's always there buried deep within me more noticeable some days than others. But it is always constant. I am still trying to understand this new life. *God, I believe you have carried me through so many dark months. I believe you have allowed me to cope and see rays of sunshine in my new life. I believe you are trying to take away my anger but, it is hard to pry from my fingertips.*

I have tried to do the best I can with coping with all of this. I am trying. When I hear of other people having tragedies my heart explodes for them in a way that it didn't before. So dearly, I don't want anyone else to hurt like we have. I know that I have a long way to go in my healing. I know that this is a terribly long process and I have a lot of mountain yet to climb. I have slipped but I haven't fallen yet. My progress is slow, steady, and oh, so humble.

"Dear Peyton,

I miss you so much. I wonder if there will ever be a day where I don't. I can't imagine that. It feels like yesterday that I last held you, changed you, fed you, rocked you, and cuddled with you. I know you are looking out for daddy, Trinity, and I. Have you forgiven Anna? I am trying not to let the hate take over. I am trying not to become toxic. When you were born, I always felt there was something special about you, like you were too good to be true. I think about you all the time, with everything I do. I am torn between missing you desperately and feeling so lucky to have had you. It is hard to feel the latter when my feelings of loss are still so strong. I am trying to be more positive; I am trying to continue living. I am trying to remember all the joyousness you made me feel. You smiled all the time. You made me so happy. I smiled all the time. You wanted me all the time, my special boy. How lucky I am to have had you. But, trust I will always carry you so deep in my heart. I will never exist without you. Baby boy, I am doing my best in this life. I can't wait until I will get to hold you so tight again. When that day comes, I will never let you go. I'll love you for forever sweet baby boy. ~Mommy"

The First Holidays Without Him

11-21-2012

Tomorrow will be our first Thanksgiving without Peyton. I have heard how the "firsts" of everything are so terribly difficult. I know the holiday season will be difficult for us as well. But I am also trying not to have any expectations of how we should be dealing with it. Today it has been exactly ten months since Peyton was declared dead. Ten months gone by and still we wait. No charges, no answers, no direction of movement. Still, we are stuck here in this place of unknown. For ten months we have heard nothing. How is this acceptable?

This weekend was Jeremiah's parents' Thanksgiving. My brother was also home for two days due to a business trip. On Sunday when we were all sitting in the living room watching football Trinity was playing and entertaining us. She was pretending to be a teacher. She grabbed one of Peyton's pictures and continued to tell her make believe class that "Anna throw Peyton James on the ground and she shake him and then the ambulance came and took Peyton to the hospital and Peyton died." She said "We really miss Peyton." That was all she said and then, she continued talking to her pretend classroom about other things. My brother sat there, hearing this from her for the first time in shock. He couldn't believe what he had just heard. He said, "We weren't even talking about Peyton, you didn't prompt her or anything. I can't believe she just said that just like it's no big deal and then she moves on to the next thing." I sat there wishing that my brother would have been the county attorney or the detectives or any of the "important people", whoever they are. All of those people have no idea what we deal with every day. They haven't heard it over and over again. I just wish they could sit and hear her and maybe then they would move or take a chance on prosecuting Anna. I just wish they would make her pay in some way.

How can she live with herself? How can she lie about what she did to my son? Ten months out, if I saw her, I still don't know what I would do. I wish I could go to her and beg her to tell the truth. As Peyton's mother I just wish I could bring justice and clarity to his name, his death. I want peace for him. I want peace for myself. I want peace for our family. I think we are getting there. We're doing the best we can. But I would never wish my worst enemy this pain, suffering and traumatization.

I have found myself reading spiritual works since Peyton's passing. I am currently reading *Proof Of Heaven* by Eben Alexander III. It is about a neurosurgeon who has a near death experience and while in a coma for seven days experiences Heaven. Ever since Peyton I yearn for some comfort that Peyton is happy and being taken care of. It haunts me that I couldn't keep him safe and I so desperately need to know that God is taking care of him; that God is tending to him like I would have been. But I miss him in this way that is so constant. Last night when reading I worried that maybe I didn't pray enough, that maybe I didn't beg for him hard enough. But I thought I did. I hope that God took him because he needed Peyton's joy in Heaven more than he thought we did here on Earth.

"Peyton,

Mommy misses you so much. We are trying to heal healthy. We're trying to miss you in healthy ways. However those ways are. I find myself taking breaks. Please know it is not because I stop missing you but because in order to stay healthy, I must. I just miss what "could/should have been". I miss the way my life was supposed to be. To outside people I look "normal", like maybe I've dealt with your loss. But our secret is that I will never be over losing you. I am trying to let go of some of the hate for "her" and maybe I am little by little. Of course, some days are better than others. And some days I am more hateful than others as well. Your sissy still talks about missing you, but her nightmares are fewer, as are her breakdowns. She will always love her Peyton James. She loved you so much and I know that in her little mind she wished she could have saved you. She was such a good big sister. Some of my anger/hate for this "woman" is that she took away so much from Trinity as well. She took away Trinity's pride and joy; you. I love you so much and I can't wait until I get to hold you and snuggle with you again. - Mommy"

12-06-2012

This afternoon I had a sonogram appointment at 4:00 p.m. I met Jeremiah there after school. For the last two months I have had this feeling that this baby is a girl. I had a feeling with Trinity and Peyton and was right with both! Since I was about six weeks along and we hadn't even confirmed to Trinity that we were having a baby she kept telling Jeremiah and I that mommy was going to have a baby girl. We got to the sonogram appointment and they escorted us back to the room. Now the third time going through this I didn't have the butterflies that I had the first two times. The technician moved the wand all over my belly and took all these measurements of the baby and the umbilical cord. At the very end she asked if we wanted her to check the gender. I looked up at Jeremiah and we both nodded. I told her that I had been having a feeling that it was a girl. She moved the wand and after some strategic aiming of the wand her response was "I agree". I smiled as this sense of peace came over me. Trinity was right! Trinity knew that we were having a baby girl. At that moment I knew that Peyton had been talking to her. I also felt like maybe this was his gift to our family. Maybe he gave us a girl as he knew how we were so deeply still mourning for him and that a baby boy now would be too painful. Maybe he knew that a baby girl would be different, yet joyous for our family. My baby boy still surrounds us!

After the sonogram I went to pick Trinity up from school. Her teacher asked to speak with me and said that Trinity had "talked" at nap time. She said it was nap time and Trinity sat up straight in her cot and proceeded to tell her that her mom is having a baby. She then went on to say, "I had a baby brother. His name is Peyton James. At my old daycare Anna hit him and then she throw him on the ground and then she shake him. The ambulance and the police come and take Peyton to the hospital but he died. We go visit Peyton at his grave now. I wanted to do something but I didn't know what to do. I wanted to save Peyton but I was watching TV. My mom and dad didn't know Anna was a bad person. I hope my mom has a baby girl because baby boys die."

I stood there and read all of this as her teacher had written it all down as I had asked her to do if Trinity talked. I just started crying. We are almost eleven months out and Trinity continues to tell the same story, although the order is sometimes reversed. I was surprised that Trinity talked to her teacher as she's only been her teacher for two weeks. Obviously, Trinity feels comfortable around her so that is good. There was nothing prompted or rehearsed about what Trinity said. She told her teacher this at around 1:00 pm. and hadn't last seen us since 7:00 a.m.

That bitch will never know the depths of her traumatization. She will never understand how deeply she has affected us all. She will never understand how deeply she has affected Trinity. It tears at my heart to hear Trinity talk about what happened or know that she is trying to process it all. She is my little warrior girl. She is so strong. She is so special for handling this like she is. I believe Peyton knew it would be easier for her to welcome a baby sister. *Thank you, my dear boy, for taking care of your sister.*

When we got Trinity home, we ate dinner and then asked Trinity to come in and talk to us in the kitchen. Jeremiah talked and told Trinity how mommy went to the doctor and we found out what mommy is going to have. We told her that the baby is a girl. She smiled big and got excited and then looked at me and said, "Mom, I tell you that." I said, "Trinity, I know, but how did you know?" She said, "I don't know, I just know." I said, "But how?" And impatiently she replied, "Mom, I just know."

12-12-2012

This afternoon at work I had a meltdown. I had to leave a meeting and go straight to my office. I just started bawling and I needed to talk to my dad. It has been almost three weeks since my last counseling appointment and I think it is evident. Maybe this is a reminder that I still need it and that I can't go any longer than two weeks between each session.

The Loss of a Child

"The moment that I knew you had died
My heart split in two,
The one side filled with memories
The other died with you.

I often lay awake at night
When the world is fast asleep,
And take a walk down memory lane
With tears upon my cheek.

Remembering you is easy
I do it every day,
But missing you is a heartache
That never goes away.

I hold you tightly within my heart
And there you will remain,

*Life has gone on without you
But it never will be the same.*

*For those who still have their children
Treat them with tender care,
You will never know the emptiness
As when you turn and they are not there.*

*Don't tell me that you understand
Don't tell me that you know,
Don't tell me that I will survive
How I will surely grow.*

*Don't tell me this is just a test
That I am truly blessed,
That I am chosen for the task
Apart from all the rest.*

*Don't come at me with answers
That can only come from me,
Don't tell me how my grief will pass
That I will soon be free.*

*Don't stand in pious judgment
Of the bonds I must untie,
Don't tell me how to grieve
Don't tell me when to cry.*

*Accept me in my ups and downs
I need someone to share,
Just hold my hand and let me cry
And say, 'My friend, I care.'"*

Author Unknown

12-14-2012

Today I had my counseling appointment. I have had so much anger slowly creeping back into my mind. For a couple of months, I had tried to let that go and was doing good. But lately that anger has re-emerged. During our meeting I talked about how someone working with our family had a conversation with one of the detectives. This person started off by saying to him, "I have been working with Courtney and Jeremiah Pottebaum and I can tell you that they didn't do this to their son." Supposedly they had a conversation about our polygraphs and how their department received mine and I passed with flying colors but that they never received Jeremiah's. I told the person working with our family that Jeremiah's was at the county attorney's office and to please let Brown know this. Aren't any of these departments working with or communicating together??? The officer then said to our representative that they still wanted us to come in and take a polygraph through them. He then made the comment that there are more people that are innocent that fail polygraphs then guilty people fail them. This comment by him really bothered me. Why have any of us do them in the first place if they don't mean anything? I believe that it is a control issue with the department. The only thing I can think of is that by us doing it again it gives them another opportunity to interrogate us. That's the thing, I would handle another one much better this time. All the pent-up anger that I have would come out on them. I would tear their damn heads off! I would question them why they can't break her? I would question why Anna and Brett were treated so differently than Jeremiah and I? I felt like so many things he was saying were mixed messages. Our representative made the comment that he told her, "It's not me that needs convincing, it's the county attorney". It seems that all of these departments just deflect any attention away from them and blame the other one. He also made the comment to our representative that he had heard that Anna and Brett were having marriage problems. Our representative said that their gut feeling without him directly saying anything was that he knows that Anna did this to Peyton. This deep part of me wants to scream, "Wake the fuck up, of course she did this!"

The officer made the comment that they are going to look at Peyton's case again come the beginning of the year. I hope we have an answer back from the state by then. I'll never understand everyone's complacency about the death of my child.

My Mommy is a Survivor

*"My Mommy is a survivor
or so I've heard it said,
But I can hear her crying at night
when all others are in bed.*

*I watch her lay awake at night
and go to hold her hand,
She doesn't know I'm with her
to help her understand.*

*But like the sands on the beach
that never wash away,
I watch over my surviving mommy
who thinks of me each day.*

*She wears a smile for others
a smile of disguise!
But through Heaven's door
I see tears flowing from her eyes.*

*My mommy tries to cope with death
to keep my memory alive,
But anyone who knows her
knows it is her way to survive.*

*As I watch over my surviving mom
through Heaven's open door,
I try to tell her that
angels protect me forevermore.*

*I know that doesn't help her
or ease the burden she bears,
So if you get a chance, go visit her
and show her that you care.*

*For no matter what she says
no matter what she feels,
My surviving mommy has a broken heart
That time won't ever heal."*

My Daddy is a Survivor Too....

"My Daddy is a survivor too
which is no surprise to me,
He's always been like a lighthouse
that helps you cross a stormy sea.

But, I walk with my daddy each day
to lift him when he's down,
I wipe the tears he hides from others
He cries when no one's around.

I watch him sit up late at night
with my picture in his hand,
He cries as he tries to grieve alone
and wishes he could understand.

My daddy is like a tower of strength
He's the greatest of them all!
But, there are times when he needs to cry
Please be there when he falls.

Hold his hand or pat his shoulder
And tell him it's OK,
Be his strength when he's sad
Help him mourn in his own way.

Now, as I watch over my precious dad
from the Heavens up above,
I'm so proud that he's a survivor
And, I can still feel his love."

Author Unknown

12-14-2012

I talked to my sister today after work. I know the next obstacle will be taking down Peyton's room and getting it ready for Tenley. That is going to be so hard for me. I have only been in his room 6-7 times since January. I keep his door closed all the time. His six months clothes are still in his drawers, new clothes still hang in his closet, and everything else is as it always has been. Part of me just wants to avoid this part. A friend of mine suggested talking to our pastor and asking him to come and bless Peyton's room and ask him to look over Tenley. My sister offered to fly home in the spring to help me if I needed it and truly, I might need it. I am so lucky to have such a wonderful family. What would I have done without them? How would I ever have gotten through this? To my family, I am forever indebted to all of you. Thank you for loving me and carrying me through this.

12-15-2012

Today we had Jeremiah's family's Christmas. Trinity had so much fun playing with her cousins and opening presents. I sat there with an emptiness today. My boy was not there, he was missing. I just looked around imagining what it would have been like with him still here. I long for the days where I don't feel this heaviness in my heart. I long for the days when Peyton was still here. I long for the true happiness I used to feel before all of this happened.

Jeremiah and I are getting through this, somehow. The pain has started to become manageable as life has continued, but it never goes away. There is this black hole that exists deep within our souls and it can easily consume us if we are not careful. We struggle everyday trying to balance continuing while still grieving the loss of Peyton.

"Peyton James,

Today you would have had fun playing with your cousins. I imagined hearing your deep belly laugh as you ran through Nana and Papa's house. I imagined sitting with you and helping you unwrap your presents and then having Trinity beg to help you. I love you so much. Thank you so much for being my perfect baby boy. Not a day goes by that I don't think about you. My heart strings long for you in a way that I cannot explain to anyone else. - Mommy"

01-03-2013

Today Jeremiah and I had a sonogram appointment to see Tenley and get our 3-D video. She looks like our baby! She has the thin upper lip and a full bottom lip, the button nose, the small chin, and the round cheeks. She looks like Trinity and Peyton in their pictures. It was good to see her moving and kicking and made me excited for the days when I get to hold her! Once she arrives, I may never want to put her down. I may never want to share her with anyone else.

When we got home, I noticed that our answering machine was blinking with a message. I played and listened as a man from the Sioux City Journal called saying that he is working on a piece and in a couple of weeks it will be Peyton's one-year anniversary from his death. He made a comment about no charges being filed and wondering how we were helping police and wondering if there was any information that could help to lead to an arrest. I stood there frozen and played the message a couple of times. WHAT??? I wanted to pick up the phone and agree to meet him and tell him everything but then, reality came flooding in. What could we really say? I know that our victim advocate will tell us that we can't say anything, and we would never want to jeopardize Peyton's case. But we have been silent and professional for almost one whole year. But now I just want to tell them everything. I'm sick of holding this in, I'm sick feeling like we have to protect her. We deserve an answer. We deserve some decisions by the "people in charge". One year later, how can they continue to give us nothing? I am so angry, bitter, frustrated. It's not FAIR!!! Why won't they advocate for us or our son?? Why do we, as secondary victims have to be put in the position of watching what we say? *God, I haven't asked for your help for many months. I've tried to do this on my own. But now I need you. This month will be very hard for me and I need your help. Please give us some sign or some direction on how to handle this. Please help us now.*

01-04-2013

To: Captain Cowell, Sergeant Brown, Detective Johnson, & Detective Anthony

My name is Courtney Pottebaum and I am Peyton Pottebaum's mother. In approximately three weeks it will be the year marker of Peyton's death from injuries he acquired at daycare. I never thought I would ever lose a child, nor would I ever have imagined that a year later I would not have resolution to his death. My son died almost one whole year ago and the daycare provider has still not been held accountable for what I believe and know she did to him. I have no closure to what happened to my son. I visit Peyton at his grave without understanding why I had to bury him. Why was my son taken? Why did this happen to our family? I have sent this December's Christmas card with this letter. We tried to act happy for our daughter's sake but deep down the anger and devastation resonates deep within us because as we struggled to get through the holidays, the daycare provider got to spend it happily with her family as if my son never died.

After Peyton died, we were in such a state of trauma, denial, disbelief, numbness, and terrible shock. For months we wanted to believe that Peyton's death must be due to some terrible accident that "she" was covering up out of fear. An accident is an easier pill to swallow than having to admit that someone you trusted hurt your child. We thought we knew her, and we trusted her. As a mother it haunts me that I took my children to someone like her and that whatever signs there were, I missed. I will never know if Peyton's injuries were a one-time event or if there were other accounts to either Peyton or my daughter Trinity. Unfortunately, I now believe the latter as Trinity has made statements to confirm this.

Peyton's trauma and death significantly affected our daughter Trinity. Almost immediately she started talking about what she saw the daycare provider do to her brother and she would demonstrate it on baby dolls at home and at school. Her teacher had to remove the babies from her classroom to protect the eyes and ears of the other kids in her class. She was having constant nightmares and night terrors. Do you know what it is like to run into your daughter's room numerous times a night as she wails and shakes and says that she doesn't want Anna to hurt her baby brother anymore? I would hold her tight, weeping myself and tell her that she was safe at home and that she would never go to Anna's house again. We couldn't even escape this trauma in our sleep. We got Trinity into a play therapist, Erin White who has much expertise in working with children who have been abused or who have witnessed abuse. We don't know exactly what Trinity told or demonstrated to her therapist, but her therapist did indicate that Trinity had talked to her and that the therapist was sure Trinity had witnessed what happened to her brother. We desperately needed direction in how to help our daughter through this trauma. I understand that one of your detectives has told our victim advocate, Shelly Martin that anything Trinity has said is unreliable and inadmissible due to her age. The bottom line to us is that Trinity's consistent story, her consistent demonstration, and her emotional and physical reactions only confirm that Trinity witnessed what happened to Peyton. Trinity has consistently told us, our family, friends, her teachers, and random strangers in the Wal-Mart check-out line that, "Anna hit Peyton James in the head, she throw him on the carpet, and she shake him." (Sometimes the order is mixed around.) This is our reality.

In the recent month a message was also given to us that one of your officers wants us to come in and do a polygraph through your department. Currently, we have no interest in jumping through any more hoops when it appears not to affect the outcome. Please understand the most traumatizing thing I have ever gone through is pulling my son off life support and watching him turn blue from head to toe. The second most traumatizing thing I have ever gone through is your interrogation in which your officers suggested and questioned if Jeremiah and I had anything to do with our son's death. The third most traumatizing thing I have ever gone through is doing a polygraph examination in which we had to prove we had nothing to do with our son's death. We shouldn't have had to go through any of those hoops. We never did anything wrong. A few months back Detective Johnson made the comment that you have three suspects: "Me, Jeremiah, and Anna" and that you couldn't prove anything. Please understand that the mere fact that Jeremiah and I are still labeled as suspects in our son's death makes us angry, outraged, terribly offended, and to me, it's unacceptable. I understand that there is a difference between knowing who did something and being able to prove it. But, just because "the important people" can't prove it, why are we still being punished?

There is a topic I feel we need to address. During my own interrogation I was the one that volunteered wholeheartedly to do a polygraph and had every intention of doing so. But I need to explain why my lawyer refused to have me do one with your department. What you may not realize is that I feel you biased Peyton's investigation by allowing Tori Henderson to be on his case and do my interrogation. Many years ago, when I was in graduate school and worked at a local gym, I would watch Tori Henderson and Timothy Black, Anna's brother-in-law, come in at nights together and shoot hoops, work out, and then leave together. I knew they had a close relationship and that she was a friend of his family. After my interrogation I also learned that Tori was/is a social media friend of Anna Black's. Please understand that I was outraged that one of the officer's that did my interrogation and made suggestions of me hurting my son was "friends" with the person that I believe hurt my son. Tori's mere presence in the investigation put us on the defense. Right or wrong, it made us feel like your department was protecting the sister-in-law of 'one of your own.' Tori Henderson should never have been allowed on Peyton's case due to her past relationship with members of the Black family. This is the reason that our family advised Jeremiah and I to seek counsel. After informing our lawyers of all the background information we knew, they were adamant that we do not do polygraphs through your department.

It has been almost one whole year since I have seen Anna Black. I believe that God has provided this small miracle as he knew that for many, many months if I saw her that something bad would happen. What does a parent do when they come face to face with the person that killed their child? Almost one year out and I can't promise how I will react when I see her again for the first time.

The bottom line to any of this is that we doted on Peyton while he lived, and we will continue to fight for him now that he's dead. We want peace and justice brought to his death more than your department could ever imagine. But more than anything we want "her" to be held accountable for Peyton's death and the trauma that she has inflicted on our entire family for the last twelve months of our lives. I hope "she" has nightmares about what I believe she did to my son every night for the rest of her life.

Please don't stop fighting for our son. Please find a way to break her so that the truth comes out.

Respectfully,

Jeremiah and Courtney Pottebaum

Photo Credit: Lola's Hope-Stop Shaken Baby Syndrome

PEYTON POTTEBAUM

07-23-2011 – 01-21-2012

"Our story, Peyton's story, and the accusations we assert have made some people uncomfortable. I say, if you're uncomfortable hearing it, imagine living through it. This should NOT happen to any child and in a perfect world, if it did, there would be consequences. In Peyton's case, the people 'on the top' remain motionless and that is wrong. If all cases were wrapped up in a bow, we wouldn't need lawyers."

01-14-2013

I can't believe I am already 26 weeks pregnant tomorrow! My belly is so big, and I feel so huge. Most likely, only 11 weeks left before we get to meet baby Tenley! Trinity has been really excited about Tenley. She hugs and kisses my belly all the time and tells me about all the things she is going to do with her little sister. In a way, Tenley has become a sort of therapy for Trinity. She gives her something to look forward to and be happy about.

In this weird sort of 'flip of the coin' this pregnancy also brings back memories of Peyton for Trinity. In the fall Trinity wasn't talking as much about what happened to Peyton. But, more so recently Trinity has been talking about what she saw Anna do to her brother and about missing him. She has also started to have nightmares again and ends up in our bed almost every night. When I asked her what her nightmares are about, she said, "sometimes about what Anna did to Peyton and sometimes about monsters." I suppose all the talk about Tenley brings back so much with Peyton. The other day on the way home from daycare Trinity said, "Mom, please don't take Tenley to Anna's house. I don't want Anna to hurt her." I just sat there and felt sad for Trinity. She is so happy to have Tenley, but she is so afraid that she will lose her too. She is afraid that the monster known as Anna will take Tenley away like she took Peyton. Trinity will be so protective of her little sister and I will probably worry in a way that I didn't worry before Peyton's death.

My father talked to the county attorney's office last week who told my dad that the state has hired someone that is a neuropathologist and forensic pathologist who specializes in 'shaken baby' and 'traumatic brain injuries' d to review Peyton's case. He said that pending her review, IF the county decides to prosecute that this doctor would be the lead witness. I guess I felt good that I know that they are truly trying to do everything they can. Maybe my frustration with the county attorneys has to do more with my frustration with the system or lack of it in my mind. In five days, my son will have been dead for one whole year and yet here we are still waiting for answers.

Yesterday I had a training to go over reporting of suspected child abuse. As a counselor we often do these reports. After the training when this woman was on her way out of the building I ran after her and asked to speak with her. I introduced myself and explained that I was Peyton Pottebaum's mother. Her eyes got big as she realized who she was talking to. She went on to mention that she has our report on her desk and was just on the phone with the county attorney's office asking for a meeting to go over Peyton's case. I just started talking. I told her about Trinity seeing Ms. Erin and what she said to her about what she saw happen to her brother. I told her about the documentation that Trinity's teachers have been keeping pertaining to what she has said to them. I told her about her teacher having to remove the baby dolls from the classroom because she would demonstrate what she saw Anna do to her brother. I explained that all of this was turned in to the county attorney's office and that I would like for her to have a copy of it for her records. She said that was information she needed.

I bawled the entire time and told her everything I could think of. She was very sincere, and I felt like she was trying to comfort me. I just had this feeling that she "knows" it was Anna and what she likely did. She said that she was going to obtain all the information about what Trinity has said. *Please let this connection be a positive step for Peyton's case.*

One Year Later

01-21-2013

One year ago, today, down to the hour and minute Jeremiah and I were confronted with the overwhelming decision to take our beautiful baby boy Peyton off life support as he was declared "brain dead". We laid with him in his bed as the doctor unhooked the tubing and turned off the ventilator. We waited for his chest to rise but it didn't. Peyton laid there lifeless. He started to turn blue quickly, his eyelids, his lips, his fingers and toes. Our beautiful baby boy was dead. We had spent the last two days in the hospital clinging for any sign of hope, praying for a miracle, hoping the doctors had missed something, and begging and pleading with God to save our son. But even that wasn't enough. Peyton had sustained such traumatic head injuries that he couldn't be fixed. Doctor after doctor explained that if he did live, he would be severely disabled. But that didn't matter, we just needed our son to live. We needed him to be given the chance of life.

For reasons that I will never understand, our deck of cards in this life were stacked against us. After two days, Peyton lost his life. We laid there in disbelief and shock. How did this happen? What happened to my beautiful baby? We had left him and his sister in the care of someone we trusted and an hour and a half later I was notified that he wasn't breathing with no indication of head trauma. There was never a consistent story provided or an explanation of what happened to him. Approximately six hours and eleven minutes after being admitted to the hospital doctors discovered that Peyton had a severe closed head injury. My baby laid in a hospital bed for six hours while his brain continued to bleed and swell because nobody knew there had been head trauma. By the time doctors discovered Peyton's injuries, his prognosis was very grim, all because the person that hurt him remained silent about what had happened to him. Because of that omission, that silence, my son never had a chance.

Twelve months later and this person has remained silent, acting as though they don't know how my son was injured. My four-year-old daughter was present when my son was injured and witnessed what happened to him. She has had a very detailed, consistent story for twelve months but because of her age she is considered an unreliable witness. My daughter experienced such a state of trauma from what she saw happen to her brother. For months she didn't sleep and had constant nightmares about what she saw happen. She would wake up numerous times a night crying, trembling, and saying that she didn't want to go back to Anna's house.

The anger and resentment I have for this person is unexplainable. For months we were in such a state of denial and disbelief that we defended this person, trying to believe that there must have been some tragic accident and this person was just too scared to say what happened. We couldn't believe that someone we trusted our babies with could hurt them. I mean we would have known if this person was capable of that, wouldn't we? We would have seen signs, right? But at the time, we saw nothing. Someone we trusted hurt our baby boy, traumatized our daughter, traumatized us, and has continued to lie about having anything to do with our son's injuries.

Due to the circumstances, Jeremiah and I had to undergo interrogations and polygraph examinations for authorities to understand and believe that we had nothing to do with our son's injuries and death. How dare the perpetrator put us through that? This person took our son and by remaining silent, directed the blame of Peyton's injuries on us, his parents. I never knew I could feel hate like I have felt for this person. This person has put us through hell and by continuing to remain silent they do that every day. Our son is dead. One year later and we have no closure to his death. More than anything

I want justice and peace brought to Peyton's death. For twelve months the person that hurt him has gotten to go about their life, enjoying their own family without having to acknowledge that my son is dead. I hope this person has nightmares every night about what they did to my son.

Much of my anger has been directed at the County Attorney's office and the police department, because they are the only ones that can hold this person accountable. I do believe they are doing everything they can, but on my very sad days, that's not enough. I pray often that GOD will give them the resources, tools, and abilities to prove who harmed my son. More than anything, I want this person to hurt like I do but, no matter how severe the consequences would be, that will never happen. She could never comprehend the detriment of loss and trauma she has caused our family to feel. Some days the only thing that keeps me going is knowing that in the end, God knows what she did.

I can't wait for the day when I can scream on the rooftops and tell everyone what I believe happened to my son. But, now I can't, and I won't. I wouldn't jeopardize the chance that the person responsible for Peyton's death could be held accountable. On my bad days it's hard to do that. It's hard to be professional and "politically correct" when what I really want to do is scream to everyone everything I know.

We will continue to fight for our son forever, for always.

"Peyton James,

Exactly one year ago, daddy and I laid with you as the doctors unhooked you from the ventilator. We watched as your chest no longer raised. My heart was ripped out as we realized you were gone. Our beautiful, happy, perfect baby boy was gone for reasons we still didn't understand. We had spent the last two days in the hospital begging and pleading with God to save you, for God to provide you life. We would have done anything to save you. Our worlds were shattered. Daddy, Trinity, and I think about you every day. Our hearts will never be the same. We long for the day when we will get to hold you, rock you, feed you, and snuggle with you. When that day comes, I will never let you go. Daddy and I will never stop fighting for you. More than anything, we so desperately want justice and peace brought to your death. We will always fight for you, forever, for always. I love you so much. - Mommy"

01-27-2013

Last Tuesday one of our family representatives called up Captain Cowell and asked him to meet with him. He did and told our family representative that Jeremiah and I weren't suspects. He also said that "they" know that Jeremiah dropped off a healthy baby boy. He made several comments to our family member explaining that "in order to arrest Anna" they would need to do this or that. He also explained that he needed to meet with Jeremiah and I to cover up some holes in the investigation.

We were relieved to hear some of this information but our trust issue with the police department runs very deep. I know they can lie to anyone to get what they ultimately want or feel they need.

On Friday morning Jeremiah and I went to meet Captain Cowell. He never said the things to us that he said to our family representative. I suppose he can't. He also said quite a few things that were very hurtful to Jeremiah and I. He said that our behavior was not typical of parents who have lost a child. He was very concerned about this as if it was "weird" or odd and he still questioned us. He said that on that Saturday morning at the hospital Jeremiah and I were supposed to be there at 8:00 and didn't arrive until 8:30 and that I walked in with a cup of coffee in my hand. Supposedly this made them suspicious of us as they didn't think this was normal behavior. *Jesus Christ, I hadn't slept in two days, was an emotional mess and barely functioning. I was doing my best.* We were also waiting to pick up family at the airport to bring them to the hospital with us. I don't get it.. How were we supposed to act through this last year? Nobody gave us a pamphlet or book telling us what to do, how to act, and how to cope with our son's death! We've done the best we can. How dare anyone else tell us what is right or wrong in this situation! Captain Cowell was very adamant that we do the polygraph with them. Whatever I guess, Jeremiah told them he'd take his next week and I will take mine after the pregnancy. Again, through this whole thing we are jumping through hoops. He mentioned that Jeremiah and I weren't interrogated, that we were questioned. I made the point of telling him that wasn't my perception. He said, 'you either trust me, or you don't." He made the comment that, "guilty people get lawyers." He had an array of other so-called holes.

I left more pissed than when I arrived. His comments bothered me so much. Our advocate ran into Cowell later that day. Cowell didn't seem to say much to her except again, that our behavior wasn't typical of parents who have lost a child. I guess what I am sick of is his insinuations against Jeremiah and I. Why don't they or can't they focus on Anna? The whole process is shitty and very re-traumatizing to the victims. Our justice system sucks because really, there is no such thing as justice.

01-29-2013

One year later and my emotions are still so day to day and so up and down. I am having more good days than bad ones, but the bad ones still hurt so badly. Losing a child due to homicide changes the whole healing process for grieving parents.

01-31-2013

Jeremiah had his polygraph with the police station scheduled this afternoon. Ever since Peyton's death the only thing we ever hear from the police is that we have never done a polygraph through them. To appease them and make the case hopefully push forward Jeremiah got his scheduled. He didn't even let his lawyer know he was doing it. He just wanted it over with. The polygraph detective through the police station said he won't do mine until after I give birth to Tenley, which I respect so much. I was so nervous for him to have to take one again. I have had people say, "you didn't do anything wrong, just go in there and answer questions and be done with it." Of course, we know we didn't do anything wrong, but taking a polygraph is terribly frightening. In the back of your mind you are so afraid that something won't register right.

Jeremiah called me a little after 5:00 pm. to let me know he was done and that he passed. I could tell he felt so relieved and inside I felt so relieved too. To me, it is another hoop that we jumped through that hopefully will help get us closer to them arresting Anna. Now Jeremiah can say that not only has he passed a polygraph but that he has passed two of them.

A year later, another hoop we jumped through. Peyton, we won't stop.

Cuddled in Heaven

"We had so little time to share
Too soon, I had to leave,
I know how much you love me
I know how much you grieve.

I know how sharp your pain is
I feel the aching in your hearts,
My life so quickly ended
Before it barely had a start.

I remember how you held me
And kissed my face and hands,

*You cuddled me so gently
But, God had other plans.*

*I was your perfect angel
From God you knew I came,
Suddenly he called me home again
And now God holds my hand.*

*I know you'll always miss me
I understand your pain is hard to bear,
Just remember that I'm in heaven
And we'll see each other there.*

*So smile when you think of me
And wipe away all of your tears,
I'm cuddled now in heaven
By our family members here.*

*I'm waiting here in heaven
And on the day we meet again,
I'll be the first to smile and greet you
When God calls you home to him."*

Author: Charlotte Collins

02-10-2013

Last night Jeremiah and I went out to eat and to a movie with a few of our friends. I don't know how long it's been since Jeremiah and I actually went out on a date and actually laughed and had fun. It felt really good. We have had such supportive good friends. They are always supporting us no matter and they are so easy and fun to be with. For most of the conversation we talked about normal day to day things but of course, talk soon turned to Peyton's case. That's the thing I appreciate so much about our friends; they never act like they are sick of hearing or talking about Peyton's case. They realize that this is our life, our reality and that no matter what we can't escape this either. They talk to us passionately about our son every time we bring him up. We can never repay them for all of their support.

During part of the conversation Anna's social media page got brought up. I never look at her page, as I can't. The anger I have for her is too much. But last night we all looked at it and this terribly consuming rage for her took over within me. To see her happy on her page made this rage inside me want to explode. How dare she experience any sort of happiness or bliss. We all had heard rumors that Anna and Brett were having marriage problems, but on her page there was a recent picture of them posted together three days ago. I felt instantly sick to my stomach. So badly I have wanted all the rumors to be true. I have wanted some type of validation that they are hurting or struggling. I want their lives torn apart as ours has been. I want that bitch to lose this semblance of life. I want her to have everything taken from her including her marriage and her son, and I want that bitch to rot in hell. That is what I want.

Jeremiah handles this disappointment better than me. I become so focused on it that I become removed from my normal daily life. I constantly think about it, dwell about it. He made the comment that he holds firm that her day is coming, that her world will crash. *Please dear God, please let this be correct. I have tried to deal with my son's death professionally and with hope. Please make this woman pay in a way that we can't. Please let her hurt like I do.*

I am getting to that place where I want to post on Peyton's page (Justice for Peyton Pottebaum) what happened to him. I want to tell about Peyton's injuries and say what he died from. I want to tell people that Trinity witnessed this happen. Without telling "who" harmed him I want to say what happened to him.

This morning Trinity and I went into Peyton's room and we took the clothes out of his dresser. I tried to do this last weekend, but I just couldn't. We brought up boxes of newborn girls clothes for Tenley and went through the clothes and placed them in the dresser. The room is starting to resemble the idea that a little girl may be inhabiting it. That's the hard part for me now because to me, it's still Peyton's room. Right now, I can't say it's Tenley's room. Sometimes when I go to say the name of the room I am torn between saying "Peyton's room" or "Tenley's room". Trinity started talking about the morning at daycare and how Peyton was hurt. This time she said, "That Anna hit him in the head, she shake him hard, and she throw him on the carpet. She said that Anna left him on the carpet crying and she left the room. She said that Peyton stopped breathing and Anna was carrying him and breathing into his mouth." I felt so hopeless and so hurt for her. Then she started crying harder.

She said, "Mom, why didn't you save Peyton? Why didn't you come to Anna's house and save Peyton? Mom, I tried but I didn't know what to do because she was bigger than me. I was crying and Anna say that 'it's going to be ok'. Mom, where were you? Why did you let her hurt Peyton? Mom, I was really scared. I wasn't a good sister because I couldn't stop Anna from hurting my baby brother."

I started crying and reached over to her and hugged her so tight. I said, "Trinity, I am so sorry Anna hurt Peyton. I didn't know she was a bad person. I never would have taken you and Peyton to her house if I had known. Mommy drove as fast as she could to the hospital to be with Peyton. I wish I could have saved Peyton too. I am so sorry you had to see Anna do that to Peyton. You were such a good big sister and there is nothing you could have done to save Peyton. Anna was bigger than you... ".

Trinity, "Mom, why did you take us to Anna's house? I wish you would have taken Peyton to Building Blocks."

Me, "Trinity, I promise you or Tenley will never go back to Anna's house. You are safe now and Tenley will go to Building Blocks like you."

I sat there holding her with rage pouring out of my pores. We are over one year out from Peyton's passing and my little girl still recalls every detail of what happened that morning. That bitch has caused so much anguish to Trinity. I hope she rots in hell.

03/15/2013

Finally, Anna has been identified as a 'child abuser' to Peyton and placed on the Central Abuse Registry for 10 years! She can never have a licensed daycare while she is on the registry! To me, this is our first victory. I want other people to know what she did to my son. I want to keep her from watching other babies. I want to keep her from hurting other babies. This is not a prosecution but at least, this protects other kids from her abuse.

Our Rainbow Baby

04/18/2013

Our beautiful baby girl Tenley was delivered today by C-section. She was 7 lbs. 15 oz.; such a big baby for me to carry!! She is healthy and just precious. We are so lucky to have this baby girl! We are so excited to have a baby in our home again. I feel so blessed to have her and feel like this baby girl is going to bring so much joy to our lives. *Thank you, God, for giving us what you knew we needed. Thank you, Peyton, for helping to deliver such a special package to us.*

Isn't she beautiful???! We are so, so, lucky to have her.

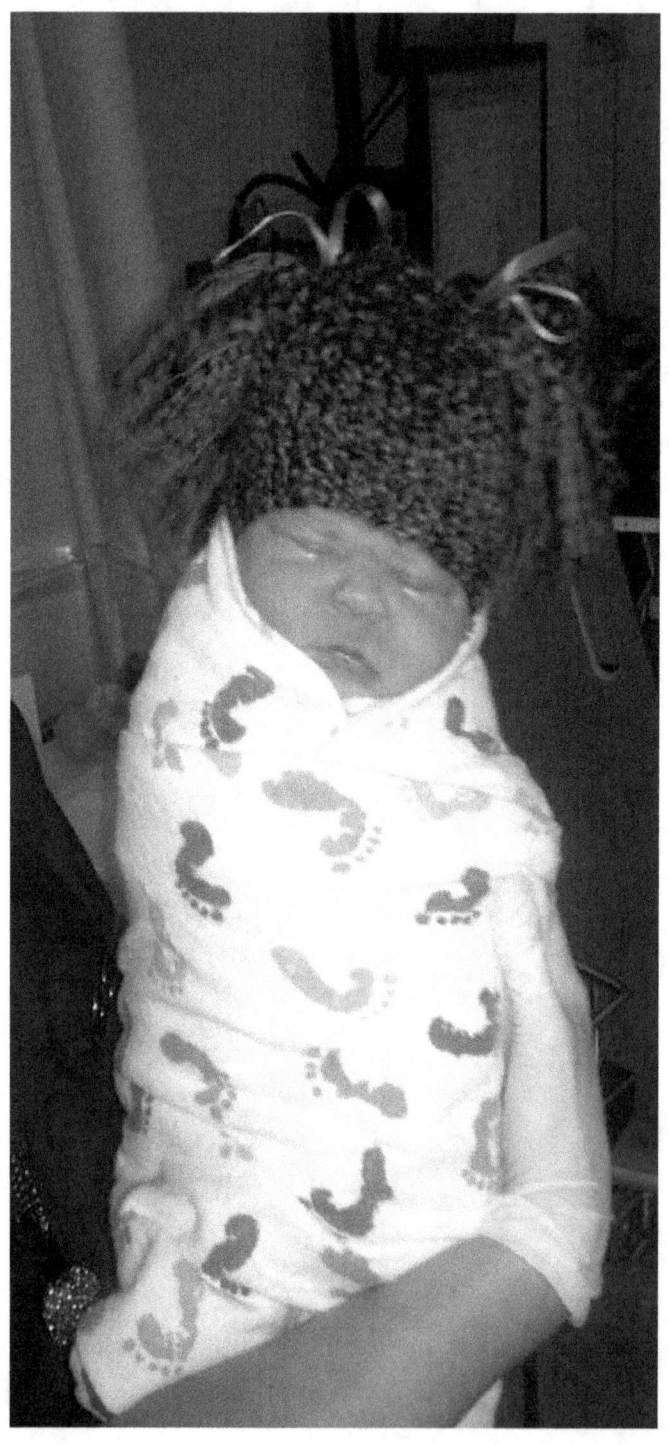

08-06-2013

"Peyton",

Eighteen months later and I have no closure on your death and all of the professionals who are supposed to be fighting for you are silent participants. To be honest, I don't know if I can even call them that.

I have so much anxiety about leaving Tenley when I go back to work full time. If I would have been home with you this would never have happened. But financially I have to work, at least for now.

Daddy and I ran the "Tough Mudder" for you. I hope we made you proud. There were so many times I thought about quitting but I didn't. I didn't because we were doing it for you, and I wanted to show you that I'll never stop fighting for you.

Do you visit daddy and I when we are sleeping? Do you watch over Tenley? Tenley is almost four months old already. I lost you at six months. I always worry about SIDS with Tenley and check on her through the night. I did the same with you. If only, I would've realized that I would have much bigger things to worry about. It haunts me that there could have been and probably were other accounts of harm done to you that I didn't know. It haunts me to think that you were being hurt and I kept taking you back there. Please know, I didn't know and still, there's so much I will never know.

I can't believe you would be two-years-old! I miss you so much. I love you to the moon and back my special boy. I ache to hold you and snuggle with you again. Those days can't come soon enough. ~ Mommy"

The Big Day

10-16-2013

Today was supposed to be the big day. The day that "they", the important people, would tell me that my baby boy was finally getting justice. But that again, didn't happen.

For weeks we have known about this meeting and waited at the edge of our seats for this "justice" to finally come. We've only been waiting for 22 months.

We walked into the county courthouse. We took the elevator to the 3rd floor and were greeted by our head county attorney. We were taken to a conference room. We were given copies of a report done by the attorney general's office and asked to read through them. I started to read the report. As I read line by line by line it became quickly apparent that this report was documenting all of the reasons that "they" would not be pursuing my son's case. I just kept reading hoping that I was jumping to the wrong conclusions. But, I wasn't. The last page of the report was very clear. According to the information they felt they did or didn't have, they would not be pursuing criminal charges in Peyton's case.

The county attorney and the assistant county attorney were somewhat transparent and maybe even slightly sympathetic. The assistant attorney general quite frankly, was an ass. He was very removed, very unemotional, very "not on our side". I felt that he was defending Anna. He showed no remorse for our son and kept making the comment that "Since they didn't know "who" inflicted Peyton's injuries." For me, as a grieving mother I was so offended and hurt by his lack of empathy or concern for the death of my son. I tried to be professional and assertive in my questions and my responses. I tried to explain my gratitude, but I am disheartened by this outcome and lack of justice for my son. I tried to be empathic to them as they stood in the line of fire of our family. I thought just maybe, that I would get the same respect back, but he gave none. Maybe out of burnout of doing this for 30 years, maybe out of defensiveness of feeling attacked, or guilt over not being able to bring justice to my precious son. But, whatever the reason for his lack of empathy, it was very transparent.

The county attorney and assistant county attorney seemed more sympathetic, more empathetic. They seemed more disappointed in the outcome. Maybe they were, maybe they weren't. As Peyton's mother I sat there so badly wanting them to feel and understand our intense pain and trauma these last 22 months. There was nothing I could say or do to make them even slightly comprehend our pain. As they listened to me their eyes remained glossed over, no semblance of pain or hurt. I would do anything to bring my son back.

For 22 months I have sat patiently waiting for "justice" to prevail and hope to drive me every day to function. But now, we are given the final answer, which is **NO**. They won't take a chance on my son. It is sad to me that one can be honest but punished, yet lie and get away scott free. This underlying principle in our legal system is wrong. I felt wronged by three. Peyton will not get justice, Trinity will not get justice for the trauma she witnessed, and Jeremiah and I will not get justice or clarity to our name.

How can Brett remain married to her? How can he believe her?

I will never understand this life. I don't understand the purpose. I believe in God, but I question the purpose of our suffering. I will get up one more day to "fight" this life. The injustice of Peyton's death is the cross that we will bear.

God, please hold my hand. Walk me through this. I am angry at you and hurt by this circumstance. I miss my son and the life that should be. I hurt for us and all the people that are fooled by her false identity.

11/24/2013

Jeremiah, Trinity, Tenely and I were all in the kitchen talking while getting ready to eat dinner. Trinity became silent and then said, "Mom, can I talk to you in your room?"

Me: "Of Course."

Trinity ran up to my bedroom and flopped down on my bed and started crying.

I said, "Trinity, what is wrong, what is going on?"

She said, "Mom, I really miss my baby brother Peyton. I just want to hold him and say good-bye to him and then he can go back to dead. Mom, I didn't say goodbye to him. Remember that night in the hospital with bandages on his head. I was scared and I didn't say goodbye."

I just sat there as tears collected up in my eyes. Oh my gosh, she remembers. She remembers the night we had to pull him off of life support. She remembers that we brought her in to say goodbye to him. And she was scared and didn't want to hug him, touch him, or even look at him. She remembers that moment and she wishes she would have said goodbye. I started crying and hugged her and explained that Peyton can't come back from being dead but that he knows she loves him and misses him.

She continues, "Mom, I think about what Anna did to him. I remember that she hurt him."

I said, "Trinity do you remember because sometimes you might hear dad and I talk, or do you remember because that is what you saw?"

She said, "Mom, I remember in my brain. Tyler and I were on the couch watching cartoons. Peyton was lying on the floor and he threw up orange on her white carpet and she get mad at Peyton. She pick him up, hit him on the head, shake him and throw him on the carpet. Peyton was crying a lot and she was really mad at him. I was scared and I didn't know what to do. I yell at her to leave Peyton alone and told her that she is being naughty."

I just sat there. I hugged her and cried with her. Almost two years out and she can still remember the trauma she witnessed. It breaks my heart every time she relives that morning. It angers me and makes me so distraught and bitter towards all the people that didn't fight for Peyton. The Sioux City police department and the county attorneys should be ashamed of themselves for not bringing justice to an innocent baby, a traumatized little girl, and a grieving family. I hope that Peyton's death haunts them and reminds them of how they messed up.

01/21/2014

It has been two years since you lived. It has been two years since I last held you. How? Why is the pain still so strong? Why do I still hurt like I do? Will I ever be free of this aching? Peyton, I miss you so much. I miss the life I should have with you. I don't think time heals all wounds. Tonight at 8:30 p.m. it will be exactly 2 years since daddy and I last laid with you as they took you off life support. Those three days will forever be scarred in my mind. You laid there in the bed, motionless. Tubes hooked up to you everywhere. Your little tongue was pushed out of your mouth because of tubes down your throat. You were so pale, so swollen. When they unhooked you, you became so cold, so fast. You quickly started to turn blue. Right before my eyes your spirit was leaving. Sometimes I wonder if there was any more I could/ or should have done. Should I have begged louder or prayed harder? What else could I have done?

I wonder if you visit me and daddy. I just wish you could visit me, and I could hold you one last time. It could be our secret. In Heaven are you still 6 months old or are you your worldly age of 2.5 years? I still have no answers in your death. I continue on with life because I have to and because I can tell some people aren't comfortable with me continuing to talk about missing you. Those people have never experienced trauma and I wish I could tell them how lucky they are. Sometimes I wish the grief away but then I stop and almost fear losing hurting for you, as though somehow that would take me away from you.

I need to learn to celebrate this date, celebrate your life. I can do that on your birthday but not on today. This date is too tragic for me. I resent this date. And deep down, I resent all the people that did nothing to fight for you.

I believe that you sent us Tenley and as individual as she is, I still see characteristics of you. I believe you sent her to us to try and heal us, to save our lives. Please know how much I love you and how much I think about you. I miss all the little things. I never knew they would mean everything to me. I miss you and I wish you were here. Please look over your sisters. Please ask angels to protect them. I wished I would have asked the angels to protect you and I am so sorry that I didn't. I didn't know...

Someday I want to be more happy that you lived and less sad that you died. But now, I am too far from that place. Will I ever get closure to your death? Maybe, maybe not. I guess the bottom line is that regardless, you still aren't here with me. I miss my boy. I miss my mommy's boy. I miss the years that were erased. I miss everything that would have/ could have/should have been. I miss it all. My family is short by one.

I love you so much and would do anything to have my boy back. I count down the moments until I get to see you again. Until then my sweet boy.

I Felt Him

01/30/2014

It is over...

Jeremiah and I finally had our depositions today. "Her" lawyer started out with me. In a way I wanted to go first and get it over with. On the way this morning I prayed. I prayed for the angels to keep me calm and confident. They did, and I thank them for that. Her lawyer's strategy is to try and cast blame on me, which we knew would happen. He asked all the things that I thought he would ask. I am glad it is over, not that it changes anything. Doesn't he have to know that he is defending someone who is guilty? How does he sleep at night? How can he justify his position?

Jeremiah did well, as I knew he would.

When we went to eat lunch, a song played over the speakers. As I listened closer, I realized it was Eric Clapton, "Tears in Heaven", which was Peyton's funeral son. This song is never on the radio as the station playing is a popular station with "new" music. Peyton was sending me a message, **he was there, he was with me**. I immediately got goosebumps all over and felt this overwhelming sense of emotion. He was there and he was sending me a sign. It couldn't have been more direct. *"Baby boy, I felt you and thank you. We are doing this for you. I love you and I think of you daily. I know a trial will be hell, but I've already been through hell and back with losing you. At this point, what's a little more?"*

As I sat there, I felt this warm, tight sensation as if being hugged. I couldn't speak and my breathing was shallow. Peyton was hugging me tight, like a toddler squeezing his mom tight as he's happy to see her. I knew then in that speechless moment that Peyton was telling me it was ok. He was there and he knew what I had just gone through. And, him knowing that I was trying to fight for him was enough.

05/16/2014

"Hi baby boy,

Your dad and I are struggling a bit. We had a big fight a couple of weekends ago. I am now understanding why people who lose children often eventually end up splitting up. I know that won't happen to your dad and I but now, I get what happens to these other people. The first year was easier because we were both so numb and so on auto-pilot, and we clung to each other because nobody else knew how we felt. This second year has been harder. The numbness has worn off and this reality has sunken in and it's easy to take our anger out on each other. Like what they say, it's easier to hurt those you love. Your dad and I will be ok but again, it's just another layer of trauma from this whole messed up situation.

I never miss you any less and it still hurts as much, and I still replay that morning over in my head often. I just hide it better. I hide the pain. "

Another Blessing

08/31/2014

Hello! It's been some time since I've written. We have been in full swing with summer now ending and going back to work. I always look forward to going back to work for the routine, but I dearly miss spending our time as a family and just hanging out. That's one thing I hope the girls will remember is that mom and dad spent a lot of time with them. Not necessarily doing big things but just hanging out with them. I was supposed to have my period last week but didn't get it. I just had a feeling, so I took a pregnancy test. And, we're PREGNANT. We have been "trying/not trying" for 8 months. We took the stance that whatever would happen, would happen. Normally, we get pregnant right away. This time it has been a little different because for 8 months of not being careful nothing was happening, until now! There must have been a reason that God wanted us to wait.

Tenley just turned two so these two will be close in age. The thought of that overwhelms me a little as I think about Jer's coaching season but know that deep down I'll be fine, as I am every year. I haven't quite processed this yet and we won't tell the girls until farther along, that is, unless one of them "knows" before I have a chance to tell. That's happened before!

Please let everything go along ok and the baby to be healthy. That's all we have ever asked with each baby, just be healthy. We have never cared if it was a girl, a boy. We just wanted health!

10/26/2014

I haven't said much to anyone at work about expecting yet. For some reason, I feel protective of this baby. Like, I just feel like I want to protect him. That's the other thing, I keep feeling like it is a boy. I guess we'll see if I'm right. So far, my batting average is 3/3! Somehow, I just know. I feel it and I just know. I am starting to have to wear maternity clothes and my belly is getting harder to hide so I will need to "announce to people". For some reason, I am just feeling so private about this baby and I'm not sure why.

11/11/2014

To Captain Cowell, The Police Department, and The County Attorney's Office:

It has been 2 years and 10 months since my son was killed by someone that we deeply trusted. And to date, Peyton's murderer walks free. She gets to enjoy her children, her husband, and the rest of her accountable-free life. She got to walk away from killing my son and "pretend" in her mind that what happened, didn't happen.

I wish that we could do that but we can't because there is nothing about how my son's case ended that is "ok" or acceptable. Essentially we were told about all of the things that your departments didn't like about our grieving and that it is what it is and we need to move on.

Please know there is not a fiber in my being that can ever move past what happened to my son and what hasn't happened to his killer. As a family we have "moved on", we have continued our family, and we have continued to function. But, we can never move past the accounts of our son.

The other day when picking up my now six-year-old daughter Trinity from after school daycare this conversation took place.

As I was talking to a female teacher who is not familiar with our family she asked, "So, is Trinity your only child?"

Me, "No, we have an 18 month old little girl and we had a 6 month old son who died almost 3 years ago. And, I am currently pregnant with our 4th."

Mrs. Longing, "What happened to your son?"

Me, "He was injured at daycare and died two days later of his head injuries."

Trinity interrupts, "Mom Peyton wasn't hurt at daycare.."

Mrs. Longing, "Well, maybe God will bless you with another baby boy."

As Trinity and I loaded into my car I asked her, "Trinity what did you mean when you said that Peyton wasn't hurt at daycare?"

Trinity, "Mom Anna hurt Peyton, not daycare."

Me, "At the time that you and Peyton were going to Anna's she was your daycare."

Trinity gets tears in her eyes and stares out the window.

Me, "Do you want to talk about anything?"

Trinity, "no", with tears streaming down her cheeks.

Two minutes later as we pulled up to the post office to get our mail Trinity started crying heavily and said, "Mom I watched her. I saw what she did to Peyton. I was on the couch with Tyler watching cartoons. Peyton was laying on the ground on a blanket and he threw up orange on her new carpet. She yelled at Peyton and told him he has a naughty baby and she picked him up. She hit him on the head, she shaked him, and she threw him on the ground. I heard a thump when he hit the ground. Mom, he was crying so loud I had to cover my ears. Anna told me it would be ok, but it wasn't mom."

I sat there turned around in my seat, fighting back tears and said, "I am so sorry you had to see that. Mommy and daddy wish we would have never taken you and Peyton to Anna's. We didn't know she was like that. We love you Trinity and you will never be around her again."

Trinity, "Is she in jail?"

Me, "No."

Please tell me as the "experts", how do I deal with my daughter? The truth of the matter is that none of you have ever listened to her or validated what she says. In my heart I know that Trinity saw what happened to her brother. What nobody has recognized is that Trinity and for that matter, even Tyler are secondary victims. As Trinity gets older and her cognitive and verbal skills get better more details of that morning are exposed. Trinity is 6 years old and she remembers in detail the death of her brother. Some of you questioned Jeremiah and I's action of coping after Peyton's death. What you failed to understand is that we had a living, traumatized little girl still at home that we had to care for and attend to. She came before us. She came before any of you.

Please understand that having our son killed and our daughter traumatized left us with nothing, not even for ourselves. We were never given a user manual that instructed us how to behave or feel after the murder of our son. Trust me, I would have paid any amount of money for one. All I wanted is for someone to tell me what to do as "functioning" and getting through each day was almost impossible. So please understand that I have no time for judgements from anyone that wasn't beside us helping us through it.

Even though I know you will never admit it, the police department was wrong. Whether your officers consciously meant to or not, they displayed actions that gave the impression that they were "protecting their own." In those first seven days we were treated very differently than Anna and Brett Black. In my heart I believe your officers assumed that because of Timothy Black being in the police department and your officers knowing Brett Black that their family couldn't be the guilty party. I believe your officers focused on Jeremiah and I. By doing that they protected Anna Black. Their opportunity for a confession from her was thrown away because they were looking in the wrong direction. I believe once Anna failed the polygraph your officers realized that they were wrong, but it was too late for them to get a confession from her. I will never understand why you didn't have a female in Anna Black's interrogation. If you had, I believe you would've gotten a confession. As you know, your officers made sure there was a female in mine. A female who had relations with Timothy Black. Again, that only reinforced to us the feeling that your department was "protecting their own." The first night we were questioned in the hospital while our son was getting a craniotomy, your officers split Jeremiah and I up for questioning. That same evening at the Black home you didn't do that for Anna and Brett. Your officers didn't split them up for questioning and they even allowed Brett to tell Anna of Peyton's injuries later in private after they had left. Why would you allow that to happen? Why wouldn't your officers separate her to tell her of his injuries to gauge her reaction? One ball after the other was dropped.

Am I a bitter, bereaved mother? Yes, I am. Over what did happen, what didn't happen, and what should have happened. I am bitter that so many "good" people aren't doing what is "right" and "just" and standing up for my son. Unlike many other people who suffer a traumatic loss, I have no closure. The system has essentially told us that "they can't do anything and to move on". O'brien's reasoning of not being able to prosecute Peyton's case without a confession is ridiculous. In fact, according to Dr. Kip Whitehouse, a professor of pediatrics from the University of Utah and a Shaken Baby Syndrome advocate, O'brien's reasoning is 'ludicrous'. Prosecuting cases shouldn't be about how many "wins" one has for their record, it should be about doing what is morally "right". If all cases were tied up in a bow, we wouldn't need lawyers.

I also understand that there is much blame to go around. Looking back maybe there were signs that I should have "picked up on".

Maybe there were signs that I missed. As Peyton's mom, I will live with that the rest of my life. How did I NOT know she was capable of hurting a child, my child at that? But, the truth is that I trusted her more than anyone else. I put my most precious gifts in her hands and depended on her to keep them safe. Initially after hearing doctors' diagnoses I couldn't even fathom what they say she did, she did. I defended her because I couldn't accept that who I thought she was, wasn't really who she was. I couldn't accept that I allowed someone like that to care for my kids. I didn't know and that will haunt me for the rest of my life.

My most scared issue is that you will all forget him or that you will forget about what she did to him. I know that you have so many cases you deal with but please don't ever forget about Peyton. He deserved so much more.

01/06/2015

Here is the good news that I posted on social media tonight!

Jeremiah, I, Trinity, Angel Baby Peyton, and Tenley are making it "social media" official that we are adding a baby boy to our family in May. We are experiencing such a "bittersweet" moment as we are excited to have another little boy but yet, all the feelings and emotions of losing Peyton come rushing back. I never want Peyton to feel like we are replacing him or for our new son to feel like he is a replacement of Peyton. Jeremiah and I both think that maybe God and Peyton thought it was time to give us a boy. I wish I could explain how truly "bittersweet" this feels, so much happiness and so much sadness all in one.

02/13/2015

Just saying, Tayden Joseph Pottebaum is taking over! Baby #4 and only 26 weeks. I look like I am due in a couple of weeks!! We're taking the girls to the movies today as this may be our last "outing" as a family of 4! He feels just like I am carrying a little basketball, so perfectly round. This has been such a special time with our second boy. The girls are so excited, as is our entire family!

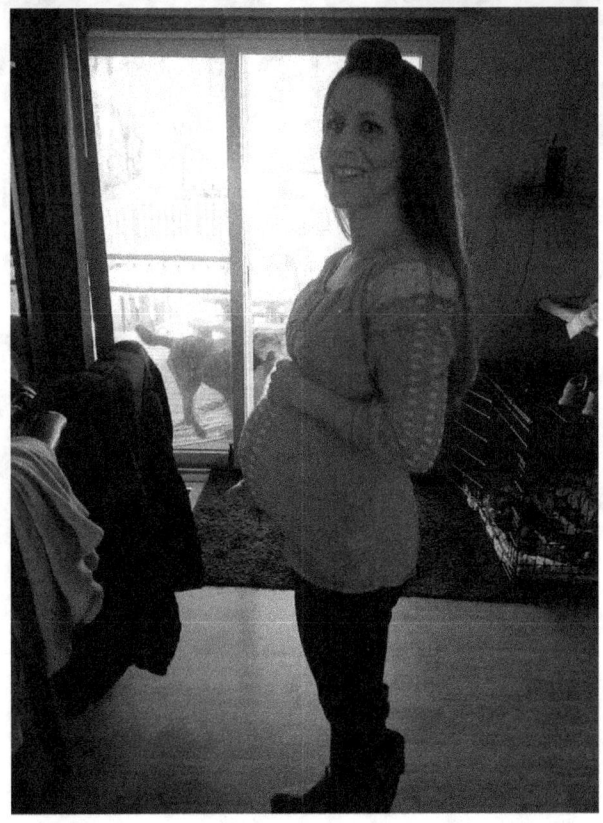

02/16/2015

Look at our boy!! He's beautiful! I am so excited to be adding this little boy to our family. He will complete us. I am excited for the girls to have a brother and for us to get to experience the light that a boy will bring. I know Peyton is helping to bring this little boy our way. We feel so extremely blessed. I am 27 weeks pregnant and so far everything is going well. I can't believe we will already be into the last trimester.

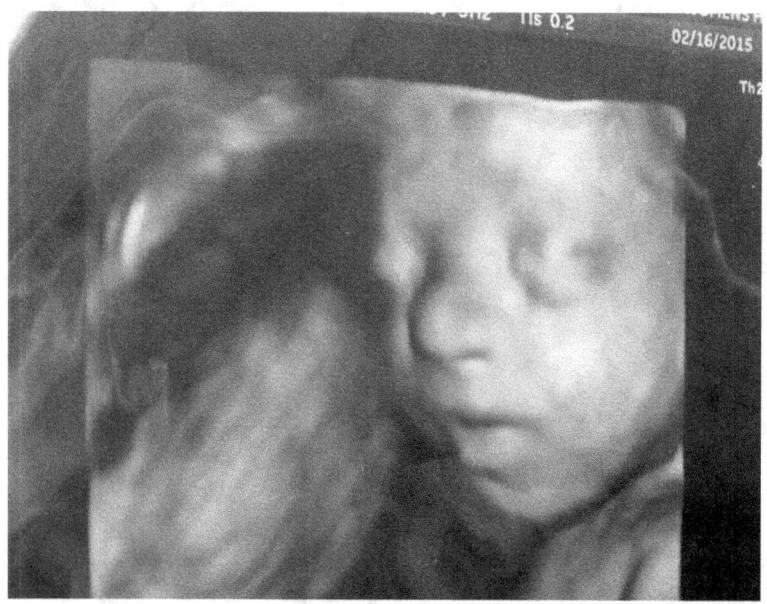

03/03/2015

This last week I feel like Tayden has grown so much. I feel like in just a few short weeks I have gotten so big, so fast. I am almost uncomfortable and feel like either he just grew a bunch or I just put on a bunch of weight. Otherwise, I have been feeling fine. I also know I am starting the "hard" trimester of pregnancy! Please keep us all safe!

03/06/2015

This week I have been struggling a bit. I am having quite a bit of stomach discomfort like extreme stretching. It feels as though I have grown so much this week and it's not slowing down. I feel way bigger than 29 weeks. I am trying not to worry but there has been a feeling all week that maybe something is wrong. I am a worrier so I am trying not to worry. Today I took a group of girls to an event for my job. It is an event with professionals around town who speak to girls about going into the math and science fields. I was so uncomfortable all day. One of the speakers for the day was actually my doctor. After her presentation I went and grabbed her and told her about my discomfort. She told me to call the office and she could see me on Monday. I felt better just talking to her. My regular appt. is still a week and a half out so at least this way I can get in and have peace of mind! I feel like I am 37 weeks pregnant, which just doesn't feel right. I don't think I should be feeling like this already.

Please, Not Again

03/10/2015

Today I had my doctor's appointment at the end of the day. Normally Jeremiah doesn't go with me. Most appointments I just go by myself. He must see how scared I am and maybe he's just trying to calm me down. We both arrive at the clinic and wait in the waiting room. I'm nervous but am trying to calm myself. A nurse calls us back to an exam room and does the routine questioning about how everything has been going and how I am feeling. She leaves the room and then my doctor comes in. We chat a bit about the event that we just saw each other at and then talk about what I've been feeling. I mention how I know this is the 4th baby and you tend to be bigger with each one but that I feel like I am 37 weeks pregnant and that I have severe stretching pain around my abdomen. She has me lay on the table and she gets out her measuring tape. She measures me the first time. She then measures me again the second time. She is very quiet which is somewhat abnormal. She mentions calmly that I am measuring "big" and that I am measuring 37 weeks pregnant. She is calm when she explains this but she mentions that she is going to have them do a sonogram of my belly to just make sure everything looks good. This makes me kind of nervous because normally you only get the one sonogram that tells you the gender of the baby. She walks out to go talk to the sonogram person. Jeremiah doesn't say it but I can tell he's nervous. We're both nervous. I'm sure we both have some PTSD from Peyton, so I'm sure that doesn't help. She comes back in and walks Jer and I to the room where the sonogram is. She steps out while I visit with the tech and get prepped.

The tech gets me settled and laying down. She puts the cloth at the bottom of my tummy and squeezes the warm gel on my belly. She starts moving the wand around and is looking at different things. These pictures are always so hard for me to see. She is measuring different things and clicking on her keyboard. She then gets somewhat silent and I all of a sudden feel something different with her. I can't explain it but it is like a "feeling" thing. I just get a feeling from her, that something is wrong. She is quiet and then mentions that she is going to go get the doctor. At this moment, I KNOW something is WRONG. They never just "go get the doctor". Immediately I am panicking inside. Jeremiah grabs my shoulder and I can feel how tense he is.

My doctor opens the door and the moment I look at her face I can tell something is wrong. My stomach drops and then knots up. She proceeds to say that in the sonogram it looks like the baby has fluid in his body. It looks like he has fluid in his stomach and lungs. She is very careful what she is saying and I can tell that she's terrified of what she sees. I start crying and ask her, "Is he going to be ok?" Her response was, "I don't know." I ask her, "Can he live with this?" She responds again, "I don't know." I just start crying, and Jeremiah is crying. She explains that she is setting up an appointment for me to start seeing the maternal fetal medicine doctor up at the hospital as they will be able to find out more about what is happening. She explains that an appointment is being set up now and that I will see him as well as continue to see her. She gives us a sheet of paper that she has printed that talks about what "hydrops" is. The fluid inside the baby is called hydrops. She walks out of the room so I can change. I just started crying....

Please God, please heal my baby. All we have ever prayed for is a healthy baby. We have gone through so much, please heal my baby. Please fix this hydrops.

Jeremiah and I leave with so many questions. We just got slammed with terrible news and we walked out of the clinic in shock. We both get in our separate vehicles and call each of our parents to let them know, even though we don't have much to tell them. I called my dad and let him know that something is wrong with Tayden. My dad tries to be positive and reassuring and I can tell he doesn't understand how sick Tayden might be. The energy I felt from the medical staff told me all I needed to know.

I drove home in tears. What is happening? Why is this happening? Will my baby be ok?

03/11/2015

For the last 24 hours I have been researching constantly what hydrops is. I have been bombarded with information trying to understand what is happening to our son. From what I have read so far there are immune hydrops and non-immune hydrops. But neither condition looks good. The outcome of healing from it does not look favorable. *How did he get this? What caused this?* Everything was perfectly fine a few weeks ago when we had the gender scan. This wasn't there then. Or they didn't see it then. How can it just all of a sudden be there?

I didn't sleep at all last night. I've had constant diarrhea today all day because I'm so anxious, worried and angry. I cried off and on at work. I'm trying to be positive but I have no idea what we're working with. I don't have any information to go on. I go back to my normal doctor next week and then I see the maternal fetal medicine specialist next week as well. But what do I do until then? Except worry....

03/13/2015

I've done everything they say you shouldn't do. I've googled this condition and keep reading everything I can. I feel at such a loss. I just can't sit here and just wait until my next appointment to learn more.

Jeremiah has been really quiet. He's not saying much. I don't know if he's trying to be strong for me, or if he is having a hard time wrapping his head around this like I am. I've been more disconnected at home with the girls because I'm so anxious. My patience isn't great but I also am not ready to talk to Trinity yet. She's so intuitive and I need to know more before I talk to her. *Oh God, I am dreading that talk. She's had such a hard time with Peyton's death. Now to have to talk to her about this. How? What would I say? What shouldn't I say? Right now, I have nothing to say..*

03/15/2015

Today was hard. I can't eat because I feel so worried. My belly is consistently larger and swollen and I am so uncomfortable. I feel huge. The skin around my stomach is so tight and just feels like it is ripping.

From everything I've read, the non-immune hydrops is the most common. I've also read that many different diseases and medical complications can cause hydrops. I also read that about half of babies born with hydrops fetalis do not survive. This is just too much. I'm trying to be positive. We're trying to hold positive that we can find out why Tayden has this and what that means for us. Does he have a condition that caused this? Was I exposed to something that caused this?

Jeremiah is so quiet. I can feel the pain that he tries to hide. He's nervous but I can tell he's trying to be positive.

03/17/2015

I had an appointment today with my normal doctor's office. They did another sonogram to look at Tayden and according to my doctor it doesn't look much different than a week ago. There is still fluid inside of him. My doctor explained that this would be non-immune hydrops and that from here on out I will continue to have my normal OB appointments but then also have appointments weekly with maternal fetal medicine. She said he will be the expert to try and determine why Tayden has this and our outcome. We have our first appointment tomorrow with him. This is agony.

03/18/2015

Today we had our first appointment at the specialist. I am currently 31 weeks exactly. The doctor seemed very genuine and sensitive. He was very approachable and there was a calmness about him. He went over what had been shared with him thus far. He talked to Jeremiah and I about what hydrops is and that it's hard to say what will happen. He was honest that some babies live with this but that some babies die. He said that there is often a medical condition that can cause this. He had the sonogram tech do all kinds of measurements of Tayden and my placenta and everything. I explained to him the pain I feel in my abdomen, all of the stretching, the pulling, and the aching. After the tech was done with her measurements he came in and talked to us. He talked about seeing fluid in Tayden's abdomen and his chest cavity. He also said that I am carrying a lot of additional amniotic fluid called polyhydramnios, likely due to Tayden being sick. He called it 'mirror syndrome' where my body is mirroring what is happening to him. He talked about doing something called an amniocentesis, where he would put a needle in my stomach to drain the fluid to relieve both me and him. He said he would then send the fluid to Mayo to be tested to see if any specific conditions could be found to help explain the hydrops. He also talked about the risks of doing this and that it could cause premature labor to start. Jeremiah and I both agreed that I needed to do this to try and relieve both me and Tayden but also possibly get answers.

We left feeling really heavy. I mean really, really heavy. We were given so much information. There was also hope. There was a plan for relief for me and to get answers. For a baby that is so sick he looked beautiful in his sonogram pictures.

I'm trying really hard to be positive but I am a worried mess.

03/25/2015

Today was a long day...

We had our appointment with the specialist. Dr. Scott had scheduled for me to have an amniocentesis done to try and take some of the fluid out of me. He specifically called it 'polyhydramnios'. I checked into the clinic and then they took me to the sonogram room. The tech was really nice and she started doing her normal measurements and scans. The doctor came in and started to look around as well. He stated that it didn't look like much had changed. He also asked if I was ready to have some fluid drained and again just voiced the risk for complications. He stepped out to let his nurse prep. Once ready he came back in. He ended up using a very small needle and piercing it into my abdomen. He then slowly started sucking out fluid. It felt like he just kept taking more and more out. It was amazing how quickly I started to feel relief. Each time he pulled some out I could feel a little less weight on my rib cage. He ended up taking about 2.5 liters of amniotic fluid out of my belly. The relief was instant and my belly shrunk so much. The nurse got me situated in a "watch" room when they were done as I started having contractions. She kept coming back and checking on me and eventually she loaded me in a wheelchair and they wheeled me over to the hospital through the underground walk-way. The contractions were more regular. The nurse wheeled me over to the maternity wing and a nurse let us in right away and got me set up in a room. They hooked me up to the monitors and gave me a shot. This shot was supposed to help stop the contractions.

I felt so worn out and truly I was just numb. I sat there crying because all of this was just becoming too much. Jeremiah called his mom to pick up both of the girls and get them fed dinner. My doctor ended up coming in to see us. She must have been on the floor with another patient. How lucky I was to have such a good doctor, a good friend. The nurses gave me a second shot and that seemed to help slow things down. The nurses had me stay for a while to monitor me just to make sure everything was alright. Eventually, they let me pack up my stuff and leave. As we walked out, Jeremiah and I just looked at each other, this look of "what the hell are we going through?" Luckily, the nurses were able to stop my contractions but all of this uneasiness. It was a lot...

04/02/2015

Today we had our specialist appointment. The doctor first had us come to his office to talk. He explained that he had my amniotic fluid sent to Mayo and that the results had come back. He said that according to my results this showed that Tayden had Down's syndrome. He had given me an envelope and had me open it and pointed to the number '21' where it showed that Tayden had three chromosomes, instead of two. He said that Tayden having Down syndrome is likely what has caused his hydrops. Again, the doctor was honest that he wanted us to "prepare for the worst, but hope for the best." Part of me was relieved to have an 'answer'. He then took me to the sonogram room and did my normal measurements. I am 33 weeks today. Every time I come here I get to see my baby moving on the screen and for that quick moment it is solace to me. While I am looking at him and he is moving about, all of my worry and concern go away. As long as he is moving, everything is ok.

The doctor also made a call to a specialist doctor in Omaha and talked to him about my case. This doctor had suggested that we keep Tayden inside of me for as long as possible and try to carry him to 36 weeks and then do the C-section. The specialist doctor also said that he could do a special procedure with him down there to pull the fluid out of Tayden's chest cavity, before they deliver him, while he is still inside of me. My doctor said that the plan is I would deliver Tayden down in Omaha at 36 weeks. If I went into labor before then they would have me 'life flighted' to Omaha as the NICU here doesn't have what Tayden would need for support. I felt good with this as this was an official plan. It was something for Jeremiah and I to work from. It was some type of guidance, some type of idea, some type of preparation.

On my way home I called my parents just to inform them of the news about Tayden, that he has Down syndrome. I felt relief that I had an answer but then this new fear of what that would mean. When I called my dad his comment was, "Oh shit, that's no big deal. He will be a little ray of sunshine". That resonated with me and made me feel hopeful. I have no idea how to take care of a special needs child but as long as he lives that doesn't matter. I had fear that I wouldn't know what to do or how to care for him.

That night at home I sensed a relief from Jeremiah. When we talked about Tayden's diagnosis Jeremiah had no concerns about it. I felt like I had more concern then he did, but my concern came from a place of not knowing how to take care of him, as it would likely fall on me. Deep down I also had guilt that my body "caused this". That I 'caused' him to have Down syndrome. In talking to my sister she said to me, "Court, if any of us were to be able and take care of a special needs child, it would be you." And when she said that it made me feel better. Deep down I just want to be a good mom for him. I want to be able and take care of him the way he needs.

Again, we have a diagnosis and all that matters is our boy lives.

04/06/2015

Today at my normal doctor's office they hooked me up to the stress test to check on Tayden. One of the main nurses that has done my shots is a lady named Tara. Today when she was hooking me up I mentioned how we are trying to prepare for everything with Tayden and that my mother in law was going to call the cemetery and inquire if the worst did happen, and if Tayden did pass, if we could bury him at the bottom of the same plot as Peyton or if there is another plot next to Peyton to buy. Tara mentioned that her husband Brad is a funeral director with the funeral home we went through with Peyton. She said that she would call him and ask him if he could find out.

At that moment my cell phone rang and it was Jeremiah's mom. She proceeded to tell me that the cemetery said that they could/would not do that as a new plot would have to be bought for him. Jeremiah and I were worried about money as we know what it costs to pay for a plot, marker, funeral and the medical bills. We were still recovering financially from Peyton's death. Financially we were really scared. I told Tara what Jeremiah's mom said when she hung up. Tara looked disappointed and said once she had a minute she would call her husband. Within a few minutes she called him, handed me the phone to talk to him and explain our situation. He told me to give him a little time and he'd make a phone call. A little while later her phone rings and she hands me the phone. After some reasoning Brad was able to get the cemetery to agree to allow us to do this but made sure to let us know that we would still have to pay the opening fee of the grave. Brad also said that "IF" his services were needed he would be more than happy to be our funeral director and that he wouldn't charge for his services. I was crying by now and thanked him immensely and after hanging up with him, thanked Tara.

When I got home I talked to Jeremiah about what had transpired while at my appointment. As I talked to him I again teared up as I was so touched by Brad and Tara. Two people that don't really know us, wanting and willing to go to bat for us. They were willing to "take one for the team" all on just being good people and principle. I was so moved by their actions of concern and help. That act of love gave me so much hope and so much love for the people that some "higher source" is placing in my path.

04/08/2015

It has been weeks of just worrying about our boy. I am now getting monitored every other day at my normal doctor's office. They haven't really said why but I assume it's to check on Tayden to see if he is struggling or still alive. Every day I go I am so anxious as I'm always terrified that he won't have a heartbeat and that he will be dead inside of me. For four weeks I have been living in a constant state of panic and anxiety. Nobody can say anything that will make this any better and anyone who tries to preach "God's Plan" to me is lucky that I don't throat punch them. I can't hear that now, I just can't.

I'm really worried and scared and the "waiting" is wearing on all of us. Last night I just collapsed in the shower, sitting on the floor just crying. I hugged my belly and spoke to my boy. I told him that I love him and that I'm taking care of him the best way I can now. I told him that I am trying to cherish this time with him, in case, this is all I get. I told him thank you for making me a mom again. I felt him in ways I can't quite explain to anyone. I felt a calmness from him and I felt a feeling of immense love. I felt like what I was experiencing in that moment was reciprocal. I just cried and held my belly and tried to soak up this time with him. I have a hard time being able to "show" what I'm feeling at this point. It's nights like this in this shower alone that I can finally let it all out. I don't want to scare the girls and I try so hard to be strong for them. I want them to feel safe and know all will be ok. When people ask how I am I say "ok" because I don't really know how to respond. I want to tell them 'I'm a fucking mess, I can't eat, I'm not sleeping and I'm terrified'. Throughout each day I have become preoccupied with checking to see if I can feel him move, just to make sure he hasn't died inside of me.

Because we don't really know what to expect we're trying to prepare for every scenario. And living in that emotional state for so long is exhausting.

Today I had my specialist appointment, which I love because I get to see my boy on the sonogram. He looks beautiful. How can he be that sick? Dr. Scott basically said that at this time nothing has changed. I have not gained back anymore amniotic fluid after he drained some, which is good. But everything as far as Tayden's condition and the hydrops remain the same. Dr. Scott explained that the problem with the fluid in the lung cavity is that it gets in the way of his lung tissue being able to grow. I've read about other babies in this situation who had drains put in utero but that is not something that has been brought up at this point. The girls got to go with us today, which was exciting to watch them "ooh" and "ahh" over their brother. Tenley is only almost 2 years old so she doesn't understand what's happening as much. Trinity on the other hand, understands everything. She doesn't say much but I can feel the "gloom" and hesitation coming from her. I've been very open and honest with her in order to try and prepare her for all outcomes. She has shed her own tears when I've talked about the possibility of death and I just hug her and try to comfort her, as I'm breaking down inside. She's already lost one brother. She can't lose another one...

We had gotten the girls both to bed. Jeremiah got out of the shower and was standing in the bathroom with his towel wrapped around his waist, looking in the mirror. He looked at me, with tears in his eyes and said, "If he dies, I don't believe in God anymore. The God I believe in would never allow this to happen, not again. We're good people, we don't deserve this." I was sitting on the edge of the bed and looked up into his eyes. Tears welled up in my eyes as I heard him say this. I could feel and sense his pain so strongly. He always tries to be strong and really hasn't shown any emotion thus far. He has been really positive and has been the one to keep me positive. But tonight, his guard was down and his hurt was spilling out. When he said that I felt such a loss for him. For some reason, and I can't quite explain why, it's important to me that we both believe. If we don't have some sort of faith, what do we have? Right now, it feels like nothing. I don't know exactly what I believe. I do know that what I was taught/told growing up isn't resonating with me. But, I do believe there is "something" greater than us, there has to be, doesn't there? If there wasn't, then why would we even be here? What would be the point? I don't really understand it all and whatever "IT" is, I'm extremely pissed and confused by "IT, but I still know "IT" exists.

Please find a way to reach my husband. I am just afraid I will lose him. I am afraid of what will happen to him. I always worry that his coping will turn to something unhealthy and ruin our family. Please help him cope positively. Please help him to feel something and not feel alone. I know he tries to be strong for me, but I need him to deal with all of this, ALL of the last three years. I don't want to lose my husband and my marriage too.

04/15/2015

Today I had one of my every other day stress tests at my normal doctor's office to check on Tayden. Throughout this whole time I have also been getting the P17 hormone shots to help make sure I don't go into premature labor. Due to having a history of my membranes rupturing early I have done P-17 shots with each baby to try and keep them inside of me as long as possible. The concentration in the needles is really thick and causes extreme pressure as the nurse pushes the liquid in. They alternate butt cheeks each week. I get a nasty bruise on each side and it stings after I get it done. I look like a war zone right now. I feel like I'm spending so much time at the doctor's office...

I haven't written much in the last week but honestly, I just can't. I'm so numb at this point.. I don't know what to say and I don't know how to feel and I just don't know how to be positive right now, but I'm trying.

Today while I was having the stress test done on Tayden the nurse that was taking care of me suddenly came over and started messing with the straps that were hooked up to me. Then she quickly walked away but never said a word. The next thing I know, the two doctors that I see came swiftly in with a look of concern on their faces, which startled me. They came over and started messing with the straps and then I felt a sense of relief from one of them. They mentioned that now they hear his heartbeat. They said that the nurse didn't hear his heartbeat after trying to fix the straps which is why she went to get them. They mentioned that he must have gotten into a certain position in which they temporarily couldn't hear him. They re-assured me that all was ok.

04/18/2015

We celebrated Tenley's 2nd birthday today. I can't believe our little "light of hope" is two! I felt blessed today to celebrate her and it was a good distraction for Jeremiah and I. I was able to find a rainbow cake which was perfect. We've always said she was our "rainbow" baby after losing Peyton. It was fun watching her try to eat her cake and open her presents.

I also spent the weekend packing our bags for the hospital. I have had our bags packed for a few weeks just in case something happened. Knowing Tayden's arrival is three days away I spent the weekend packing the rest of what I felt we would need. I packed extra stuff for me as the plan would be that I stay behind in Omaha and Jeremiah would come home to care for the girls. I also packed bags for the girls as they will go to Jeremiah's mom's house while we are in the hospital.

It was pretty quiet here. I did sit down with Trinity and again explained that we just don't know what is going to happen with Tayden. He may live and he may die. I told her that I just want her to be comfortable and that if she wants to come back in the room and see Tayden, then great. If it scares her to see him with all of the tubes and she doesn't want to that is totally fine too. I told her that it is completely up to her and she gets to choose and no matter what she chooses dad and I will be good with it. She asked me if she can hold him. I told her if they allow us to she can. I then prepared her that if he dies, does she still want to hold him? Her response was yes. I reassured her that if she changes her mind at the last minute that is always ok. I hugged her and told her we want to be positive but that we're trying to also prepare for what could happen.

As I went back to my room I just sighed so heavy. The conversation I just had with her was so heavy, so real, so not a common conversation to have with a six-year-old but yet here she was, talking to me and responding like a teenager. Peyton's death and this situation has matured her so much. I have to be honest with her and I want her to feel prepared and safe.

04/20/2015

Today I had my normal doctor's appointment for the stress tests I've been doing. As they hooked me up with the straps a weird feeling came over me that this would be the last time I was doing this. I've spent the last month here and it's kind of become like home. I feel comfortable here. I've gotten to know the nurses and doctors and they've kind of been a rock for me. The nurse told me after my stress test that one of my doctor's would like to see me in her office. So, when it was done the nurse took me back to her office and she was sitting at her desk. She had me sit and proceeded to pull out a box and told me to open it now. I opened it and inside there lay a pretty necklace with a single "cross" on it. Her card and writing on the necklace talked about 'keeping the faith'. I started crying and so did she. She came around her desk and hugged me and told me that she wished she could be there and that tomorrow I will be in her prayers. By now the other doctor that also "saw" me came into her room and she hugged me too. She also started crying and expressed that we will be in her prayers and that she is rooting for us.

As I walked out of this office I felt like the luckiest girl in the world. Look at what amazing doctors I have. They knew tomorrow was the BIG day and here they are loving me and trying to comfort me in the way they can. I know they wished that they could be there, that they would be the ones working on me. Tears filled my eyes for the millionth time this last six weeks. But this time, they were tears of happiness. They were tears of hope. How blessed am I that I have the BEST team of people around me? How blessed am I that I am more than just a "patient" to these two women? I couldn't wait to show and share with Jeremiah. These small rays of sunshine have kept me going. There are good people in this world and somehow God is trying to show me that.

Tomorrow... is... tomorrow. I can't even talk about it tonight. I am as ready as I ever will be.

Dear God,

Please take care of my baby. Please grant him life. Please help heal him. Please wrap your arms around Jeremiah and the girls and comfort them. Please give me strength to handle whatever it is that happens. I need you now.

04/21/2015

I am so scared...

Today is the day. For six weeks we have been anticipating, worrying, crying, hoping, and praying that our littlest boy will make it. And today is the day, the day where he will either be given life or we will have to say goodbye. While he is inside me I feel like he is safe, that I can protect him. I have known that he could pass inside me but he hasn't, he has been fighting to meet his mom and dad. These have been the longest six weeks of my life. The worrying, the researching, the planning for an outcome that we have no idea...

But really throughout all of that I can't fathom the thought of losing my littlest boy, my second son. That couldn't really happen? I mean we've already paid our dues losing Peyton, right? Please give my baby boy life. Please help him fight through this. I am so scared. Today is the day. I just wish he could stay inside of me forever.

7:00 a.m. - I am up and getting the girls up and ready. Let's be honest I never really went to bed. Today is the day. *I am so scared.*

We get the girls dressed and bags finished packing to stay at Nana's for a few days.

8:30 a.m. - We drop the girls off at Jeremiah's mom's house. Now the day is getting real. We give kisses and hugs. Trinity gets teary wanting to know if mommy will be ok. I reassure her that I will be fine. She asked me, "If Tayden dies, can I hold him." I say, "Of course you can honey." More kisses and hugs and we are out the door. I feel extra emotional this morning because there is a good chance I may be spending a lot of time out of town in Omaha when Tayden is in the NICU. That will be hard for me to be away from the girls.

On the way to the hospital Jeremiah and I are so quiet, with so much fear we're holding. We're both scared and anxious. We don't really know what to talk about or what to focus on. We know that whatever does happen soon, will affect the rest of our lives in a profound way.

Wouldn't you know, of all the worst times, Jeremiah pulls over and says there's something wrong with our vehicle. He pulls off to the side of the road and walks around the vehicle. I hear him cursing and he comes back into the car. He says, "We have a flat tire." What?! You've got to be kidding me, not NOW. We are on the way to the hospital to deliver our boy, our complex situation of a delivery and THIS happens??? He tells me to bunker tight as he attempts to change the tire and put on a spare. He gets the job done but when he comes back into the vehicle he mentions that he doesn't know if we'll make it to the hospital on the spare. We pull over on an exit as there is a car dealership here. Jeremiah goes in, only to come out frustrated that it'd be an hour before they could help us. We are scheduled to have this C-section at noon and were asked to be at the hospital at 11:30. We just don't have time to wait. We continue on our way and pray that the tire holds up. Now, we are even more on edge. Seriously, of all days, this has to happen today? In the same breath, this is the least of my worries.

We get to Omaha and Jeremiah uses his phone navigation to get us to this hospital, as we've never been here nor met the specialist that is going to do this special procedure to try and save Tayden and then deliver him. We are already behind schedule and I'm stressed but then, it's that much more time with my baby.

Jeremiah lets me off by the door, parks the car and walks in with all of my bags. We ask for directions and are escorted down the halls to where we need to be. The nurses greet us and they immediately get us in a room, mentioning that we are late. I spoke up quickly to let them know we had a flat tire. They have me undress and put on a hospital gown, hat and socks. They have me sit in the bed and hook me up to monitors for Tayden. I hear his heartbeat pounding and I smile because he's still with me. They start preparing me for surgery by placing my IV and doing paperwork. The nurse working with me mentions that she worked with my doctor when she was doing her residency. She said that my doctor had contacted her knowing this is where I was coming to and asked her to take care of me. In that moment, tears filled my eyes as I knew God was sending little signs along the way.

The doctor comes in and introduces himself, again commenting that we're late, to which we reply about the flat tire. He scoots up to the monitor and starts using the handheld device to move around and look at Tayden. He explained that he is going to go in with a large needle, through my belly while he's still in me and in through Tayden's chest cavity in an attempt to relieve some of the fluid inside his chest to make resuscitating him easier/possible. He explains they will use the sonogram to guide them so they know where they are entering on Tayden. I cringe inside as I think of this long needle puncturing his little body but I know that this is an attempt to save his life.

There is a knock at the hospital room door and Jeremiah opens it. It is one of the pastors from our church. My insides just burst. When we found out Tayden's diagnosis 6 long weeks ago we were put on a prayer chain with our church. One of the pastor's Chad reached out to us to offer prayer and ask what he could do to help. He offered to drive down to Omaha, an hour and a half from Sioux City to be with us. And, here he is. Although he offered, how many people really follow through? Or are so compelled to want to be there for someone else? Tears welled up in my eyes as here he was. He didn't really know me and Jeremiah personally but here he is. At that moment I uttered these words inside of my head,

Thank you for sending someone to be with us, to comfort us and to bring us hope. Thank you for this man. He left his own family, his own job to come support two people that he doesn't really know all to bring comfort to us. This, in itself, is exceptional to me. This effort makes me believe in the good of people.

Our pastor was given scrubs to put on as we asked him to be in the operating room with us. With Tayden's prognosis unknown I wanted him in with us and asked him to baptize Tayden immediately upon birth. Although in our church baptizing doesn't mean "one is saved" but to me, it means a commitment to Christ. I'm not overly religious but I know there is a higher power, whatever that may be. I just want Tayden blessed by faith and to know love.

The specialist doctor continues to use the sonogram to gage where Tayden is and the nurses continue to prepare me. Soon, too soon, we will have an answer and I am terrified of this next journey.

The nurses wheel me into the operating room where a nurse anesthesiologist is waiting for me. Here they prep me for an epidural. Upon the first administration the doctor has a tough time getting between my vertebrae just right and it doesn't take. The doctors prep for a second time which doesn't take again. These are painful and now I'm feeling like I'm going to pass out. Finally, they attempt a third time and they are able to get through like they need to. Soon, I start to feel my toes and legs going numb. The nurses start preparing me for surgery with the catheter and so forth.

As they get me moved on to the table they get the sonogram machine set up next to me for the specialist doctor. The NICU team of doctors is also setting up in the room next door so that they are ready to intubate Tayden. Jeremiah is with me and our pastor is standing off to the side. Once the team of nurses and doctors are ready my doctor explains that he is going to do the procedure first where he uses long needles to go through my belly into Tayden to try and relieve fluid. Using ultrasound he does this procedure, wherein I feel pressure as the needle is inserted through me and I feel pressure from Tayden, which I assume is movement from being poked by the needle.

Once he's done with this he starts my C-section. He has a resident doctor with him who is helping with my surgery. The doctor is talking to Jeremiah through the whole thing and talks as he's moving organs out of the way. As he gets close to cutting through my uterus he is talking to the NICU doctors who are next to me ready to take Tayden. He now is pulling Tayden out and handing him off to the team next to us. I am so nervous and I don't hear anything. I don't hear Tayden crying. I start to panic.

Dear God, please help these doctors help my baby. Help them to save my baby so he can breathe. Please allow my dear son life.

Jeremiah and our pastor follow the NICU team next door as the doctors are trying to save Tayden.

As the doctors are intubating Tayden our pastor is praying to God and baptizing him. The doctors and nurses work on him while Jeremiah and our pastor are praying over him.

Once they have him intubated Jeremiah comes back to my side. I immediately hear him say that "he's alive, they intubated him, the pastor baptized him and they are taking him to the NICU". Tears of relief are streaming down my cheeks. Jeremiah announces that his birth time was recorded at 12:45 p.m., his weight was noted as 5 lbs. and 4 ounces and his height was 15.75 inches long.

The specialist doctor and resident start to work on getting me put back together. There is some conversation and mention of me having to wear a catheter for a week. As Jeremiah is talking to the doctors they mention how my bladder got nicked in the process and now they are stitching it back up which is why I have to wear a catheter for a week. They even showed my bladder and the surgery catheter tube sticking out of my bladder. I guess it's a good thing they "caught" this now before they stitched me back up.

One of the NICU doctors comes into the room and mentions that they got him on the ventilator. The nurses take me back to recovery and Jeremiah visits Tayden in the NICU. After some time Jeremiah comes back and shows me pictures of Tayden. After what seems like ions I get to be wheeled down to my sweet tiny son. As I am wheeled in, I see him so tiny in the hospital crib with tubes all over him. Unfortunately, I am not shocked by all of these as my mind flashes back to three years previous with Peyton. Who would have ever thought I would be with another critically ill child once again begging God to answer my prayers this time and grant my beautiful boy life? He was so small. Jeremiah wheeled me up to him as I couldn't stand up and I just rubbed his little fingers and the side of his face. His hair is beautiful, a lot of light blonde wavy hair. He is so gorgeous.

Please, lord heal my precious son. Please don't take another one of my children from this earth, please.

Doctors are draining more fluid from him and informing us that he is in critical condition. They informed us that they already drained a pound of fluid out of him. Our pastor Chad came into the room with us and we prayed over Tayden. The specialist doctor soon came down to check on Tayden and I. By this time my mom was there to see our precious boy. The doctors and nurses just kept working on him, which brought us so much hope.

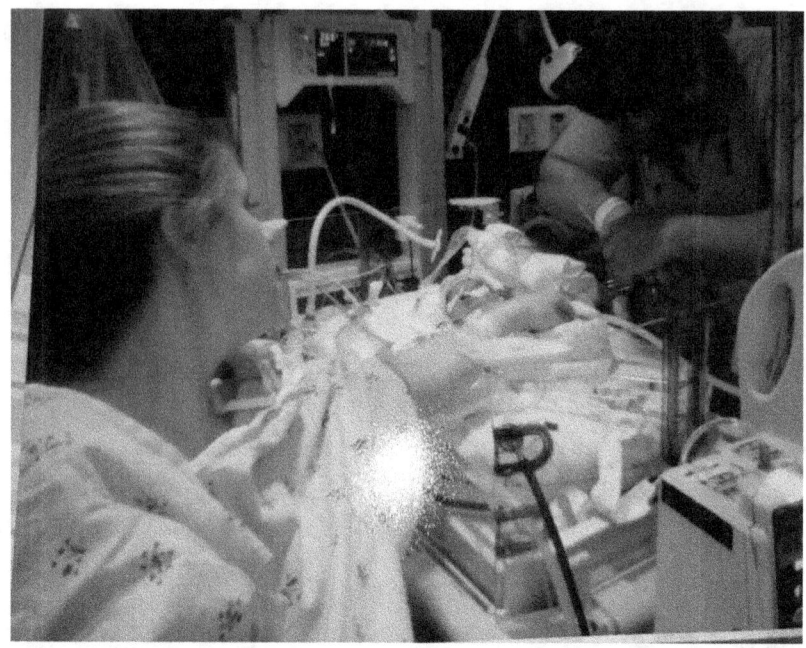
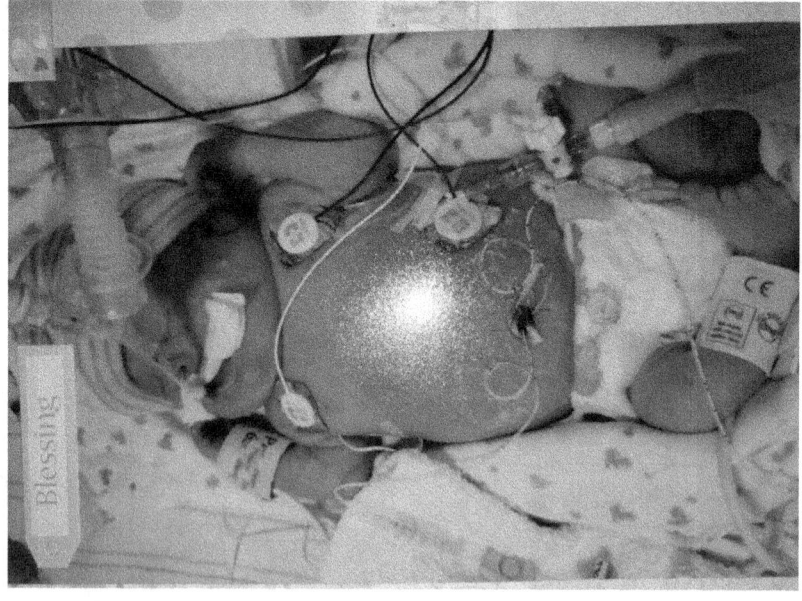

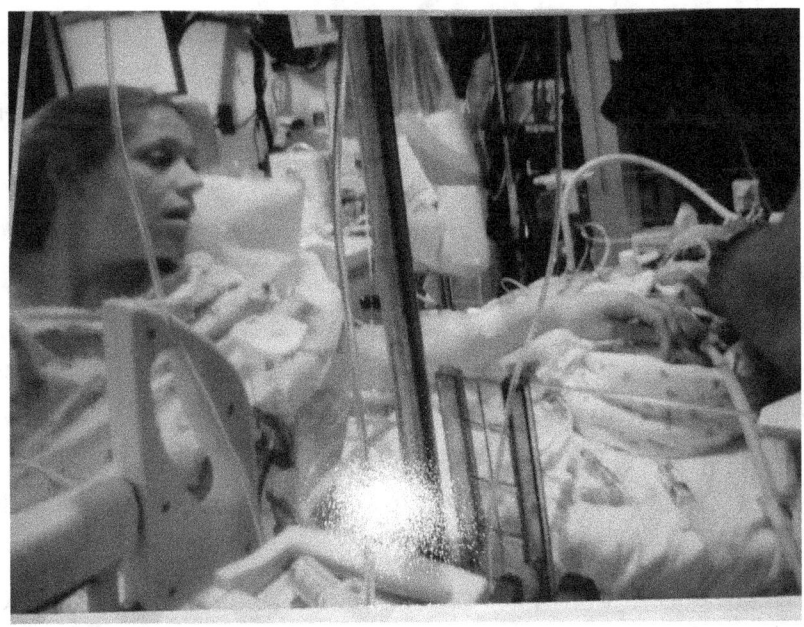

After resting for a little while in my room Jeremiah's parents show up with the girls. Tenley runs in happy to see us but Trinity slowly approaches my bed. She is scared and desperately looking around for her brother. I talk to her and explain that Tayden is downstairs and he is hooked up to a lot of tubes and that she doesn't have to be scared. I tell her he is very sick but that the doctors are trying to fix his little body. We make our way down to the NICU and everyone washes their hands. As Jeremiah wheels me into his room the doctor and nurse are talking and assessing our tiny little peanut hooked up to all of these tubes. There are tubes everywhere on him. Our little man is so beautiful, but he looks so vulnerable.

Please God, let the doctors heal him. Let the doctors heal him and allow life for our sick little boy. Please let his hydrops clear up and drain. Please don't make me lose another boy. I don't think I can handle burying another baby. Please, dear God, please allow life to my son.

Jeremiah wheeled me up to his incubator. There lay our beautiful Tayden Joseph. I couldn't hold him because of all of the tubes, so I sat there and through one of the small holes I rubbed the side of his face, temple to chin, temple to chin, telling him how much daddy and I love him. For the next day this was what I did. This was the only way I could show him my love.

All of these thoughts are going through my mind. Will he live? How long will he be in the hospital? Where will I stay in Omaha? How will Jeremiah manage work and the girls at home? How is all of this going to unfold? How long will our boy be in the hospital? How much care will he need when he gets out? Will I be able to care for him?

It doesn't matter, as long as I get to bring my boy home, we will do *ANYTHING*.

I'm really sore from my C-section, more sore than the previous C-sections. The pain is almost excruciating but maybe the stress of Tayden's status is causing my physical pain to be more intense. I really can't stand for long and I'm thinking this pain MUST be due to my bladder being cut. I didn't have this much pain with my other two C-sections. It just feels like something is wrong...

Dear God please heal my second beautiful boy.

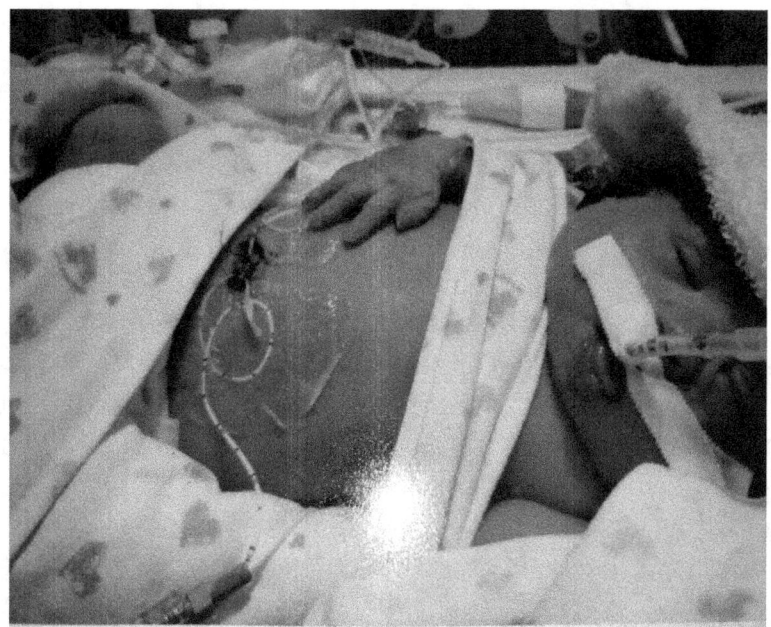

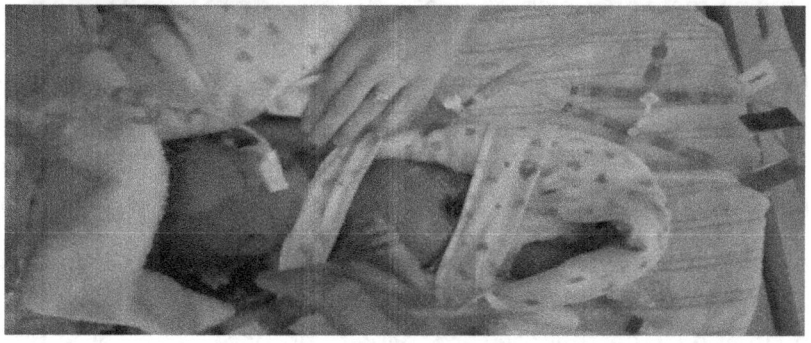

04/22/2015

I couldn't really sleep through the night, or at all. I just laid there trying to guess what might happen with our family. I am running on so many emotions. I am trying to be hopeful but I have a nagging feeling that my boy may be struggling more than we can see. The doctors and nurses are working around the clock on him trying to help him. He's so tiny. He has the face of our babies and his beautiful blonde wavy hair. It's gorgeous. His frame is so small but yet I can see the typical features in our other babies.

I find myself going down to be with him but when my emotions are so overwhelming I excuse myself and have Jeremiah wheel me back to my room. This happened while Peyton was in the hospital too. I would sit with him but as the emotions became too much I had to leave, I had to go out into other parts of the hospital or take breaks back to the hotel. Deep down I think I needed these breaks because I was trying to be strong for Peyton and now Tayden. I didn't want them to feel me as a complete mess or fear coming from me because I didn't want it to scare them. When I was with Peyton and now with Tayden I want them to feel that mommy is confident, as a way to bring them a sort of comfort or peace. I didn't want to alarm them and feel that I was a mess. I didn't want them to feel like I had broken down, that I had given up on them or that I had submitted to the ultimate of outcomes, death. I wanted them to feel hope from me. But this amount of holding it in forced me to leave for breaks often to release the feelings and energy. Again, a second time, I am here trying to be strong, trying to bring comfort to my second boy that he can fight through this and that mommy and daddy are here and that he is so loved.

As we continue into the early afternoon I notice that the dialogue between the nurses and doctor is one of preparedness towards Jeremiah and I. I feel that they are trying to prepare us for something.

Tayden Passes

Now, it is late afternoon and the doctors and nurse talk to Jeremiah and I that Tayden is on the highest level of intervention they can provide and yet his little body is having trouble fighting with this. His coloring is becoming darker, a little more bluish tone which the doctors explain is because his body is having trouble with his oxygen and carbon dioxide exchange due to Tayden having such little lung tissue developed, due to the hydrops. The doctor starts the "talk" that I so vividly remember from 3 years ago. They start to tell us that Tayden is starting to decline and to prepare for his death.

This cannot be happening to us, not AGAIN. I cannot lose another little boy. *Dear God, please don't make me go through this again. I cannot endure this pain again. This has to be a bad dream, a nightmare. Why would God bless me with such a beautiful little boy only to have him ripped from my arms? Why would he tease me with another baby boy only to take him too? This feels like such a cruel game. We are good people. We are great parents. Why is God allowing this to happen to us?*

By now our friend couple is here. My in-laws have brought the girls back to the hospital. My mom and step-dad had come and gone. My friend from long ago stopped to see our sweet boy. My sister-in-law called a local photographer who is part of an organization called 'Now I Lay Me Down to Sleep'. There was only one photographer in the whole Omaha area that was part of this. Through the organization he volunteered to come take pictures of babies as they were dying, as a momento to the family. We did not know this service existed when Peyton died but my sister-in-law found out when we got Tayden's diagnosis. I can never repay her for finding this service for us. She called the photographer and before we knew it they were there setting up for our "last shoot".

I had asked Trinity if she wanted to be in the room as Tayden was dying, or if she would rather stay out. I wanted her to feel comfortable and didn't want to cause her any more trauma then what she's already experienced in this life so far. She was adamant that she be in the room with me and daddy. She even asked if she could hold him. I knew Tenley wouldn't really understand what was going on but I also asked her and she said she wanted to stay with me.

We were all there around him in his little incubator, his little body struggling. His breathing was getting more labored. I asked the nurses if I could hold him. I needed to hold him while he was alive and I needed him to be in my arms as he died. I needed him to know what it felt like to be held and loved. I needed him to know that he belonged with me. The nurses placed him into my arms carefully, carefully adjusting all of the wires and tubes. He felt so light, so tiny but he melted into my body. I just started bawling. Here was my beautiful baby boy, dying. Tears streamed down my face and onto his beautiful porcelain skin. I felt like he could sense me, he knew I was there. The photographer was in the background taking photos as we were in this raw place. It was so surreal, but I knew those photos would be the only piece left of my boy.

The nurse moved Tayden into Jeremiah's arms and he too broke down, overcome with these raw last moments. And then Tayden slightly opened his eyes, which were gorgeous. I knew that he had just given us a gift. He had opened his eyes for us, to tell us goodbye. We had lived this moment with Peyton and here we were living it again with Tayden. *Thank you dear boy.*

Jeremiah eventually moved him back to me. Deep down I think Jeremiah knew it was getting closer to his physical death and he knew that I needed to be the one to hold him. The nurses placed him back into my arms with Jeremiah and Trinity at my side, all of us talking and touching him. His breathing got more shallow and then slower. He then took a few more breaths that were more spaced apart, and then had a little gasp and breath, and then I heard no more. The nurse came over and listened to his chest and nodded that she no longer heard his heartbeat. *My beautiful, tiny little baby was gone*...

I am broken, I am shattered. I don't understand, my baby is gone. My special little boy is gone. I had already prepared to take care of all of your special needs as you aged. I had plans to take care of you the rest of my life. *Please God, not my second precious boy. Why is this happening? Why do you continue to punish me?*

Trinity asked to hold him and so a nurse helped to move him over to her arms. She held him and I just sat there devastated that once again she has lost a brother. She wanted to cry but she was trying to be strong. When she was done we let Tenley hold him. Tenley was giddy and talked about him as a baby doll. She held him so tight and when it was time to take him back we had to practically pry him from her tiny arms. We just sat there with him and took some more staged pictures with the photographer.

Eventually my in-laws loaded up the girls to take them home. The nurses took Tayden to clean him up for us so that I could sit with him more later. Jeremiah wheeled me back up to my room where the nurses had brought in sandwiches, food and pop for our family. How sweet that was of them?

After it quieted down and everyone left the nurses brought in Tayden. They had bathed him and dressed him in the pj.'s that I had given them. He was swaddled in a little blue blanket that I had brought for him. I laid in the bed with him and just held him... and cried... and cried... and cried. I smelled him and kissed him knowing that this was it. This was all I was ever going to get of him. I would never get this moment with him ever again. I caressed his little head, his beautiful blonde hair. Jeremiah took him and held him in the chair. I couldn't look at Jeremiah holding him for too long as it broke my heart. To see my husband with his second deceased boy was devastating. We didn't care that Tayden had Down syndrome, we didn't care about any of his medical issues. We just wanted him, all of him. To us, he was perfect no matter what. He would have been our little boy with Down syndrome that brought so much light to the world. He would have been our littlest light, our beautiful ray of sunshine. He would have brought so much happiness to our family and we are devastated...

As bed time approached the nurses took Tayden for good. Jeremiah and I slept there broken again, trying to understand what was happening in our life. My brother stopped over to the hospital to give his condolences. But really, what do you say to someone whose baby's just died?

The next morning the doctor that performed my surgery came in to express his condolences. He also said he would be willing to let me out of the hospital a day early so that I could go home and not be surrounded by all of the moms and their new babies. During the C-section they had accidentally cut my bladder so I had to be in a catheter for a week to let my bladder heal so I would see my normal doctor in the next week to have it taken out. Jeremiah and I packed up our stuff. We thanked the hospital staff and just like that we left. On the way home we were so quiet both unsure what to say. We were both still in shock as I think deep down we both believed Tayden would live. We had prepared for a long haul but not this, not death. But once again we drew this shitty deck of cards. *I feel like we are cursed.*

PEYTON'S PASSING

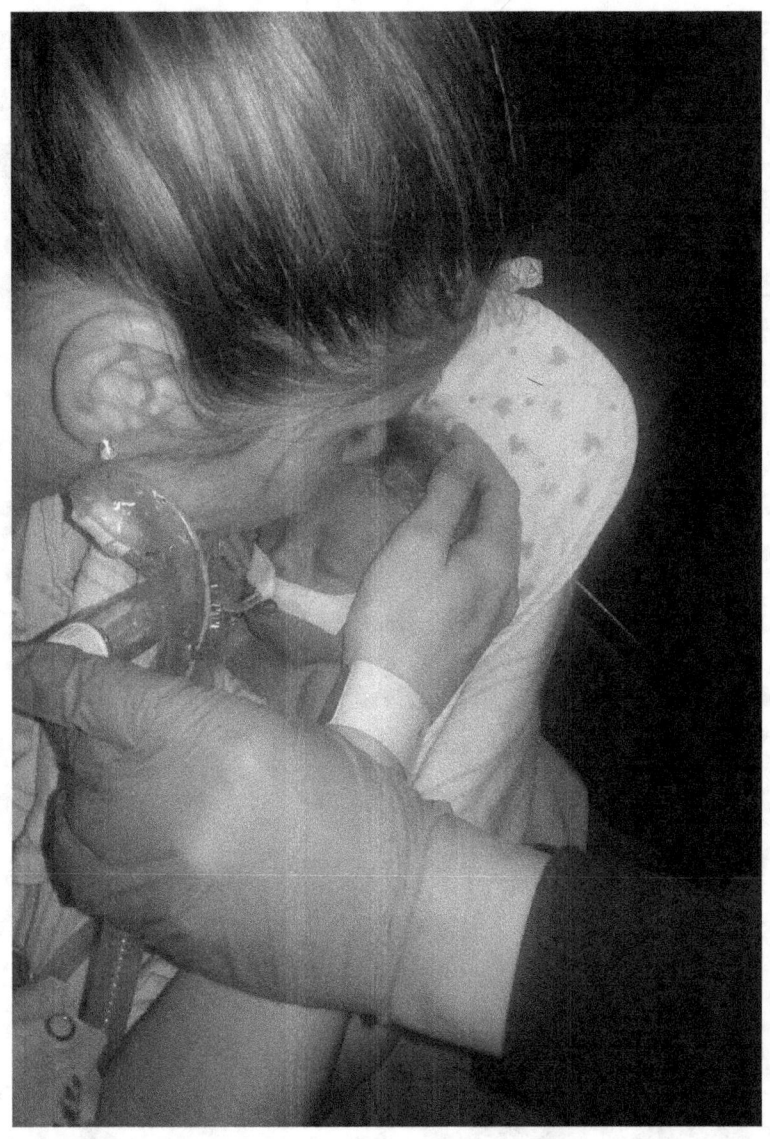

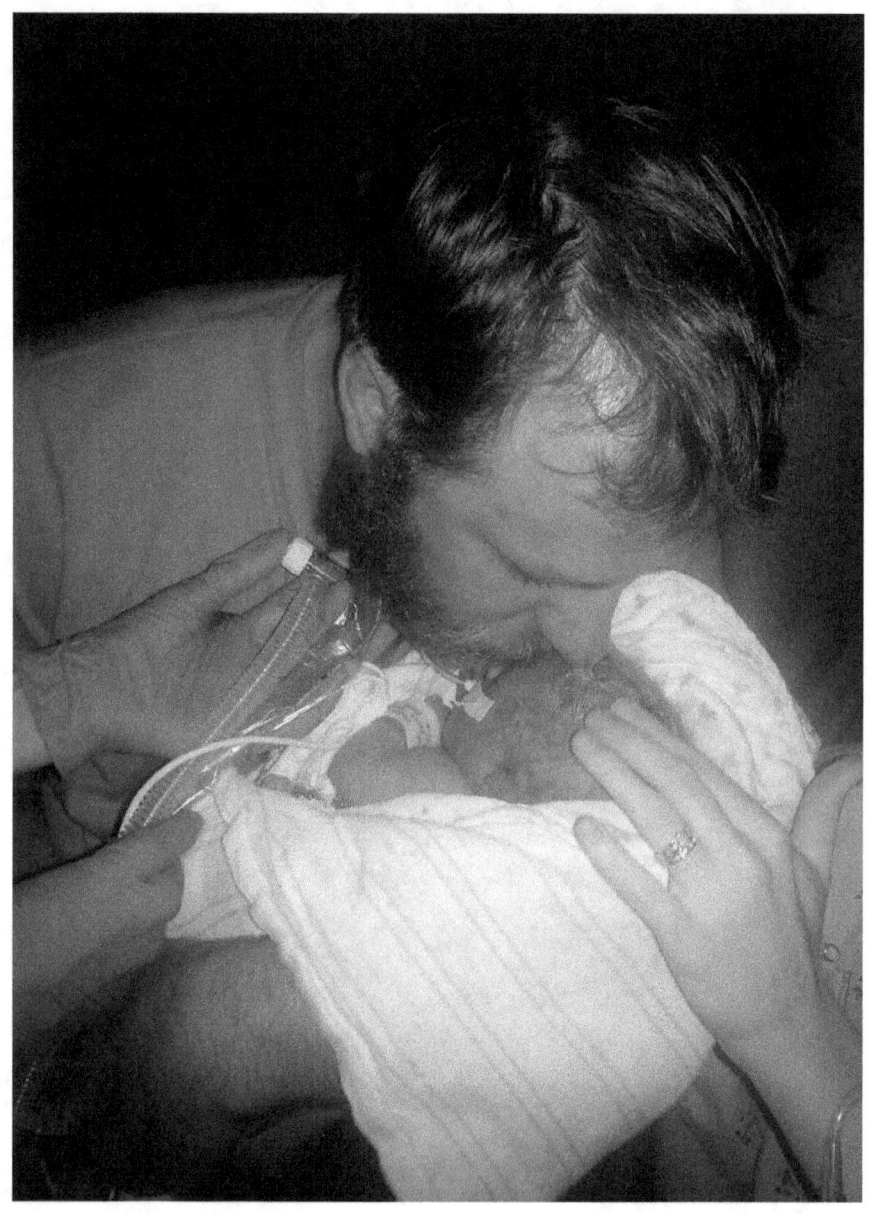

Jeremiah posted this on his social media account.

"Courtney Pottebaum and I have another Angel in Heaven. Tayden Joseph, born 4/21/15 joined his brother today, 4/22/15. Tayden had his mother's short stature and my rugged good looks."

04/23/2015

Today I posted this on my social media account to update our friends and family that live far away:

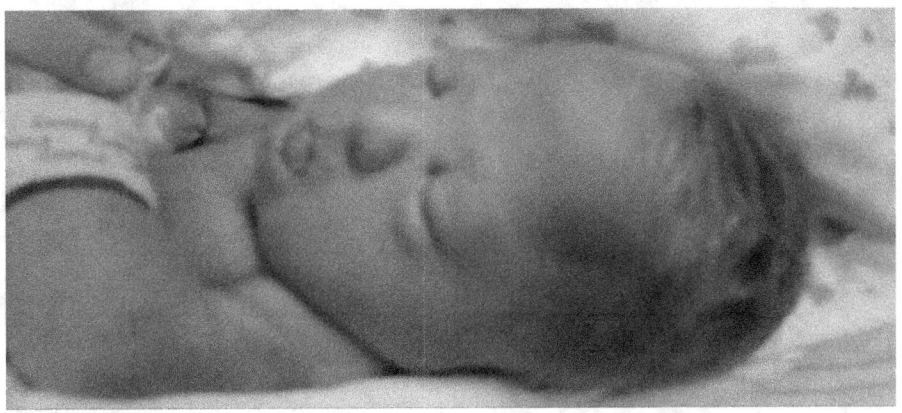

Approximately 6 weeks ago Jeremiah and I received the news that I was suffering from a condition called polyhydramnios (massive amounts of amniotic fluid). Doctors also discovered that baby Tayden tested positive for Down Syndrome and had a great deal of fluid around his little lungs and stomach, making it unknown to doctors if he would be able to sustain life outside of the womb. The next 6 weeks consisted of waiting and being monitored. We never posted anything about what was going on as we needed time to process the possible outcomes. I delivered Tayden @ 36 weeks by C-section in Omaha on Tuesday the 21st. He held on for one day but passed away in my arms at 8:06 p.m. on the evening of the 22nd. As we

have told our girls...his older brother Peyton has gained a sibling and playmate in heaven. Tayden has been our only baby born with blonde hair. If love could have saved him, he would have never died. ~We love you Tayden Joseph Pottebaum. ~

We will have a visitation on Wednesday the 29th @ 2 p.m. @ Meyers and a 3p.m. Graveside service at Memorial Cemetery. He will be buried next to his brother Peyton.

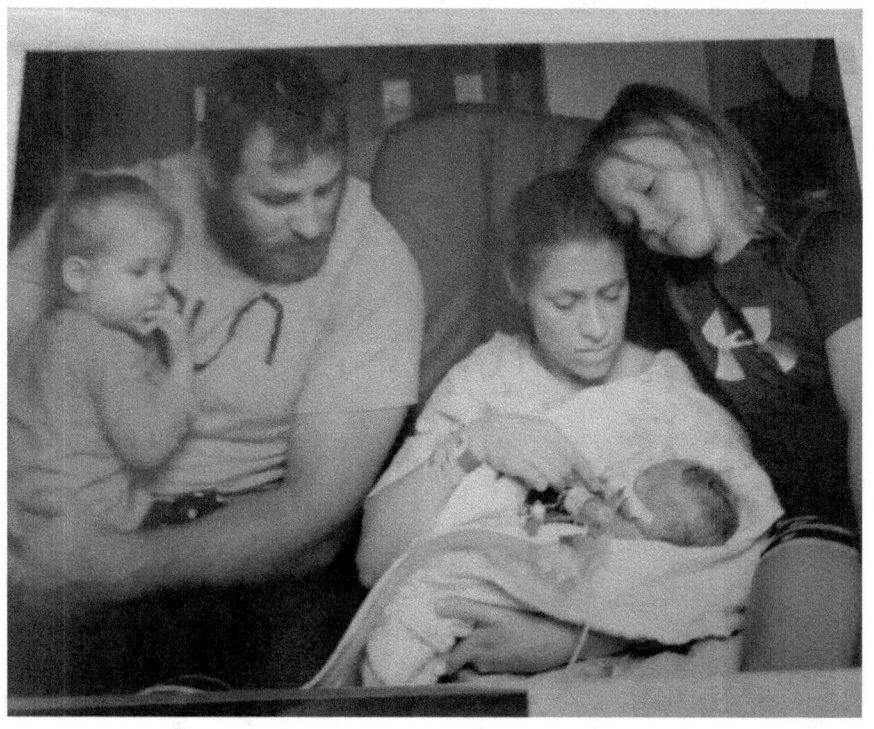

04/27/2015

Our amazing funeral director called today asking if we could drop off the clothes that we wanted Tayden to wear for his service tomorrow. I picked out his outfit, which is a Chicago Bears sleeper that his

Aunt had gotten him. It was the exact same sleeper that we buried Peyton in. *How fitting....*

On our way to the funeral home I was so self-conscious as I was still having to wear a catheter from my bladder being cut during surgery. I kept trying to figure out how I could hide the catheter. I brought a big purse that I put the bag in, even though the tubing would still show.

As we walked in Brad met us. He was so warm and genuine. He had expressed that he was the one who had driven down to Omaha to pick up our boy and bring him back to the funeral home. He expressed that he wasn't going to charge us for this service and that he wanted to do this. *Dear God thank you for this amazing man who is helping us. How can we ever repay him?*

Brad then looked at me and asked me if I wanted to dress Tayden myself to get him ready for his service. We were never offered this option with Peyton but Peyton had an autopsy so I suppose that would have been too traumatic seeing my boy's body all cut up. Tears filled my eyes and I said, "Yes, please". Brad led me into a private room and there lay a table covered with a covering. I took out Tayden's outfit and the blanket I would wrap him in. Brad walked in holding our boy and laid him gently on the table. There he was ... my beautiful, tiny little baby boy. He lay there so calm and so precious. Tears streamed down my face as I started to dress him. I undressed him from his hospital outfit and put a clean diaper on him as well as his Bear's sleeper. I moved so slow as this was my last time to be with him. My eyes soaked in every little detail of my dear boy's body and begged my memory never forgot what every detail looked like. Once I had him dressed I bundled him in his blanket and then I just sat with him in my arms. THIS TIME was the best gift anyone could have given me. I just sat there holding him, tears streaming down my face onto his beautiful cheeks. As long as he was in my arms I could pretend that he wasn't dead.

God I have been so faithful. I have tried to believe in you through all of the last three years. How can you take my second boy? What am I supposed to gain by burying my second boy? I am broken, I am tired, I am struggling to understand your purpose. What have I done to deserve this ... ALL of this?

When I feel that it's time Jeremiah gets Brad and we hand our sweet boy over to him. Who am I kidding? No amount of time would ever feel like enough when this is **all** I'll ever get. We pack up and drive home. A silent, defeated, exhausted drive home...

04/29/2015

Today is the day that I have to bury my second son. Today is my second funeral. My belly is still swollen from your birth. My breasts are now leaking milk but you're not alive to feed. I am so broken, so empty and so hollow. I just don't understand. My legs are like cement and they will not move. I don't want to get ready, I don't want to do my hair, I don't know what I'll wear. I have to dress my girls for an experience that they might not want to go through. I just don't want to do this... not today, not ever..... **NOT AGAIN**.

I get myself dressed and get the girls dressed and ready. We pack in the car and silently drive to the funeral home. As we pull in there are already vehicles present, many family members are already here. We unload and start to walk in and I remember that feeling, that feeling of needing to be kind to others. The feeling of needing to be able and converse with everyone enough, even though I am numb and miserable. The feeling of having to entertain others when I am the one that is broken. Why do we do funerals the way we do? We place the grieving people in a position to have to entertain all of the visitors when we can't even function. Why do we do this? I have to act like I am "ok" when I'm not. I have to act like "He's in a better place", when I completely disagree. I have to say, "Thank you for your thoughts and prayers", when I really want anyone to bring him back to life. I sigh heavy, ready to "act" like I'm doing ok and that somehow I will get through this. Here I fucking go again....

There were some people already here as we walked in. I immediately unpack our stuff and family members start to interact with our girls. I head straight to the room and there at the end of the aisle is a little white casket. As I get closer I see his beautiful hair, in his cute little Chicago Bears footed jammies. He lays there so peacefully. "*Gosh, Tayden, you are such a tiny, beautiful baby. Your features are so sweet.*" I instinctively pick him up out of the casket and cradle him in my arms. His jammies are so long that the legs are tucked behind him. He's cold to the touch. I pull him into me and the tears stream from my eyes. I just tuck him into my chest and I feel my breasts ache, for a baby that they cannot feed. This is what I should be doing with him. I just hold him as my long hair falls around my shoulders and over him. It's as if I am guarding him from this cruel world, as if I am trying to keep what is left of him safe... even if it's only his body. I don't know how long I hold him but it is getting evident that Jeremiah is waiting for his boy. Trinity comes up to me and is standing near me waiting for her turn to hold him as well. I pass him to Jeremiah who holds him as tears are streaming down his face. I can feel how broken he is...

Dear God, I don't understand this plan, if there is such a thing. I don't know why we have to endure this again. We are good people who love our children deeply. Why are we being punished? Why is this happening? Why do we have to endure this pain again?

Trinity asks me to hold Tayden and so we have her sit on a chair. Jeremiah carefully passes him over to her and helps to make sure she is stable. She has tears in her eyes as she holds him. I am instantly so angry again. Why does SHE have to experience this **again** a second time? I can feel her pain as she sits there trying to be strong. Tenley is petting his head like a little doggie and saying she wants to hold the baby. She is trying to pull at his little legs and arms in an attempt to take "this baby doll" from Trinity. We have Tenley sit next to Trinity and we help Tenley to hold him. She holds him like a baby doll and when it's time for her to give him back she clutches on tighter. We have to carefully pry him away from her. I can tell there are other family members that want to hold him. And I guess I should let them but deep down I just don't want to share him. I don't want to give anyone else any of this small amount of time we have with him. But, we offer for Jeremiah's mom to hold him and we also let my mom hold him. I can tell Jeremiah feels like I do… we don't really want him to be with anyone but us. The clock is ticking and soon he will be buried where we will never be able to see him again.

The pastor of our church speaks at the service and many family and friends are present. So many wonderful people are there to support us. But my energy is below zero and it is near impossible to carry on any meaningful conversation. We try our best to 'keep it together' and the service comes to a close. My brother is the casket bearer and is called up to carry baby Tayden down the aisle. We follow behind. As we approach the doorway, the funeral director that has been so loving to us hands me a stack of envelopes and says, "These were mailed to the funeral home for you. You are both very loved." I then inquire about our bill with the funeral home and he said, "That has been taken care of. There is no bill for you to pay". I asked him, "Who paid for this service?" His response was, "The person has asked to remain anonymous." I begged him to tell me but again he said, "I'm sorry, but the person requested to remain anonymous." And just like that the tears that had dried up now came rushing down my cheeks. WHO could have paid for us and our boy? God bless this person for they just lifted a huge debt from our shoulders. I had no idea how we were going to pay for our second son's service. Relief and gratitude overwhelmed me. *Thank you so much to whoever you are… you have no idea the gratitude I feel for you.*

As we approach the vehicle that would hold the casket, the funeral director asks me if I would like to hold on to the casket myself and drive it over to the cemetery. I look at him with big eyes and say, "Please, and thank you so much." He knew the gift he was giving me, the gift of TIME. Every extra second with my boy was the best gift anyone could ever give me. And for that, I will forever be grateful. Me, carrying our boy in his casket in the front of our vehicle and Jeremiah gets the girls buckled in the back. We drive over to the cemetery which is literally a mile or two away. As we approach our very familiar spot we see the tent over Peyton's grave, where Tayden will also be buried, at the foot of Peyton's grave. I would never have thought this but this place, this cemetery has become a sort of home, a sort of comfort for me. This space has witnessed more tears, more begging, more prayers than any other place I inhabit. This place has become my solace. So, even though I am now getting ready to bury my second baby I am calm... broken definitely, but calm. I cling to the thoughts of what he looks like as this is my last opportunity to sneak a peek at my boy.

Our pastor does a great job at his service and incorporated Petyon into his service. I didn't ask him to but he did; I think he knew I needed it. After the service as people are separating to leave, I look at my brother and instantly I know that he is the person that paid for Tayden's service.

When the seconds have been long enough or long enough to take, we load up the girls. We head home and a few members drop by the house to see us. I approach my brother and ask him, "It was you, wasn't it? You paid for Tayden's service? The director said the person wanted to remain anonymous, but I know it was you?"

My brother just stared blank at me and responded, "No, it wasn't me." But I could tell... I said, "I know it was you and I will pay you back. You don't have to do this, this is not your burden to bear."

With tears in his eyes he said, "I just couldn't let you do this again. I know how independent you are. You've always done everything on your own and you take pride in that. If I could help this way, it's what I want to do."

I cried, "Thank you so much James, you have no idea how much I appreciate this" and hugged him.

Our family members brought over some food for anyone at our house. Our couple friends came over and they brought treats as well. As I sat there in the kitchen talking to my good friend I said, "Here I sit after my son just died and all I can think about is having another baby. There was damage done physically to my body and I don't think I can. I feel guilty that I am already thinking of another baby... I just wanted him, no matter what."

My friend's response was so genuine and loving and she simply said, "That's ok to feel that way. I don't think there's any wrong or right way to feel right now. You're allowed to feel however you do. And maybe, that will be an option in the future and whatever you decide, Tayden would approve."

I felt like I had just confessed such a "weight" to her about wanting another baby. I fear that anyone hearing that would tell me, 'listen, this baby thing isn't really working out for you. So, rather than cause yourself anymore pain, you just need to stop while you're ahead. Be grateful for what you have and move on. Let that dream go.' But she didn't say that, she didn't say any of that.... She said exactly what I needed to hear. And for that, I am forever grateful to her. She didn't judge me. She just accepted that 'where I was' is 'where I was'.

04/30/2015

Jeremiah had a few work friends come over to see us. This friend gave Jeremiah a bible and tears swelled in my eyes. I am so afraid that Jeremiah will turn away from God, faith, a belief in anything greater than us. I am afraid that he will become bitter and angry and through anger turn away to whatever is "above" us all. I don't understand why this has all happened and I'm angry and bitter that God has allowed this to happen but I still believe. Something deep in my soul knows that there is a force greater than us. I just don't know exactly what it looks like. I call it "God" because that is what I was taught in CCD class growing up. I am faithful but I am pissed...

I'll never forget some time ago while Jeremiah was in the bathroom looking in the mirror, he looked at the mirror and said, "If Tayden dies, I no longer believe. The God I believe in would never allow something like this to happen." And when I heard that, my heart dropped to the floor. For I feared the destruction that Jeremiah would create within himself that would ruin himself and our family.... All from pain....

Dear God, Please don't let that happen. If the bible is a place where he can try to find meaning then at least it means he's still holding on. If this is what can hook him, please just let him believe in SOMETHING.

05/03/2015

Visiting my two beautiful boys.

Do I Stay?

05/04/2015

I woke up around 10:30 p.m. feeling delirious and weak. I was so light-headed and in extreme pain in my abdomen. Jeremiah was not in our bed and then I remembered him earlier going to walk Tenley back to bed. I got up shakily to go to Tenley's room to get him and I collapsed in the hallway. I crawled to her bedroom to where he was in the rocker with Tenley. I grabbed his leg and said I needed him to take me to the ER and to call his mom. He put her in her bed and helped me back to the bedroom. He called his mom and his voice shaking asked her to come to the house because he needed to take me to the ER. I dressed myself and he helped load me in the car. I felt like I couldn't breathe and the pain in my abdomen was excruciating. His mom pulled up in the driveway and we were off.

Jeremiah drove me quickly to the ER and tried to talk to me on the way. Once there they immediately started working on me. I was hooked up to an IV and fluids were immediately given. A nurse got a urine sample from me and the ER doctor came in and started talking to us. He ended up doing a vaginal examination and said that there looked to be some leftover tissue in my uterus. They took blood samples and it was determined that I had gone septic due to leftover placental tissue that was inside of me. They also took x-rays to see what they were looking at. I also was severely anemic since I had been hemorrhaging for two weeks and didn't realize it. My uterus hadn't started to go down yet but I was so numb from grief that I was just doing my best to function. I had been in a catheter for a week since the doctors cut my bladder. I was miserable in every way... physically, mentally, emotionally, spiritually. But, I had just lost my baby... so I thought it was the grief. The doctors admitted me immediately with IV fluids and antibiotics hooked up to me.

Jeremiah got me settled into a room. Once I was settled he asked me what I needed from home. He left some time into the morning hours to relieve his mom from watching the girls and to pack a bag for me. I was so numb...

I knew that my body was failing. I was weak, extremely weak. I knew my body was dying. And something inside of me wasn't scared. I wasn't nervous, or sad, or terrified. I was **EMPTY.** There was nothing left inside of my well, the water was dry. There was no concern for what would happen to my family once I left. There was a calm inside of me that they would all be ok. I had begged God to take me after Peyton died and now after Tayden, he was finally fulfilling my request. *I am done 'fighting' in this life and I'm ready to be with my boys.* And with that I drifted off to sleep...

05/05/2015

Jeremiah came back up closer to mid-morning. He had gotten the girls up and ready for their day. He put the dogs out and kenneled. He got Trinity to school and Tenley ready and dropped off to daycare. It's a lot of work to keep our household running.

He brought me up a bag, my toiletries, my tablet, my chargers and comfy clothes. In that moment I missed my girls as I had never really been away from them. Being away from them made me feel sad, that I was failing at doing my job to take care of them. Jeremiah called his work to inform them of what was going on and reached out to one of my coworkers so people at my work would know. He called our family members and informed them.

Then he sat next to my bed... He looked tired from having no sleep the night before. But more than tired, he looked concerned. He asked how I was feeling. Sometime through the morning doctors consulted with me that they were going to try and give me a pill to see if that could help my uterus contract enough to expel the tissue that was still inside and infected. They explained that if that didn't work then they would do a D&C to expel it. We would know more in a few days. I also knew that the doctors didn't know how sick I really was. They didn't know I was on the verge of dying...

Jeremiah sat there and I could feel him just staring at me. I wasn't in for much talking... words just weren't coming to my mind. At one point he moved the chair over closer to me, grabbed my hand and said, "Courtney, please, I need you to fight through this. I know right now, after losing Tayden, it would be easy to give up. Please, fight through this. I cannot lose you too." As he said this, tears came to his eyes and I felt the stirring of his soul. He was pleading with me because he could see that 'fighting' was not what I wanted to do. I was devastated after losing my second son. I was angry that my hopes were elated, only to be crushed on the ground.... Again. I have been fighting for three straight years since Peyton. Now losing Tayden, it took all the rest of my "fight" with him. I was done fighting and just wanted to go be with my boys. I knew in that moment that I was being given a choice. I could die or I could choose to stay... *How do I choose between seeing my sweet boys or staying with my husband and girls?* I felt intense energy, light and emotion all around me. *Dear God, What are you trying to tell me?*

Jeremiah brought the girls up this evening. They were happy to see me. Trinity was scared and nervous. She didn't understand what was wrong with me. She stayed away just enough so she didn't get "it". I tried to muster up enough energy to interact with them. I was sad I wasn't home with them. Jeremiah was tired, I could see it in his eyes. He had a home to go care for, girls to feed and bathe and a bedtime routine to start. He kissed me deeper than he had in a long time.... Almost like he was afraid that it would be the last. *He's praying that I make the decision to stay.*

05/06/2015

I have had a few visitors over the last few days just checking on how I have been doing. Word got out fast that I was hospitalized. Jeremiah took off of work to be here every day. He has brought the girls up each evening. He has tried to make sure I have what I need. The doctors talked today and decided that the medication they were hoping would contract my uterus didn't work so I am now scheduled for a D&C tomorrow.

My family members all live away. And right now, I just wish they were here. I feel so lonely and I wish Jeremiah had more help. For some reason, we haven't told anyone how sick I really am... Sometimes, it's easier to suffer alone.

05/07/2015

Today I am scheduled for the D&C at noon. For some reason, I am really nervous. Please pray that it all goes ok. I googled complications of this procedure, which I shouldn't have, but obviously it makes me really scared. I've already had a D&C years ago with a miscarriage but that wasn't after just giving birth and having a recently operated on uterus.

Of course, Jeremiah was there but my aunt also came up. She's been a pretty constant for me these last few days. She called my mom for me. I just couldn't ... I don't know why. My mom then did call me to check on me. I told her about today's surgery. She said that she was busy with 'work' and so she wouldn't be able to come up. I knew that really meant that she was working but that after work, she would be 'busy drinking' and nothing can get in the way of her drinking. And as she said she was 'busy' my stomach turned and rage filled within me. Because I was really sick, and instead of being here for me, she could only be there for the bottle. I am educated; I understand the physiological happenings of addiction but I will never understand that 'desire'. I can't imagine something having such a hold on me. I can't imagine choosing that over my child. My son died and here I am sick in the hospital and even that isn't enough for her to 'love me enough'. If I ever needed her... it was now. Addiction has taken my mom and stolen her away as well.

A chaplain met me upon the entry into the surgical room. I looked at her and instantly I knew her. She was familiar. And then it hit me.... She was the chaplain at the hospital the day Peyton was rushed to the ER from daycare. She was in the room with us. I knew she recognized me too. She said she recognized my name on the surgery registry so she thought she'd come to greet me. How thoughtful.... How special. I told her I was scared and she said a prayer. I slipped off to sleep.

When I awoke I was out of surgery and back in my normal hospital room. Jeremiah was next to me. He explained that surgery went well. I was scheduled to have it done by a doctor that I don't typically see. Jeremiah said that the two doctors I normally work with showed up to help with the surgery. He said that he spoke to one of them who said that with a sweeping motion of her hand felt all along the inside of my uterus making sure they had gotten everything out. She said that they pulled out leftover placental tissue that was the size of a small ball. He mentioned that the two doctors that normally saw me weren't scheduled to do the procedure but I knew that due to the care they had for me, that's why they showed up to help. They have always been amazing doctors to me. Since Peyton, they have supported and comforted me all along this whole journey. I knew they were heartbroken for me... again. They are such amazing people and I am so lucky and grateful that they are my doctors. There are people here on this earth plane that are fighting for me.... *I guess that means I have to decide to fight for myself.*

05/17/2015

I came home from the hospital a day and a half ago. Today I went to church. I was so hesitant. Would I be able to sit through a service and act like I don't have anger, confusion, and sadness pouring out of my pores? I was there, but not really "there". Tears poured down my cheeks. *What is the purpose of this pain? Is there something that I didn't learn with Peyton's passing and you felt it necessary to make sure I learned it this time? Why were both of my boys taken?* I wanted a baby to snuggle with, kiss, embrace with love and dote on. I wanted Tayden. I didn't care about his needs. He would have been my mommy's boy for the rest of my life. I would have adored every minute of it. I just don't get it, nothing about his loss makes sense to me.

He was so beautiful. He would have been my little peanut...so tiny. His beautiful blonde, thick hair. He was beautiful and precious. I took care of him the best I could while he lived inside of me. I believe he held on like he did so he could see his daddy and I. While in the incubator the day before he died he never opened his eyes. But, as we held him, as he was dying, he opened his eyes. I know he knew he was with us... I also know that he knew I needed to "see" him. *Thank you sweet boy.*

I am so confused by Tayden's loss. How is it possible that my second, tiny baby was also taken from me? Did Peyton need him more than me? Most parents don't ever have to experience losing one child, let alone two. *Why was I chosen to experience this pain and what am I supposed to learn or gain from losing my second, precious son?*

I think Tayden would have been just a little guy who dearly loved his momma and all he touched. I think he would have brought so much joy and love to our life. Tenley would have been such a good big sister. He would have been doted on by all of us.

Sometimes I feel guilty as when we first learned of Tayden's diagnosis I was scared as I didn't know what to expect. Tayden's loss is different but still there isn't really closure. There's just no one to blame this time. But, he's still his own self, his own little being, and another life that should be dependent on me to care for and love. I was scared of his special needs only because it is a road I am not that familiar with. It was more of the unknown that I was scared of. I was afraid that I wouldn't know how to care for him. What are the chances of our family losing another baby...who had so many rare conditions against him? Inside I feel like there is something I am supposed to learn, gain, or understand with Tayden's loss.

"Tayden Joseph, you were beautiful and perfect. I loved you from the day you started growing inside of me. I would have doted on you and cared for you with all of my heart. I would have adored you, snuggled endlessly with you, and loved you beyond loving. I love you so much and long for you in my arms. I wish I could rock you, kiss you, and show you off to the world. Mommy loves you so much. I hope you are having fun with your brother. I know Peyton is taking care of you. I would give anything to see my two precious boys snuggling and playing together. That day can't come soon enough for me and one day I'll get all my babies together. I imagine what chaos it would be like if both of my boys were alive. I would love every single minute of the craziness. I love you dear son...so, so, much....my beautiful, tiniest son."

05/25/2015

A friend of mine that I knew from high school came to our house and brought Jeremiah and I an apple tree to plant in memory of Tayden. Such a special gift to give us. She has reached out to Jeremiah and I with such compassion and genuine concern. It's something that can "remain here" long after my sweet boy has been gone. THAT is what is so precious to me.

06/7/2015

"Dear Tayden,

I can't believe it's been almost six weeks that I got to meet you, hold you, cry over you, fall in love with you, and be struck with the notion that I won't get to watch you grow up. Six weeks out and I'm still numb. My youngest little boy, you were perfect and so beautiful. I look at pictures of you often and I imagine those moments of having you here. I also replay holding you... and losing you. It will forever break me into a million pieces as I recall holding you and hearing three little gasps from your tiny body. You had fought and you were trying, but you just couldn't anymore. You gasped as I held you and then you were silent. You were gone... you were still... you were beautiful. No amount of tears from my eyes or pain from my heart could bring you back. I so dearly wished I could breathe life into your lungs and bring you back. I was so in love with you and wished that I could fix your little body. I was ready to have my little boy that needed so much of mommy's love. For months I waited for your presence and I dreamed all of the big dreams. I made memories of what it would be like to have you here in our family. Oh, how bad daddy and I wanted you... Please know for those months I carried you daddy and I felt so happy, so healed, so excited about life. We were getting a little boy! Oh, how badly we yearned for you. Please know I took care of you as best I could while you were inside me and how well I would have doted on you if you had lived. You were born to a family that deeply loved you from the moment that we conceived you. You were 'our happy ever after'. But,

> I grieve for all the unsaid words that you will never say. I grieve that I will never see you happily at play
>
> — sayinggoodbye.org

life or the devil have taught me that really there is no 'happily ever after'. And even though I have experienced this twice, I still have trouble accepting this. I don't believe that there is this magical plan that God has so intricately inscribed for each one of us. How could he let your brother be murdered or you die of sickness? The God I believe in wouldn't promote or arrange suffering. I just can't accept that. But, people for fear of what to say or for fear of realizing that life could actually be random tell me that God has this plan. Bless them for trying to comfort me but that theory cannot be this life. Randomness seems to make more sense... but even then, what would be the odds that I would lose my two beautiful boys? I have to believe that for some reason the devil wants to break me and I must say he has gotten so close. I can't let him win and I don't know why he has chosen me. As I did with your brother, I have armored up ready to dig out of this trench solely for the purpose of not allowing him to win and defeat me. I am far from understanding my losses. I am far from being content with the life I have. I am far from accepting your deaths. I am far from happiness. I would be lying if I said that I look at families with multiple healthy children, or mothers with their new babies and feel happy for them. I look at them and the deep pain underneath my smile wishes that was me. It makes me resentful of them, that it is so easy for them, that they don't know my pain, that their life is so easy, that they can believe so faithfully, that their heart isn't broken like mine. Why my boys? Why me? Why my family? I am not that strong... or at least I didn't choose to be. All I ever wanted were my four healthy babies, but two were stolen from me for reasons that I cannot grasp. My body mourns the loss of you Tayden in ways that I wasn't prepared for. Milk still runs from my breasts not realizing that there is no baby to feed. My baby weight holds onto me thinking I need the weight to nourish a baby. This whole process has been so lonely, so unreal, and unfortunately so familiar. I love you so much baby boy. You were beautiful and I miss you so much."

07/07/2015

I sit here at the grave... my place of solace. It's beautiful today. Grandpa is doing a good job of keeping your grave trimmed up and wiped off. It tears me apart if your grave isn't looking its best with decorations and care. I guess it's my way of taking care of what's left of you here. I sit here, Tayden's marker isn't in yet, but I sit between you two. One boy on each side of me. That's the way it should be. I can't believe it's been 12 weeks since Tayden was born. How can that be? I feel like this time I am not grieving like I did with Peyton. Like, it won't come out... doesn't know how to come out... can't come out. I don't know... I just know it's not the same. Tayden would be three months old by now. Surely, smiling and cooing. I can't be around babies. My heart just aches. At church last Sunday a mom sat by me with her infant. As she got close I thought, "Please don't sit by me, please don't sit by me, please don't sit by me." But she did, right next to me, as if to rub salt in my newly opened wound. The soul inside of me just bent over and bawled and collapsed and said, "why me, why me again."

I find myself looking around wondering 'what is my purpose?' What exactly am I supposed to accomplish in this life? What am I supposed to contribute to this world? How do I use my pain to impact people in positive ways? Will I ever get over feeling so bitter? Will I ever stop comparing our shitty hand to all of our friends who seem to have it so easy? It's not their fault... it's not our fault... but, that doesn't make me any less bitter. It's just a shitty hand no matter how you look at it. The cards were definitely stacked against us and I can't help but think that someone stacked the deck against us.

In college I remember visualizing and feeling so positive for some reason that Jeremiah and I would always have two girls. Was that some sort of message for me to remember now? Like in some way, was that a warning? I still think about having another... and medically/emotionally that also seems absurd. Why would I push our luck anymore? Because I deeply wanted a baby. I wanted our family to feel complete. And maybe my cross to bear is that I will never get to feel that...

What I do know is that I miss my boys terribly and there isn't a second that goes by that one or both of them aren't on my mind. I am not afraid of anything in this world because I have done the unimaginable, twice. While I say this I also think of the parents who have lost children much older than mine... How have they survived? How did they make it through? How were they strong enough to continue to live? What magic do they possess? I do not want my sons' legacies to be that their deaths completely destroyed me. For that alone, I need to get better, get healthier, be present for my girls, and attentive to my husband. Somehow, I have to look up and feel grateful that I got to hold them at all and continue clawing my way out of this pit.

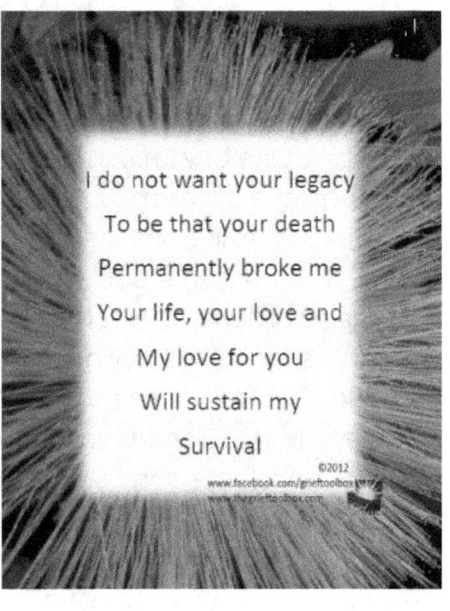

~I love you sweet Peyton James and precious, tiny Tayden Joseph.~

https://www.google.com/search?q=I+do+not+want+your+legacy&hl=en&sxsrf=ALeKk00VBNEBdomzx-onqnAAFErv6Sk2nAQ:1614027091302&source=lnms&tbm=isch&sa=X&ved=2ahUKEwj25ry7r_7uAhX0dM0KHf5PAtUQ_AUoAnoECBcQBA&biw=1536&bih=666#imgrc=gJ9i8JtXeSkBEM

07/23/2015

"Happy 4th Birthday in Heaven to my sweet Peyton James." Somehow, in some way you would be four years old here on Earth. Gosh, how cute you would have been. I have a friend that was pregnant with a little boy the same time I carried you. Her little boy was born three months earlier. I see him every now and then. When I look at him I envision what you would have looked like. He's stocky like you would have been with blonde hair, blue eyes, and smiley. I saw him on the 4th of July and stared at him longer than I ever have before. In my mind I see you...

How has Tayden been doing with you? Have you shown him all around Heaven? I am so grateful that he has you to show him around and take care of him. Do you talk about us down here? We are always thinking about both of you. We are always wondering what you two are doing. I hope you know how often you are thought about and how deeply missed you are. I can't wait to hold both of you on my lap... and kiss you... snuggle you both... and just soak you up. What a joyous day that will be.

We had a cake for you two days ago when your aunt and cousins were in town. We sang you happy birthday. Tonight we met Grandpa and Grandma at the cemetery and released balloons to you. Did any make it up to you? We also took a picture at your grave. As we were getting our picture taken by Grandpa a car was driving by. Two older females were in the front and there was a boy in the back with the window down. The boy was anxiously waving and I waved back noticing he had Down syndrome. My heart just froze and then skipped. I just feel like this was a sign from you and Tayden that you were with us. To think of that just fills my heart with hope and tears of happiness.

All I ever want in this life is for both of my boys to know how loved, cherished, and missed you are. I just want to live my life in tribute to my boys and make you proud of the kind of mom you have. I would have done anything if it meant saving both of you. As long as I live I will never understand why either of you and both of you were taken from me.

I hope your birthday in Heaven today was fun with Jesus, relatives, and friends. Your dad had a dream about your Great, Great Grandpa the other night. Maybe that was Grandpa checking in to let your dad know that you are both well and safe.

Since you died a sensitivity inside of me has opened up. I sense Spirit and energy in a way that I didn't before. It's almost as if I was cracked open through such extreme pain and now I'm being shown a 'world' that I didn't know existed before and most others can't see. But really, all I want to see is you.

07/25/2015

Last night while lying in bed I just started sobbing. I was thinking about Tayden and missing him. I was so sad. Jeremiah just hugged me and held me as I sobbed. I asked, "Do you feel the same?" He just replied, "Yes". At this point we have had many of these moments. He knows he can't fix me... so he just consoles me... he holds me until I stop sobbing. Then we roll over and go to bed. We have had many, many nights like this in the last 3.5 years.

We went to church this morning and tears just started rolling down my face. It's like Tayden's grief is just now hitting me. Why now? I don't know.

> "Other people are going to find healing in your wounds. Your greatest life messages and your most effective ministry will come out of your deepest hurts.
>
> — Rick Warren

I believe after the losses of my boys, that there has to be some basic principle in this life. I don't

https://www.google.com/search?q=other+people+are+goign+to+find+healing+in+your+wounds&tbm=isch&ved=2ahUKEwi-Igby8r_7uAhUOL6wKHceYB9QQ2-cCegQIABAA&oq=other+people+are+goign+to+find+healing+in+your+wounds&gs_lcp=CgNpbWcQAzoHCCMQ6gIQJzoICAAQsQMQgwE6AggAOgUIABCxAzoECAAQQzoHCAAQsQMQQzoECAAQHjoG-CAAQBRAeOgYIABAIEB5Qo_wIWOXDCWDzxAloAnAAeASAAbw-

BiAGnR5IBBDcuNzGYAQCgAQGqAQtnd2I6LWItZ7ABCsABAQ&sclient=img&ei=VRk0YMiCF47esAXHsZ6gDQ&bih=666&biw=1536&hl=en#imgrc=KbuggPg7YcERwM

know why we're here? I don't understand the 'point' of this life when the ultimate life is Heaven. But, I do know that this life can be painful, hard, bitter, unfriendly, lonely, hurtful, devastating, and unbearable. But, I do believe that in order to 'sustain' this life we have to show compassion towards one another. That's it, that is the only way to truly get through this life. To show each other compassion, sympathy, and empathy. Life can be wonderful but it can also be ruthless. We can't fix each other but we can show compassion towards one another. We can send cards, leave thoughtful messages of compassion, we can bring each other food, we can give hugs, and simply say 'I'm thinking of you.' Those small gestures can change the world ... if not for others, for ourselves. This world is hard enough on us, we don't need to exacerbate that pain with hurtful words or actions towards one another. We don't have to love each other, or even like each other. But, we can simply respect each other and recognize that deep within each one of us we are all struggling to some degree with something. We all have felt pain and we all have crap. Big crap, small crap, neat crap, messy crap, hidden crap, crap laying out in the open, crap that's crippling, and crap that is functional. At the end of the day... we all have crap that causes or has caused us pain. What we do with that crap... and how we show compassion to others through their crap is what matters. We are not better than each other, more important than each other. We are just who we all are trying to make it in a world full of pain. I believe God gave us compassion to help us survive this world. It is the one small gesture that we can all show...

I say this out of love to all of us! If you know me, you know my motto:

"Everybody has shit. Some of us have big shit. Some of us have small shit. Some of us are open about our shit. Some of us are afraid of judgement because of our shit. Some of us don't even know we have shit. And for the lucky few who haven't gone through the shit yet.... At the end of the day, we're all just people trying to manage our shit!"

08/09/2015

Today I shared on my social media the pictures that we had taken while Tayden was in the hospital and dying. They are precious to me. I have had them for some time but I wasn't ready to share them with the world until now. The photographer that took them did an amazing job and he is such a beautiful soul to volunteer his services for a program like this. How lucky are we that this photographer volunteers like he does? What would we have done without him? He will forever be such a special person in our hearts.

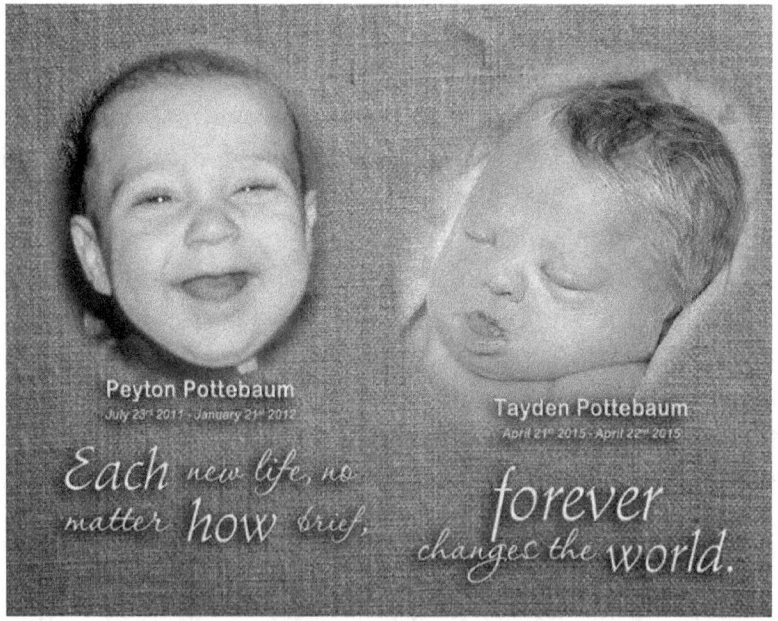

Photo Credit Ron Shankland Photography

Photo Credit Ron Shankland Photography

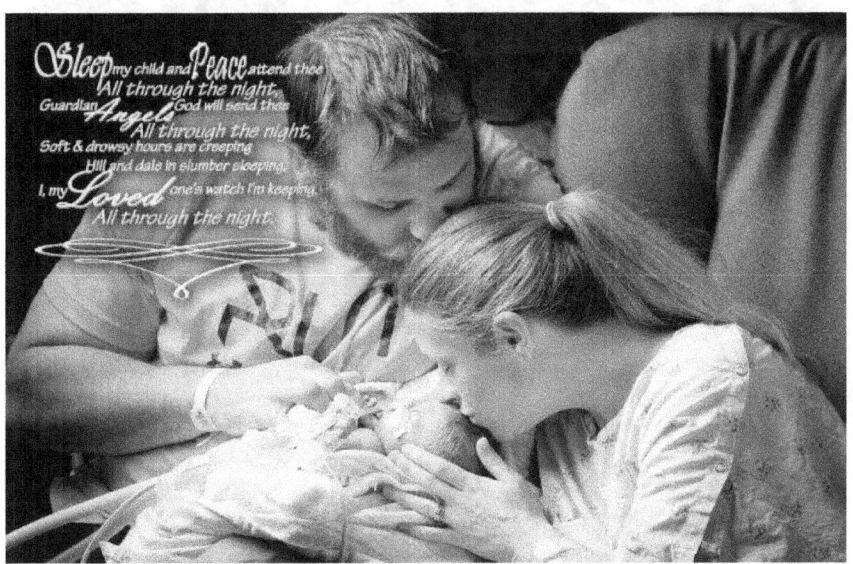

Photo Credit Ron Shankland Photography

Photo Credit Ron Shankland Photography

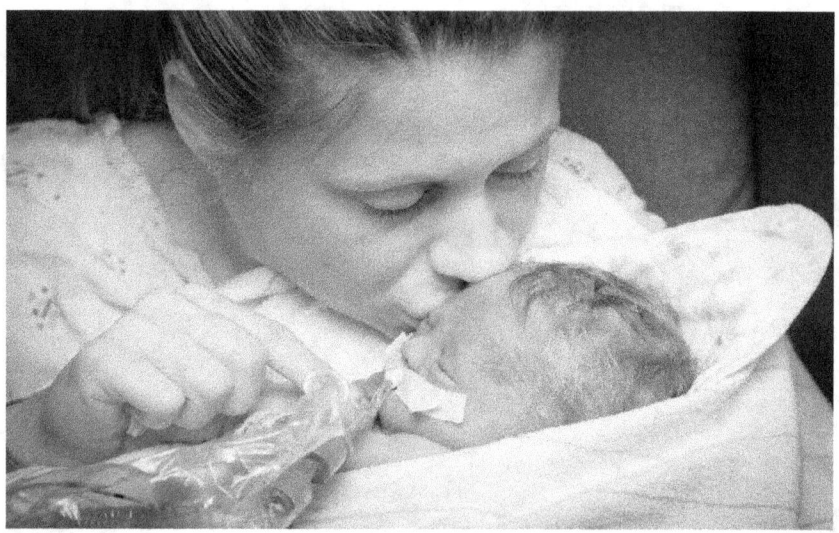

Photo Credit Ron Shankland Photography

Photo Credit Ron Shankland Photography

08/11/2015

We go back to work in one week. How can that be? An entire summer is already gone! We spent every day with our girls. Some day when they are big I hope they remember every summer with mom and dad; sleeping in, staying up late, going to the park, for walks, swimming, ice cream, visiting the zoo, seeing cousins, and a whole lot of nothing at home. We may not have all the fancy things, drive the newest cars, or have a bunch of money in savings but, our girls will always have 'TIME' and memories with us. We get by and the girls will never know what it feels like to be 'unloved'. They are our world. Truly and deeply, our children are our everything, all four of them.

At church on Sunday the pastor talked about the idea of envy and jealousy. He gave many examples of what some of us may be struggling with or have struggled with concerning envy. And then he talked about the couple who just had a baby and while you should be happy for them even if on the inside you are sad or envious of their glory. Unfortunately, I sat there while I sank deeper in my chair. I do feel envious and jealous of friends of ours who have had or will be soon having a baby. Because, why do they get to have a baby to keep but I couldn't? Why does having babies seem so easy for some people but yet keeping them for Jeremiah and I has been so difficult? Why is it that two of our babies were taken from us? Why two? How are we supposed to be happy for those around us that so easily have what we want? Will we ever get to a place where we can let that go? If I'm really honest... I dread that day. Somehow, in some way as long as I still hurt and yearn they are still here with me.

The other challenge I face is my lack of sensitivity. Don't get me wrong, I can be the most empathetic person you have ever met. But deep down in my core where I am broken from the losses of my boys I harbor a sense of disgust over other's weakness or self-pity. In other words, it is difficult for me to watch someone drown when all they have to do is stand up. I am a counselor and I know this sounds heartless. This is the part of me that needs the most work... again. I also know that pain is pain. I know that, I believe that, but some days it's hard for me to accept that. In ways, going through the losses of the boys I have become desensitized to life in general I suppose. I also recognize that this could destroy me if left unattended. This time, this is the part of the trench that I may need to call on others to supply rope, ladders, or hands to pull me out. I am not this person and the best of me is in here but I may need help burying her out.

> The worst thing is watching someone drown and not being able to convince them that they can save themselves by just standing up.

Author Unknown

https://www.pinterest.com/pin/43558321370487576/

12/02/2015

Since losing Peyton, I cling to rawness. I cling to people who are open, raw, genuine, and just plain honest no matter if those experiences aren't always the most comfortable. You see, I trusted the person that babysat my kids thinking I knew who she was and I trusted the environment they were in. I believed the fake facade that she wore every day. She always seemed like she was perfect. But now, I know that she learned how to show people what she wanted them to see to ultimately get what she wanted. She learned how to be very fake... and she did it very well. What I know now is that nobody can be that perfect all of the time. We all have bad days, opinions, and times when we just don't feel the best. My safeness now comes from knowing when I feel someone is just being 'real'. When there's no show... no production... Like it or not, I know how they feel. Give me that all day long. I don't have time, trust, or any interest in some fake facade of well- being.

HOLY Crap!

12/04/2015

It Happened Today... I Have Waited Four Years. They're Here.

It was a Friday and I was so ready to leave for the day. I was going to hit up the gym that I had slacked at all week and then pick up Tenley to go home. Jeremiah called me during the day and surprised me by offering to pick up Tenley on the way home. He said maybe I could stay late and finish anything at work that I needed to and then hit up the gym on the way home. I was so ecstatic that I was getting this time! I stayed a little after my normal contract time and was finishing one last job before I left so that it was done when Monday rolled around. I was in the office filing some information when out of the corner of my eye I saw a woman approach the main office asking one of our secretaries something. The secretary sent the mother and her daughter up to talk to one of the other staff members. I kept on working on what I was doing. A few minutes later the mom was back down at the front office counter talking to one of the secretaries. I just had a feeling that maybe I might have to help. To be honest, it was after my normal working hours and I stayed late with the intent of getting this extra work done. I really didn't want to be helpful! I wanted to get my work done and then leave. I never stayed late.... Ever. I was normally always rushing out of the doors to pick up my own children. Everyone in the office always knew that I NEVER stayed late. The secretary, not seeing me working at the back of the office, turned around and looked at me and commented that, "Oh look, she is still here... Mrs. Pottebaum, this mom has a question."

Inside my head with a smile on my face I thought, 'Geez this is what you get for hanging around. You should have left when it was the end of your contract time'. I was done helping for the day and didn't have any more "help" left in me. I responded, "Yeah, just come around to the counseling office and I can help you"(deep down hoping it wouldn't take too long). I went around to the counseling office entrance and held the door open as the mom and daughter walked through. We walked into my office. The mom gave me the demographic information of the young girl so I could look up her information on my computer. The mom was really nice and very talkative. I responded back and found that she was really easy to talk to. I explained certain things about our classes. I took down mom's information and explained that I would start the channel of communication and get back to her with more once I knew the next steps. I had never met the mom who introduced herself as Malia before. She was very talkative. I was tired and ready to go home for the day. I recognized her daughter but hadn't yet gotten the opportunity to get to know her. Malia noticed the pictures of my wiener dogs and continued to talk about her dachshund and some of the issues with hers. I talked about mine. Throughout our conversation she mentioned that her husband had died a few years earlier.

I stood up trying to be polite but initiate the parting of our ways. She stood up continuing to talk. She then initiated, "You have 2 living... (hesitation) children."

Me being me, turning to look at the pictures of my kids behind me stated, "Actually, I have four kids. My first son died in January of 2012 at six months of age due to head trauma that he received at an in-home daycare. My littlest baby boy died in April. He had Down's but that wasn't what took him. He had non-immune hydrops which... (getting ready to explain as nobody ever knows what this is)..."

She interrupts, "which is fluid in his body."

Shocked that she knows what this is I continue, "Yes, and his little lungs couldn't keep up or sustain life."

She says, "You seem like you're doing well, considering you just lost him in April. I'm sorry to make you talk about it."

Excited that someone asked me about my boys, I say, "No I love talking about them."

And then she says, "He knows you didn't know."

My eyes big and paralyzed, she says, "I'm a medium. Peyton, he needs you to know that he knows you didn't know. He says, 'Mommy, sometimes monsters dress up as Barbie dolls and you didn't know.'"

In shock and disbelief with tears streaming down my cheeks I said, "I didn't know she was like that. I never would have taken my kids to her if I had known she was like that. I have so much guilt as his mom that I took them to that woman."

Malia, "He knows this. He says, 'mommy sometimes monsters dress up as Barbie dolls. You have been carrying around a guilt and responsibility that isn't yours to carry. Mom, that burden to carry in this lifetime is hers. You did a good job working through your grief after me, but now, after Tayden you have more work to do. My mom is the best mom and my mom isn't by nature a bitter person. But now mom, you have pockets of bitterness. That's not you, you have work and healing to do. You were born to be a mom. You love babies, they're your thing."

Malia, "He says he's ok. They are ok. He is smiling. He says tell my mommy I'm ok. She needs to know I'm ok."

Malia, "He wasn't dropped."

Me, "What...."

Malia, "He was laying on the floor, the door was on this side (pointing to the left side) and he was crying. He sensed animosity and deep anger from her towards him and didn't understand why. It was intentional."

Me, "Was he shaken?"

Malia, "They are showing me her house, the living room. Trinity is sitting over here on the couch watching TV. Peyton was on the floor, in front of the TV on a blanket. He was picked up like this and shaken (shaking her arms) as he was yelled at to stop crying and then thrown down to the ground. She left him on the ground crying. Sometime after he was hurt I hear the doorbell ring. Either a delivery person or another parent dropping their child off. I wonder if the police could find out who was at the house and give any information about what they noticed?"

Tears running uncontrollably down my face I asked, "Was my other child, my daughter, was she ever hurt?"

Malia pausing said, "Not abused as bad as Peyton... but there were things. She never wanted to deal with her. She just pushed her to the side. It was more of the 'I don't have time for you' ".

Malia, "There is a woman about the same height as you... you are about eye to eye. She is petite like you. She is holding your son, Peyton. He is smiling and coo-ing and she is rocking him in her arms saying, 'Look at him, look at his smile. He gets his smile from his mom.' I am sensing that this woman is from your mom's side. That's where you get your petiteness. Ask your mom, she will know. She keeps saying something about potatoes. You come from this woman. You need to learn about her and you will find out a lot about yourself. She is one of your guides in this lifetime. She works with you on the Spirit side. You are different ... you have always known that you are different from your family members. You are very good with feelings and sensing things about people. You are a free spirit. You are an empath."

Me, "I wish I had your gift..."

Malia, "You do have a gift .... You are so good with feelings. You are an empath and you can sense things about people ... that you have an intuition. You can feel energy. Now you can put a word to it. Peyton is saying to, "Tell his mommy that she needs to let go of the guilt of not sensing what that woman was capable of doing". He says, "Mommy you are good at reading people, but she was better at hiding it. Mommy monsters can dress up as Barbie dolls."

Malia, "There is a man also... about this tall. He is very barrel chested and he is holding your baby, your newest baby, Tayden. He is stroking the right side of his face in a downward motion from temple to chin and is saying to him, "This is what your mommy did. This is how your mommy showed you love. This man is imprinting the memory of you on Tayden."

Chills and confirmation ran up and down my spine. What nobody else but Jeremiah and I would know is that after delivering Tayden he was very sick. He had to be kept in the incubator and had all sorts of tubes and the breathing machine hooked up to him. I had just had a c section and my bladder was cut so I couldn't stand up and was in a wheelchair. I wasn't able to hold him and my wheelchair would only fit next to the right side of his incubator. The only affection I could show him was stroking the right side of his face from temple to chin. This was it... I didn't get to hold him until he started getting closer to demise. That's all I got... temple to chin.

Malia said, "You wanted a baby so bad. It was devastating for you to carry him for 9 months and not be able to bring him home."

Malia, "Do you want to have any more?"

Me sobbing, "I don't know...".

Malia, "But you do, you know. You say you don't know, but deep down you do. And in fact, you will. You will have one more and it will be a boy. You will know by the fall that you are pregnant. You will be very fertile in April, May, June, July, and August. Peyton is saying, "'Mommy I want to be with you." You have a bond with both of your boys but Peyton... there was something special between you two. You were soul mates. You might not want to tell your husband that. People think that being a soulmate is only a "romantic" thing but that isn't true. That's why you have struggled with his passing so much. When he left, a part of your soul left too. He is saying that he is determined to come back to you. That is how reincarnation works. He is saying mommy I am determined to find a way... I don't know how but I will find a way. You were meant to be in this life together. "

At this point I am beyond crying... Malia says, "Right now the woman next to you... she is going like this, she is rubbing your back to console you."

Malia, "You just wait momma. In a year I will see you looking like this." (Hand out pretending to touch a pregnant belly.)

Me, "I had a C-section with Tayden and got very sick two weeks after having him because I went septic. The doctors had left a piece of placenta inside of me which got infected. They did another surgery and got that out. And they accidentally cut my bladder. Then I got another infection in the fat/muscle layer beneath my incision. I don't think I can have any more babies."

Malia pointed at my uterus, "The latter infection has been gone for ages now. Your doctor did the other surgery and she got all of that out of you. (Making a scooping motion with her hand.) Your doctor wanted to make sure it was all out. She didn't want anyone dying on her watch."

Malia, "Your boys, they visit you and they know that you know this. That feeling you get like butterflies in your stomach and then it goes up to your chest and tightens. That is them, trying to let you know they are there. If you don't sense them for some time and panic, call me, you have my number. I will talk to you."

Malia, "Peyton is saying that you have work to do. Something about an art project or writing piece or something... that you're supposed to throw yourself into this. Through this project you will continue to heal the way you need to."

When she said this I knew... I knew that what she was talking about was my journaling that I wanted to make into a book. After Peyton died, my journal was essential... and I journaled a lot. Since Tayden has died I haven't journaled much at all. I haven't gone and visited the grave as much as I did after Peyton died. I haven't done much of anything to work through my grief and in fact, have felt quite stuck. A few weeks ago I called my sister crying and upset with frustration that I know I haven't processed or dealt with Tayden's death and have the feeling like I can't get it out.

I asked Malia about her gift and if she'd always known she had it. She said yes, and that her mom knew from a young age that she was different. She told me about seeing Spirit and how it can be quite stressful. She explained how this life isn't it... that there is more. She is able to see behind the veil. She explained how what she does can be intrusive to some people and that she has to gauge how open they are.

Through all of this I think I was slightly shaking. I told her, "I have waited four years for this." In my heart I always believed somehow I would get some kind of communication from Peyton but I just didn't know how or when. Was I supposed to initiate it or was I just supposed to wait? At one time I had even looked into hiring a medium in an attempt to get some of my questions answered.

There are details I can't remember as I was so shocked. As she stood to leave I got closer to her and hugged her. She told me to have a good weekend. Like that, I grabbed my stuff and walked to my car. As I got in my car I still had a mild tremble and I kept thinking 'it finally happened.' I felt like these big thick chains had been cut. They weren't pulled off yet, but they were cut and now I needed to do the rest of the work to free myself.

I called Jeremiah with no luck. I called my sister with no luck. I called my dad.... "Dad I have to tell you what just happened to me. I'm ok...

please be open to what I am going to tell you..." and I proceeded to explain the best I could remember.

Next I called Jeremiah still crying, "I am ok... but you're never going to believe what happened to me."

I know that, that whole experience was REAL. Every part of that was real, and genuine and the beginning of my second round of healing.

I talked to Jeremiah the whole way home before the connection cut us off. I could hear the muffled sniffles in the background. Two minutes later as I approached the driveway, Jeremiah was standing in the driveway waiting. When I got out his eyes were red and swollen from crying. He said, "When I got off the phone with you Trinity asked, "Why is mom late?" I explained that you were at work talking to a lady about Peyton. Trinity then asked, "So was I right about what happened to Peyton?"

"Just let it go, just let it be. Everything's that's wrong, leave it to the breeze. Everything that's broke, leave it to the breeze, Let the ashes fall. Let it be. I think now it's time to let it slide. You be you, and I'll be me." James Bay's, *Let it Go* played on the radio the minute I got into my car to leave... It was so powerful, as they were telling me in the chorus it's time to let go, it's time to move on. I can't believe this has happened to me. As I drove home, telling my dad and then Jeremiah about what had just happened I could feel my boys sitting in the car beside me.

12/06/2015

I spent the weekend replaying the entire experience I had with Malia. I didn't sleep much because I was so happy and still just trying to wrap my head around all of it.

12/07/2015

At the end of the day as I'm walking to my car in the parking lot, there standing in front of me is Malia. She asks, "How was your weekend?" She goes on to explain that she had to drop something off at the school office so she thought she would see if I was still here.

Malia, "Was your weekend okay? Hopefully uplifting."

Me, "I have been talking about you and our conversation nonstop for the last 48 hours!"

Malia, "Did you figure out who the woman and man are?"

Me, "I think the woman is my tiny grandma, my great grandmother on my mom's side."

Malia, "With your research about her, you will find yourself. What about the man?"

Me, "I am thinking my great grandpa, her husband. A family member said that they always had kids at their house and that he loved little ones."

Malia, "That would make sense. Usually if they show up together there was a relationship in the prior life. Sometimes if one comes through it can then pave a wave for another to come through also. But, this would make sense that it was both of them together. Did you find out about the potatoes?"

Me, "I talked to my mom and she said that Tiny Grandma always fixed some type of potato at every meal. She also said that she wore a lotion or perfume that smelled like roses or floral."

Malia, "I hope I didn't make you late on Friday as I know you had somewhere to go."

Me, "I was just going to go to the gym so instead I just went home."

Malia, "I was late to meeting my friend and I told her too. I told her I was visiting my daughter's counselor and that you had lost a baby. My friend, she does in home daycare and loves kids. She said how she couldn't imagine losing a baby. I explained that you'd actually lost two and about what the person at daycare did to him. My friend was so upset..."

Malia, "It's weird how it happened. I had been putting off coming in to talk about my daughter's classes and just felt the need to come in that day. When I walked in I saw you in the office and I knew I needed to talk to you. I saw your auras which were blue and green. But they were broken and some pieces were healing or trying to heal. I could tell that you had been through trauma, multiple trauma. And I knew that we had to talk."

We talked about her late husband and about dealing with her emotions still six years later. She said that she had thought about our experience all weekend too.

Me, "What about miscarriages?"

Malia, "This is when there isn't a connection between the spirit and the soul and so it can't grow. It's hard to believe but everything does happen the way it is supposed to. We accept what happens but we have a hard time accepting that this is part of a plan or the way it's supposed to be. It is the way the creator needs it to be. Accepting that is the hardest part."

01/03/2016

I can't believe it is January already. In December I had a short meeting with Malia at a coffee shop in town. She said that Tiny Grandma visited her in her dreams the night before and was saying that she needs to check on me as I'm very worried about something.

I did go on to explain to her that I have been worried as I think about having another baby. I am very scared about my own health. I am worried that I would die from complications due to my experience with Tayden's delivery and post-delivery. She mentioned earlier in our visit that I could carry another baby and that baby will live but she never said that I would live. I had so many complications with Tayden's delivery that I am scared about my own health. If I knew 100% that my own health would be fine then, I wouldn't even hesitate in planning to have another baby.

Malia went on to reassure me that she must not have been clear enough but explained that I would be fine with another baby and my health would be fine. She said that when Peyton visits her now he is a little boy with blonde hair that is kind of combed over. She mentioned that he is determined to come back to me and that I am the first reincarnation experience into the same family and the same lifetime that she has worked with. She said that he and I were supposed to be in this life together. She said we will meet a couple more times until her work with me is done. She said it is like that saying, the one that says that friends are for a 'reason, a season, or a lifetime'. She was sent to me because I was stuck in my grief and she is here to get me moving and working through this grief. She said that things have to happen in a certain time frame and in a certain way. She said that they have to 'get me onto my path'.

This whole experience thus far is absolutely incredible. Please know that I am still hesitant. Before I move closer to 'trying' again I will meet with both of my doctors and get all of their opinions and expertise. If they give me a no for an answer I will respect that. I trust them with my life. But, I can't help but believe everything that Malia tells me. I was worried for some time after our first encounter as I know there is preaching in the bible about not following or listening to mediums or psychics. I worry that somehow it is the devil trying to pull me prey. But, deep down I believe in this spiritual realm that Malia talks about. To me, it is about God and Heaven but I also believe it is about more spiritually. I do believe that our loved ones visit us or send messages to us but many of us are too busy to stop and listen. I am also surrendering to the idea that there is some "master plan" that God has for us. Prior to meeting Malia I would have told anyone that told me this to 'shut the hell up' but now, I do believe it. I don't 'get it' and I also understand that maybe I'm not supposed to, but I will always try to understand. In my heart, there had to be a reason for the pain my family and I have experienced. I believe there is a plan but we also have free will, which can alter that plan. Malia said she will visit with me soon.

I went over to my friend's house yesterday and our kids played together. She is expecting and I am truly happy for her. In my heart she deserves this little girl. There wasn't a part of me that was jealous or sad for myself, which to me, says a lot. I am doing ok. I just think the peaks and valleys will always exist. There isn't a day that goes by where either one or both of the boys aren't on my mind. While I am cleaning the floors or doing the dishes or folding laundry I daydream about them. My mind wanders a lot and it always goes to them. I hope they know that, how much time I think about them, how much time I dream about them. I just miss them and I miss them being able to live alive in our family. I miss them getting to grow up with their sisters. I experienced two scenarios that aren't common for most to experience and somehow I had to go through both. It does bring me peace to know that they visit me and I hope that they know how much I love them. I would have been the best mommy to both of them. I tried to be the best mommy to them for the short time I had both of them.

I think about my experience all of the time and how so many people will say to me that I am so strong. That statement strikes me as so odd. To me, I haven't had a choice in any of this. The only options I have had is to give up or pull myself up. For the sake of my girls and my family the only choice was to pull myself up. Obviously, God knows that I am still trudging up this muddy slope after losing Tayden. I think about Tayden a lot and worry that he will think my feelings of loss are greater for Peyton than him. And truly they aren't, but they are different. Peyton's loss encompassed so much instant trauma whereas with Tayden I had six weeks to prepare for his death. Not that I was ever prepared. Because I wasn't, and I'm not. But, the losses were different. With Tayden there is no one to blame.

Author Unknown

https://www.amazon.com/byyoursidedecal-Forever-Changed-Moments-Inspirational/dp/B071WMFJ8Z;

"To my boys, gifts I was given for short moments in time. I love you both so much. ~ Mommy"

02/07/2016

At church this morning I just thought about everything. Part of the scripture was on the Godly purpose of our life. I have always wondered what my purpose is. What is it that I am supposed to accomplish in this life? In my heart I have always believed that I was created here to do something, to make some positive impact. I just wish I knew what that was. I also yearn to know what I am supposed to do with my sons' deaths. How are they supposed to change me, mold me, or teach others?

I started reading a book last night, "Safe in the arms of God", that was given to me by my pastor after Tayden died. I couldn't read it until now. I don't know how I feel about the book. I am half-way through and realize that I have an internal debate. I have always believed that babies and children automatically go to heaven when they die. I struggle with the understanding that 'sin is sin', and that as long as one comes before the lord and confesses they can still go to heaven. I think of the person that hurt Peyton. So, as long as that person confesses to God their assaults that they did to Peyton, they can still go to heaven? In my heart I just can't wrap my head or my heart around that. I guess deep down I want that person to have some type of accountability or payment for what they did to my son. While I am having to accept that it's not my responsibility to hold this person accountable, I do believe it is God's. I guess really, I want them to feel the pain that I have felt. I struggle because I know that I need to forgive them but.... I just don't know if I can do that. I do believe I will become closer to God once I make that last step. The hardest step for me. To forgive.... To pray for them. I know that I can't do that one alone. I struggle because to me, sin isn't just sin. I mean to me, there are different levels of sin, aren't there? I also know that I can't get hooked up into that....

I just want to feel peace. I do believe my boys are living a glorious life in heaven that they couldn't have physically experienced on this earth. For them, they got to avoid a life of pain and go straight to heaven. For them, I am grateful. For me, I selfishly grieve for the voids that their losses have created in my life. So many people have told me that I am strong. I didn't have a choice. I have had two beautiful girls who depend on me to function and be a good mom. I want my girls to feel loved and be good people who care for others. I want my girls to understand that love and compassion is what makes this world go round. That's our job. To be loving... To be compassionate... And to believe in God and live a life that would be pleasing to him. To have relationships and conversations that matter and mean something.

I do feel somewhat torn... I believe in God but I also believe in energy, nature, and that our loved ones communicate with us and send us signs. I believe that there is much more going on than we can physically see with our eyes. I believe that all the material objects in our life are just "stuff" and that it is our relationships and treatment towards others that truly matter. We owe it to our world and life to enrich ourselves and others. I guess nobody said it would be easy, but hopefully it will be worth it. So I guess I need to pull on my big girl panties and keep trucking forward.

> We're all in the same game; Just different levels. Dealing with the same hell; just different devils

Author Unknown

https://www.google.com/search?q=we%27re+all+in+the+same+game+just+different+levels&sxsrf=ALeKk01GL3cZp0FfsIh_Wj4rb5KCDnQCKw:1591286273477&tbm=isch&

source=iu&ictx=1&fir=RGb8nfe1meX-XqM%253A%252Cz282E0AgKOWQuM%252C_&vet=1&usg=AI4_-kTdt8GfT_yMjrV23mxxqJNvVGuKVQ&sa=X&ved=2ahUKEwjmxsOow-jpAhUSG80KHQBCDNUQ9QEwAXoECAoQFw#imgrc=S2m8U29REqqLwM;

02/27/2016

It was gorgeous outside today and we took the girls to the park. Jeremiah and I sat on Peyton's bench in the park as we watched the girls play and were able to look to the right at the volleyball court where the high school girls dedicated a plaque in honor of our precious little Tayden. So there we were...all of us...in one place...at the same time. Tears are welling up in my eyes as I write this...as I imagine two beautiful precious boys playing up over us and giggling at their sisters below. What our family didn't know when they purchased that bench in honor of Peyton is that they would be providing us a "place" where a joyous presence would be for the multiple children that are present in our lives in various forms. The finishing touch of our "place" was the beautiful plaque that some very thoughtful high school girls and parents put in place for the tiniest member of our clan. There are only four of us that your eyes can see, but if you watch us closely and listen thoughtfully you will see ALL of us crystal clear.

The Whole Crew 🖤👨‍👩‍👧‍👦😇

03/14/2016

A week and a half ago I started reading The Long Island Medium's (Theresa Caputo) first book. A good friend of my sister's suggested that I read this after my first interaction with Malia. I feel that was one of my loved ones planting that seed in my head that I needed to hear and ponder. The last week and a half have been the most inspiring and releasing weeks of my life. I feel like Theresa has finally explained things to me that no one else has been able to. My dots have started to connect. I am so thankful that God has blessed her with such a remarkable gift. She has brought peace to many people and even just by reading her book I feel extremely moved. I feel validated that deep down I have always known that there is more to our souls than this one lifetime on earth.

This is what I know....My boys know how much I think about them, how much I talk to them, how much I long for their physical touch. My loved ones kept me from exiting this life early after Peyton died when I was in such a state of deep despair and grief. And, when I was desperately hurting and completely illogical they kept me from doing something to the woman who killed my son. God knows it wasn't me who had the willpower to just "be". My loved ones intervened and they kept me from taking either of two terrible paths. As a mom I felt it was my responsibility to go be with my son. My loved ones knew that neither of those paths were meant for me. I still search for what that purpose might be...

After traumatic events some people find meaning out of their pain by throwing themselves into advocating for something, as a way of bringing something positive out of their loved ones death or trials. To be honest, my last four years have been full of much advocate worthy issues. I could advocate for Shaken Baby Syndrome/non-accidental head trauma.....or maybe for the rights of victim homicide survivors...or maybe for individuals dealing with the effects of trauma...or for the miraculous children born suffering from hydrops fetalis or maybe for our sunshine children born with Down syndrome....maybe I could advocate for the health and healing of siblings who have witnessed the abuse that lead to their sibling's death...maybe I could pour myself into the grieving process of children...or maybe I could minister to husbands and wives as they try to keep their marriage in tact as they try to process and heal...maybe I could reach out to moms who've experienced more than one child loss....or maybe the advocacy of greater state laws considering the licensing of people caring for children....or maybe reaching out to souls in great pain and suffering and encouraging them towards hope, faith and light by taking small baby steps forward....or maybe to families whose relationships with each other have been torn apart by the anger and blame that arises out of unfortunate events.... or maybe I could minister to people who are struggling with their faith and spirituality. I don't know what my calling is but in my heart I feel like I have to do something with all of this. Somehow I am still standing and not completely broken. And my departed loved ones believe that I have a greater path and purpose, whatever that might be.

I realize now that being here on earth is just a part of our journey. We are here to learn big and small lessons to grow our souls more to God's pleasing. What are my big lessons? I feel like my big lessons are forgiveness and unconditional love. How can I ever forgive the person that killed my son? I don't know and that thought makes me want to throw up...but deep down, someday I have to. I also have to learn how to love unconditionally. I have a tendency when hurt by someone to completely cut them out of my life as a self-protecting mechanism. It's like having an ache in my foot and rather than going to the doctor I just cut it off.

Pain is pain and hurt people, hurt people. (Yehurda Berg) By remaining broken we continue to harm ourselves and others and the ripple effect never stops. Somehow we have to rise through the pain in an attempt to contribute positively to the rest of mankind. It can't start with everyone else. It can only start with us. We have to look up and claw our way up from the trenches. We may get sucked back down and this time we dig our heels in the side of that trench and we catapult ourselves up the best we can. And we pray the whole time asking for purpose and clarity and maybe even someday, peace. From one wounded soul to the other our purpose has to be greater than this pain. ~

Your life has a purpose.
Your story is important.
Your dreams count.
Your voice matters.
You were born to make
an impact.

QUOTEDIARY.ME

https://www.google.com/search?q=quotediary.me++your+story+is+important&tbm=isch&ved=2ahUKEwiz9d64kbLrAhUKUKwKHYQoBe0Q2-cCegQIABAA&oq=quotediary.me++your+story+is+important&gs_lcp=CgNpbWcQAzoCCABQqD1YiWRgzmZoAnAAeACAAfYBiAGbFpIBBzEzLjExLjGYAQCgAQGqAQtnd3Mtd2l6LWltZ8ABAQ&sclient=img&ei=sM1CX7PdM4qgsQWE0ZToDg&bih=576&biw=1366#imgrc=jKPlsmKFdMITXM

04/10/2016

At church this morning I felt more emotional than I have in quite some time. My dad and stepmom met me at church this a.m. On our way out of service I introduced them to pastor Chad, who was the pastor that was there for us all throughout Tayden's sickness and passing. As my dad spoke to Chad I could see the tears welled up in his eyes. The pain my dad must feel to watch his daughter suffer and being powerless to stop it. As I have said many times, "This can't all be for nothing."

05/01/2016

I prayed tonight as I was in the shower. I asked my angels and spirit guides to help me. I asked them to give me a very clear answer. Am I supposed to have another baby in this lifetime? I always think about my initial meeting with Malia and how she told me I would. Whether I want to or not is not the question. I wanted the two that I had. It is more of a concern about my general health and well-being. Can my body safely endure another pregnancy and C-section? Another C-section is what I am terrified of. With all of the complications after Tayden was born it scares me so much. I prayed that my angels and guides would send me a very obvious sign as to whether I should or shouldn't. I asked them to make my sign obvious as I don't want to miss it!

Jeremiah told me this morning about a dream he had last night. He dreamt that we had another baby and it was a boy and his name was Broen. This just sat with me all day. I felt like Jeremiah was visited by Spirit and speaking to him in his dream. This afternoon I went to the gym and when I got home Jeremiah asked, "Do you ever feel like a warm sensation on or around you?" While I was gone he hung up some new ceiling lights in our house. He explained that when he was working on the upstairs light he felt a warm sensation down on his lower leg. He said he paused and then talked to Peyton to let him know he knew he was there and showing affection. Tears ran down my face from happiness.

> **Focus on the powerful, euphoric, magical, synchronistic, beautiful parts of life, and the universe will keep giving them to you.**
>
> GeniusQuotes.net

https://www.google.com/search?q=focus+on+the+powerful+euphoric+magical+synchronistic&tbm=isch&ved=2ahUKEwjcla3q-svuAhVujK0KHbjrDJoQ2-cCegQIABAA&oq=Focus+on+the+powerful+e&gs_lcp=CgNpbWcQARgBMgQIIxAnMgIIADICCAA6BwgjEOoCECc6BAgAEEM6CAgAELEDEIMBOgUIABCxAzoHCAAQsQMQQzoGCAAQCBAeOgYIABAKEBg6BAgAEBhQ9aHuU1jK4-5TYKft7lNoBXAAeAOAAasBiAGzMZIBBDAuNTGYAQCgAQGqAQtnd3Mtd2l6LWltZ7ABCsABAQ&sclient=img&ei=P6sZYJz6JO6YtgW417PQCQ&bih=666&biw=1536#imgrc=uz1nRhNPdfi7z

What a special moment for him to experience. It's finally like we are aware that our boys are still here...just in another form. It's training ourselves to think about life and death differently. It's training us to look for the signs, feel their presence and notice the beautiful synchronistic moments in our lives.

A Big Sign

05/02/2016

This afternoon I met with Malia. She asked me how I am and said she is just checking in. She asked about Jeremiah...which was different. Inside I panic asking if he is ok, is he sick? Is something bad going to happen? She hesitantly proceeds by telling me that Jeremiah really wants a baby. She says how he isn't trying to replace either of our boys but that he genuinely wants another child. She said he is throwing hints out there to me trying to let me know where he's at. I smiled as deep down I knew she was right. I have been so focused on what I want that I haven't been thinking about him. Secretly, I have felt like it should be my decision since it's my body and health at stake. I have been overlooking what he wants.

Malia explained that Tiny Grandma encouraged her to visit with me. Malia again talked to me about how my chances of getting pregnant this summer were very strong. This time when she talked she was careful and a little more hesitant, like it was important to her that I knew it was still my choice to make. I could tell she was being urged to help me understand that pregnancy was the path for me. I could also see some questioning from her as this was a message she had already given me some time ago. I got tears in my eyes and said that I had prayed last night in the shower for my spirit guides and/or Angels to send me a sign as to what was best for me. I asked for it to be a big, really obvious sign for fear I would miss it if it was anything but big! Malia threw her arms up and stated, 'Here I am, how much bigger do you need it to be?!

As we continued talking I asked Malia some lingering questions I have had since Peyton died. I wanted to know after he was hurt how long before he was on the other side. Malia explained through what she believed was Tiny Grandma's eyes what again the person caring for Peyton did to him that morning. She explained that Tiny Grandma was there that morning and when it was time she took Peyton. Malia explained how the person caring for Peyton shook him because she was frustrated that he threw up orange baby food on her white carpet. She said that this person then threw Peyton on the ground. Now through Peyton's eyes after the incident she talked about his head feeling fuzzy and that he could only see a small ray of light through his eyes. She said then he lost feeling in his arms and then legs. She said it was about 15-20 minutes before he was no longer aware of what was happening around him.

I told Malia how I was so confused because that entire day he laid in the hospital bed with a closed head injury that nobody knew about and he was not conscious that entire time. I explained to her that afternoon after Peyton's doctor found his head was fractured and they decided to do the craniotomy. As the nurses were wheeling him down the hallway to prep him for surgery Jeremiah and I followed close behind him talking to him. Right before parting with him he tilted his head back and looked at us. He wasn't conscious all day but at this moment he opened his eyes and looked at us and deep in the pit of my stomach I knew he was saying goodbye for the last time. Later when I expressed to medical personnel that this had happened they just looked at me sadly. It was a look that there was no way he could have medically done this and we must have imagined this through our pain. I pleaded with Malia that I knew I saw this and that I hadn't imagined it. She put her hand out as if to console me and told me that Peyton didn't do that. She explained that Tiny Grandma opened his eyelids and tilted his head back and reassured me that what I saw was **real**. Malia explained that it was important to Tiny Grandma that the moment of exit of Peyton be humane for us and for him. She knew that I knew this moment was him saying goodbye. Tiny grandma gave us this moment...How much I thank her for this precious glance that was seconds in reality, but forever in my heart and mind. I was allowed the gift of "good bye" and I knew it at the time, even though the medical personnel couldn't support this.

Malia explained that through the tragedy of Peyton Tiny Grandma got Archangel Gabriel involved. Archangel Gabriel said that Tiny Grandma had to allow Peyton to get to choose to stay in this world or he could choose to leave. She explained that Peyton chose to leave because he did not want to be a burden to us. She said that his inability to function could not have provided us or him with the life we were supposed to have together. Malia explained that Archangel Gabriel created a loophole for Peyton in which he would be allowed to come back through reincarnation to us in this lifetime. She said that we were meant to be in this life together. She said that is why Peyton is waiting to come back to us, hence the clarification of us having another baby.

I sat there just amazed at what Archangel Gabriel and Tiny Grandma have worked on behind the scenes. In my dark moment I thought the world was against me. Loved ones were actually trying to take care of me from this lifetime and beyond.

Malia confirmed to me that Tiny grandma is one of my spirit guides and that she chose me to work with. She said that I come from her and that I am an empath like she was. She said that Tiny Grandma is proud of the work I do in my job as I am utilizing my gifts as an empath when I work with kids and families.

Malia went on to tell me that she would be meeting my family, specifically my cousin. She said that my cousin has some questions for her and needs some closure from Malia. She said my cousin will be asking to meet her through me and that Malia's answer is "yes" she will meet her. I didn't think too much of this because I didn't really see my cousin asking to talk to her.

On the way home to coach track for Trinity I called my cousin to talk. I never mentioned talking to Malia. Out of nowhere my cousin asked if she could talk to my friend some time. I just froze! I didn't expect it that quick! I told my cousin how I had talked to Malia that day and Malia had informed me that she would be asking. My cousin gasped in shock. She asked if I was shaking!! I explained how prior to six months ago I would have been freaking out but I was now getting kind of used to this happening!!! I told my cousin I would talk to Malia sometime before summer break and I would ask her.

What a ride and blessing this has been!

05/17/2016

1:00 p.m.

We are on our way to Dr. Sutherland's deposition, who is the child abuse pediatrician from the hospital in Omaha. I prayed last night that Tiny Grandma, my other spirit guides and angels would help me today. That they would allow me to be classy and feel whatever emotions I need to. That they would support Dr. Sutherland in being as confident as she can be. Please allow me to handle today the way I need to. Please allow this to be healing for my soul. Please release my anxieties and fears and show my genuine love.

9:30 p.m.

We are home and got the girls down to bed. Dr. Sutherland was confident in her deposition. She stood by her initial diagnosis of non-accidental head trauma. She reiterated that Peyton's symptoms would have been immediate. She indicated that based on multiple people stating that he was acting normally and smiling when he was dropped off at daycare the injury had to have taken place at daycare. She also stated that it would not be possible for him to have a lucid interval lasting 90 minutes, meaning that there was no way he could have been hurt in our home before being dropped off at daycare.

At the end of the deposition we were able to thank her for advocating for Peyton. I got to express my gratitude for talking to me on the phone months after Peyton died. As we walked out I got to give her a hug goodbye.

> "The women whom I love and admire for their strength and grace did not get that way because shit worked out. They got that way because shit went wrong, and they handled it. They handled it in a thousand different ways on a thousand different days, but they handled it. Those women are my superheroes."
>
> – Elizabeth Gilbert

https://www.google.com/search?q=the+woman+whom+i+love+and+ad-mire+quote&sxsrf=ALeKk03Rafm8Cf4TffUM-wQZjp_keoLvn4Q:1598214952546&source=lnms&tbm=isch&sa=X&ved=2ahUKEwjsq5XUIrLrAhVaCM0KHaUXABEQ_AUoAX-oECAwQAw&biw=1366&bih=576#imgrc=TB7-8IQOcuRFBM

I know that she knows what the person that was caring for Peyton did to him. I felt like she was warm and caring. I hope she felt my sincerity as well.

To be in that hospital again....to relive the moments frozen in my head of what was happening while we were there with Peyton was surreal. My world was shattered 4.5 years ago in that place. But, somehow I handled it. And for a million different days...in a million different ways...I've handled it.

06/30/2016

A couple of days ago I contacted Melissa, my gifted cousin's wife and asked if we could get together and talk. We picked out this morning to meet at her house. We showed up and I could sense a feeling from Melissa... Not really a hesitation, but a waiting for me to start asking her questions and so forth. We eventually made our way inside and then into the living room. I didn't waste much time as there was so much I wanted to ask her! Not many people know of Melissa's gift and it wasn't until after I told her about Malia that she confided in me her gift as well. So many people are afraid of judgement and thus don't speak up for fear of other's judgement. Many people think they are open, but really they aren't. I am so lucky that I now have two "mediums" in my life to help steer me!

Melissa started off by saying, "Courtney, after I found out about Tayden's fate I was so angry at Spirit. I told them it wasn't fair and that you were both such good people and that you didn't deserve this. They told me that we won't be able to fully understand until we're on the other side."

I nodded my head as those statements too pierced my soul. I started out by going over some of the things that Malia has said to me in some of my interactions with her. I told her that Malia confirmed that Tiny Grandma was one of my spirit guides, and she agreed. She told me that she was in fact standing behind me at that moment. I don't know why but I reached behind me and of course, I couldn't feel her or see her. I cried to Melissa that I wish I had her ability. She explained that in times when I feel high emotion... joy, sorrow, etc. is when Tiny Grandma is with me. She reaffirmed that Tiny Grandma chose to work with me as I remind her so much of herself. There was so much that was said and reaffirmed through Melissa and the conversation went so fast. Below I will write the points that Melissa expressed to me as a way of trying to explain what was all told to me....

Melissa confirmed that Jeremiah and I will have one more baby and that Peyton or a "part" of Peyton is coming back to us. I expressed some of the guilt I still struggle with since losing Peyton and Peyton confirmed to her that there is nothing I would have seen that I missed leading up to his death. Peyton explained to her that he did choose to leave because if he stayed Jeremiah and I would have had to sacrifice so much to care for him. I asked Melissa how I would know it was time to get my IUD taken out and she said that Tiny Grandma said that it will just hit me during a very peaceful moment and I will just know. She also explained to Melissa that she will be there with me the whole time. I told Melissa I was scared to have another baby because I've lost two... And God forbid, what if it happened again? Tiny grandma reassured her that it will be ok. Peyton told Melissa that 'miracles happen'. Melissa said that this new baby and Trinity will be very close. She said that he will grow up and make it his mission to advocate for children. She said that he already has a life purpose so to speak. He told her that there is much work to do and he didn't want to waste any more time. Melissa also reafirmed that once I get the IUD taken out it will be very soon after that I am pregnant, that it will happen very quickly. Melissa explained that my grandpa visited her before I came... knowing that I was coming. He told her that he is proud of Jeremiah and I for dealing with our boys' deaths. I asked her, what was the purpose of having and then losing Tayden, after already losing Peyton? She explained that Tayden left so that I could stay. She explained that by him passing maybe it made me surrender (not her phrase but I can't remember how she said it) to accepting this spiritual intervention. In my heart I have wondered if by me losing him it forced me to surrender so to speak. It forced me to give up the control I thought I had over my life to realize the life that was waiting for me to live. Melissa affirmed that the boys speak to both girls but that Trinity realizes that it is her brothers talking to her. Tenley hears them but doesn't know that it is her brothers yet.

She said that the person that hurt Peyton and her husband are really good at putting on a show or acting like everything is just perfect with them. She said this is not true and that behind closed doors they have a very dark relationship with each other. She said that Brett knows what his wife did to Peyton. She said that they were in an argument sometime after Peyton died and he point blank asked her if she hurt Peyton and she didn't respond but instead hung her head. He knew that her silence was her admission and that he instantly felt disgust. He told her that they had to stick to the story or she would ruin his life and his career. Melissa said that some time will go by but the tension between them will continue to grow. Eventually, Anna won't be able to take it anymore and things will come to a head. Melissa explained that she felt everything will come out but I will be at a point in my healing that it won't be earth shattering so to speak (again my word not hers). Tiny Grandma confirmed that they are 'taking care of it'. I felt like this gave me permission to let go. Not let go of fighting but maybe permission to start living again, knowing that I don't have to fight Peyton's fight alone. To know that 'they' are helping to manage it while maybe, I can try to live again.... Whatever that might really mean.

Melissa told me that at Tayden's prayer service that when she hugged me she could hear Tayden say in her ear that, "I'm ok mommy." She also explained that he felt no pain and that he knew he was loved. She said that she saw him looking as a baby with wings right there in her living room. Peyton explained that it was ok that I have bad days sometimes. That sometimes we have to take a step back in order to move forward. That just because I have a bad day doesn't mean that I'm not healing or moving forward.

My life has changed these last six months since meeting Malia and then finding out about Melissa's gift. I am so indebted to these two strong women. They went outside of the box and risked talking to me... They risked judgement for me. They have to know how they are healing both Jeremiah and I. I have hope now. I have faith and now I realize that there is "the other side". I also realize that our loved ones never really go away. They just change form. I also can put a finger on my gift of being an empath. Melissa explained that I've always been this, I just didn't have a name for what it was. I feel everything when I am around people. I sense things from people without words ever being spoken.

I thank God for allowing Malia and Melissa to use their gifts to help Jeremiah and I heal. Truly this has been the most beautiful and special blessing.

"Tiny Grandma-

Thank you for choosing me to work with. Thank you for protecting me and looking out for me in this world. I know I am challenging and quite indecisive and I worry about everything. Thank you for being patient with me and giving me validation when I need it. Thank you for allowing Peyton to say goodbye to Jeremiah and I that day in the hospital before surgery. There is no doubt that you saved my life after Peyton died when I was in a really dark place. I never understood how I made it through but now I understand. Please continue to steer me and guide me like only you can." ~

07/14/2016

Last night I met with some of my family and gifted cousin for dinner. Poor Melissa knew she was walking into a meeting of all of us wanting to know more about her gift. I could feel her nervousness and maybe a little hesitation. She hasn't really told anyone of her gift as she explains that many people think they are open but really they aren't. Just in meeting with me two weeks ago she was able to bring me such healing messages that I feel indebted to her. I want her to know how much I value her and her abilities. I feel protective of her and want to keep judgements from coming her way. She and Malia have saved my life. They were able to step into my life willingly and bring me the most healing messages I could ever have asked for.

Many people go through trauma and heartache in this life, but they don't get the spiritual intervention that I got. But, my loved ones, especially Tiny Grandma and my boys have told me just what I needed to continue to live. They used Malia and Melissa to intervene in my life. I have healed more in six months than I have in the last four and a half years. I did everything the "right" way. Individual counseling, couples counseling, medication, grief groups, church grief groups, homicide victim survivor grief groups and visiting the cemetery every day for the first year. I truly did ALL of the work but nothing has healed me quite like this spiritual intervention. Please know that therapy and medication are needed and very effective for many people and they surely helped me, but I needed more.

Some of my family members started asking different questions pertaining to our family history. As we brought up something about Tiny Grandma I asked her if she was there at that moment and Melissa confirmed that she was. She expressed that the only time she's talked to her is when I'm there. I asked Melissa why Tiny Grandma chose me to work with as I am a worrier and sometimes indecisive. She must have extreme patience to be around me and work with me! Tiny Grandma's response to Melissa was, "You needed me." I just shook my head and said, "I did." When people ask me how I got through those first months after Peyton died I tell them I don't know because I didn't know. But now, I know that I did partly because of her. The talk was good and Melissa was able to explain some family things. But really, it was just nice to sit and all talk together.

Today I had my appointment to get my IUD out. The process was quick and actually I thought I might be nervous but I wasn't. Tonight Jeremiah and I were sitting outside in the rocking chairs and we were talking. I told him how I feel kind of vulnerable, knowing that I don't have the IUD in place. I started to cry a little and just explained that deep down I think I am a little scared. After losing two babies and having two miscarriages my track record for keeping them isn't exactly stellar. Me stepping out of my comfort zone and preparing to have another baby is me completely believing in the messages of my spiritual intervention. It's me giving up the control and trusting my departed loved ones. But the human, logical part of me, still holds a little fear. I am also worried about the judgments of other people. I just have a feeling that many are going to cast judgement or opinion on 'why would she put herself through this again?' Or something like, "Can't she just be content?" Trust me... The human part of me has asked these same questions. There is no doubt that my heart would always love to have another baby. But, the logic part of me after losing Tayden was settling in, to the acceptance of having my girls and this all just being the hand of cards we were drawn. Me moving in the direction of another baby came about through this spiritual intervention.

You know, I don't know how many times I would scowl to Jeremiah in conversations that if one more person tells me that God has a plan I am going to punch them in the face! That's the thing... Now I truly understand that he does. It doesn't necessarily make sense to me but I can truly say that I am ok with the fact that it doesn't. To be honest, it takes some of the pressure off of me. I know that 'they' have got this. I also understand that we have free will which may cause alterations in the intended plan. I will continue to struggle I'm sure, but at least now I know that it isn't all for nothing. That truly, there is a purpose to my pain. From now on when I struggle the bigger focus becomes, *'What am I supposed to learn or gain by going through this or experiencing this?'*

Yesterday morning I got my hair done by a wonderful woman and of course, I had to update her on my last six months. Her tears came and went as we talked. Multiple times she said, 'You have to write a book.' I have thought about that. I'm nobody... But I'm somebody with a story... I know pain... I know heartache... I know desperation...I know defeat... I know hopelessness.... I know helplessness... I know anger.... And bitterness... And despair. Maybe, my story could inspire just one other person and push them towards the light of hope. If it saved just one person my life heartaches would have purpose.

> "Other people are going to find healing in your wounds. Your greatest life messages and your most effective ministry will come out of your deepest hurts."
>
> — Rick Warren

https://www.google.com/search?q=other+people+are+going+to+find+healing+in+your+wounds&tbm=isch&ved=2ahUKEwjv67akx-jpAhVX96wKHSP4C-AQ2-cCegQIABAA&oq=other+people+are+going+to+find+healing+in+your+wounds&gs_lcp=CgNpbWcQAzoCCAA6BwgjEOoCECc6BAgjECc6BQgAELEDOgUIABCDATOECAAQQzoHCAAQsQMQQzoECAAQHjoGCAAQBRAeOgYIA-BAIEB5QkKqSqgFYzIKTqgFgvIOTqgFoBXAAeASAAagCiAHmQZIBBzcwLjE3LjOYA-QCgAQGqAQtnd3Mtd2l6LWItZ7ABCg&sclient=img&ei=Kh7ZXu-uJdfuswWj8K-ADg&bih=576&biw=1366#imgrc=wxeAsGR7J-MBPM

08/15/2016

It is almost time for summer to be over!!! How can that be already? Our summer was great...relaxing and so much time together as a family. It was probably our best summer so far 👍 Malia and I met up today just to catch up. Some of the things that we talked about...

Malia talked about how Peyton said that he was willing to come back as a female if that was the only way he could come back. She said that souls don't necessarily have a gender but can prefer to be a certain sex over the other. She said Peyton preferred to be a male but that he would come to be a female if that was the only way. She said he was confident and ready waiting to come back. Tears just fell from my eyes because what I hadn't told her at this point was that I had a dream a couple of nights ago where we had a baby girl but we were calling her a "he". When I woke up I was so confused because I have been told by Melissa and Malia that we would have a boy. When I told Malia this she expressed that this was Peyton validating the dream I had. Talk about amazing... She reinforced that Jeremiah wants a baby so bad. She explained to me that Peyton coming back is such a special blessing and just reinforced that a child coming back into the same lifetime and family is extremely rare. She said that we are so loved on the other side and that for this to happen our loved ones had to agree for this to happen. That our loved ones had to feel like it would be more detrimental to each of our souls if we didn't have this lifetime together. She emphasized what a special gift this is. She explained how my moodiness has to do with "them" getting my body ready for motherhood. I would have two more periods, that my cycle is shortening and I should know around October that I'm pregnant. She said this pregnancy will be much different than the others as this baby with Peyton's soul is also an empath. She said my gift as an empath will be extremely heightened since I will be carrying a baby that is also empathic. I will be able to walk into a room and know how anyone is feeling at a quick rate. She said I will be able to "feel" right through any verbal words said. She suggested I look into learning and teaching Reiki as my empathic ability would complement that.

When I got home I started to tell Jeremiah what she all said to me. When I got to the part of her saying that Jeremiah wanted a baby so bad he dropped his shovel in the ground. He was digging a line in the ground to run electricity to the shed. He looked at me and said, "I didn't say that, I've never said that to you. I have never wanted to pressure you. It's your body and you've already gone through four.

God, she hit that on the head." I then explained the part about Peyton coming back as a female and I saw his shoulders fall. I asked him about his reaction and he said that he really wanted a boy but that a healthy baby is the ultimate goal. After having Tayden I think we both feel that deep in our bones. We know what it means to have a sick baby and pray every day that he will get better and wait and wait until one day the waiting is over and he dies in my arms. That pain...that pain, those memories never leave. And yet that pain is what broke me enough to see what really is and spiritually save my life.

The thing is, I feel so blessed and loved that all of this has happened to me. Most people go through life with trauma and pain and never get answers like we have. For the first time in my life I know that things really do happen for a reason. Those reasons don't come without pain, heartache and struggle but it's not all for nothing. The suffering isn't for nothing...it is evolving our souls in the way we need most. Sometimes there are perspectives we have to learn. And other times it's really shitty trauma that we are dealt, at no fault of our own. And sometimes when it's trauma that is done to us we have to find our own way out.

I wish others that hurt like I did, the ones that are ready to check out early in this life like I was, I wish they could see that it's not all for nothing. Instead of allowing the pain to overwhelm and control us we can use it as an opportunity to connect with our true selves and to others in this lifetime. It allows us to become genuine, sensitive to the suffering of others, compassionate, kinder and more accepting...if we would allow it to teach us and grow with it. This is hard and the pain forces us to fight it with our legs kicking. Maybe the goal is to feel it, truly feel just how much it hurts and take it in as energy to transform us into a better version of who we were before, scars and all. The pain never extinguishes as a constant reminder of how strong we really are and what it feels like to hurt in an attempt to keep us humble and available to positively shape this world.

We're all forced to play a game that we have no chance in winning. No one in this world is free of pain but we can use this to grow us, to grow our souls. And the question of our lives can become, "What is the purpose of THIS pain? What am I supposed to learn or gain to grow my soul?"

https://www.google.com/search?q=damaged+people+are+dangerous+because+they+know+they+can+survive&tbm=isch&ved=2ahUKEwiAhIzl-PLpAhUujK0KHdoDBfgQ2-cCegQIABAA&oq=damaged+people+are+dangerous&gs_lcp=CgNpbWcQARgCMgQIABBDMgIIADICCAAyAggAMgIIADICCAAyAggAMgIIADIC-
CAAyAggAOgcIIxDqAhAnOgUIABCxAzoHCAAQsQMQQzoECAAQA1DZzBIYo5waYJepGmgCcAB4BIAB3gOIAa9JkgELNTUuMTcuNi4xLjKYAQCgAQGqAQ-
tnd3Mtd2I6LWltZ7ABCg&sclient=img&ei=ChadDeX-oDyB66YtgXah5TADw&bih=576&biw=1366#imgrc=M2vi-UXaf2zF9lM

09/05/2016

Trinity has had night nightmares often since Peyton died. In my heart I've always believed she has some type of gift just by what she experiences. Trinity can see what our "normal" eyes cannot.

Isn't it amazing how Malia came across my path for me but also to help me mentor Trinity? I also think by working with her it has forced her to deal with her own grief from losing her husband. She once told me that our relationship is reciprocal and that "nothing is for nothing" in the spiritual world. I believe we are all like a big grid and we all are affected or cross each other's paths for certain reasons. A good friend also gave me that visual description and instantly it made sense with me and felt right. I feel Spirit uses each of us to talk through to one another.

Trinity has been so constant about asking me if I can have a baby. She rubs my stomach all of the time and asks when I can have a baby. Seriously, I think she is being prompted on the other side to help move me along because her timing is incredible!

09/23/2016

Today we are on our way to my brother's wedding. Jeremiah is a groomsman, the girls are the flower girls and I am an usherette. This should be a fun weekend and I am so happy for my brother. He is such a good man and he deserves this. I am excited to see my sister as well.

I woke up this a.m. vividly remembering a dream I had last night. Except I know it wasn't just a dream, but a visitation. I remember being told by Peyton "Mom, I am coming back to you." It was brief but very distinct. I woke up feeling lighter with a peacefulness about me. I believe I will be getting pregnant soon and he will be reincarnating soon. He visited me last night to give me a message and validate what I've already been told by two different mediums. As I think about this, tears fill my eyes...I am being given a special miraculous gift and I feel so very indebted. How many people go through pain and trauma and don't get the answers and gifts that I have been given? Because of this I feel that I have to do something with this. I want others to have the peace that I have been given.

Before we left this a.m. Jeremiah went to Best Buy and took Trinity with him to get a new case for his phone. I stayed home with Tenley and continued to pack. When they got home Trinity came up to my bedroom where I was packing. She started to cry and hugged me. She said that when they were at the store 'she heard her brothers saying, 'Hi Trinity.' She said, 'it kind of scared her.' I said, "Trinity, I bet that is scary but that is such a special thing. Your brothers are just trying to tell you they love you and they are thinking about you. They aren't trying to scare you but instead just let you know they are thinking about you", as I held her. I also told her, "If it scares you and you don't want it, you can tell them to stop".

I want Trinity to feel empowered and also only allow what she is comfortable with. Our boys connect with her...I don't want them to scare her but I'd be lying if I said I didn't wish that I could experience that🥰

09/30/2016

I think I might be pregnant...

Yesterday Jeremiah came home and explained how in the last couple of months that when he finds pennies he always finds two at a time. He believes that he finds two as these are communication from both the boys. He finds them all of the time...always outside of his truck door or along his path. This never happens to me, I mean ever. He even started a Peyton/Tayden jar because it happens so often.

He said that yesterday when he was getting out of his truck at a gas station there was a penny...just one. He looked at me and said, "Are you pregnant? I always find two together and today there was just one. That makes me feel like that penny was from Tayden and that Peyton is reincarnating now as a new baby in you."

I just looked at him...with tears. I don't know yet if I am pregnant but what he didn't know was that I had bought a pregnancy test as I have been feeling different. I just haven't taken it yet...like, I think I am afraid to. I'm just not ready to yet...like I want to wait until I've at least missed a period. If I am... holy crap...

~Just waiting~ 🙈

10/06/2016

I have been feeling different this week, like a feeling that my body is working on being pregnant. I have always been really hypersensitive concerning my body. When I was getting pregnant with Tayden I remember telling Jeremiah that I was either on my way to getting pregnant or I was in the early stages of a UTI. We went to urgent care that night and I was negative for a UTI. Two weeks later I had a positive pregnancy test! I wonder if me being able to sense my body so well has anything to do with me being an empath?

Today I took a pregnancy test after school and it was negative. My stomach just sank and I felt a little confused. I know I have been feeling something. I was disappointed and went straight to grab my IPad. For some reason I noticed the time on the clock which said 4:44. This struck me deep inside my gut. From my current learnings I know that 444 means that "angels are with you" in that moment. One of the first pictures to pull up on my Pinterest feed was "The meaning of 444 and angels". I knew this moment was not a coincidence. I also knew that at that moment I was being comforted and reassured. I felt like they were telling me to just "hold on, ride this out, you don't have your answer yet." The test said negative but deep down I knew it was wrong. Spirit was trying to tell me to just hold on, stay calm, hold on to faith and sit in this moment. ~

10/09/2016

Happy 35th birthday to me! How does it go by so fast? Today I got to take a nap by myself and go on a walk by myself ;) Jeremiah sent me flowers to school on Friday from the kids. He bought me really comfy soft jammies. After my walk I was playing with Tenley in the front yard. I happened to look down and there was a little white feather. About two feet away was another even smaller baby feather. I knew that it was a sign from our boys letting me know they were there with me. I yelled to Jeremiah and told him about the feathers. He smiled and nodded his head. I am so lucky he is so open and believes like I do. We ended up loading up the girls and going to the cemetery to weed eater and clean around the graves.

When we got home that evening I was getting a lot of birthday posts. My gifted relative sent me a message that said, "Happy birthday beautiful lady. Sending a BIG hug and lots of kisses. 😚😚😚". I knew that was her speaking to me for my boys. I told her that her post made my night! She said, "The boys send you a big hug and lots of kisses. They were with you today- they said you knew that." My heart exploded when I received that text. I never said anything to her about the feathers. Her comment confirmed what I already knew; I knew they were with us.

I am so lucky to have been enlightened and awakened. If all of this spiritual awakening never would have happened we would have missed out on all of this love and connection from the two souls I miss the most.

~Peyton's death broke me; Tayden's death saved me. ~

10/19/2016

Jeremiah is still finding solo pennies. I feel like I am pregnant... After school I took another pregnancy test. I swear I could see a very faint line. Jeremiah couldn't see it. I feel perplexed... I mean Jeremiah is only seeing solo pennies. I swear they are trying to let us know that I am pregnant even before my body can tell us.

10/23/2016

I took another pregnancy test and this time the positive blue line was very visible. Holy crap!!! This has been amazing, all of this. They have been communicating this to us before my body could even physically register it! I know this is only possible because of my spiritual team on the other side.

I am extremely cautious and guarded. I just need this to sit with me a bit...

I have been wanting to go to the Theresa Caputo show here in town next week. I have been thinking about this so much but am failing to know who I should ask and feeling guilty about spending that much money on a ticket. I have thought about asking my gifted relative but I just wasn't sure. Then all of a sudden yesterday on the way home from the gym my gifted relative texted asking if I would want to go with her! She said her family member bought two tickets but now can't go and said that she'd want me to take her place. Again, my spiritual team has a way of making things that they know I need just work out!

10/27/2016

Tonight I got to go to Theresa Caputo and it was great! My gifted relative and I met for dinner first and then we went to the show.

Before I left, I told Jeremiah that I wasn't going with the intention of being read. I knew that wasn't the purpose of me going and in fact, I felt that I needed to go to validate to myself how much I've healed and how far I've come. I needed to go to Theresa to hear the life lessons that Spirit would reveal through Theresa. The experience was awesome and captivating. Many people may not have access to a medium and I have been blessed with a stacked deck of them!

Afterwards, Melissa and I talked for some time before I dropped her off. She told me some messages from Spirit...

She explained that during the show my Tiny Grandma in Spirit was on one side of me and my grandfather in Spirit was on the other side. Melissa told my grandpa that she wanted me to be read and he said that I knew that there were other people who needed it more. He told her I had Malia and her to help me. When I heard this it resonated so deep with me because of what I had said to Jeremiah before I left. I was also told when Peyton's soul would be coming back she felt like it would be a boy. She explained that the new baby we have will "shake the earth". She said that the new baby's life purpose has already been planned and that he is going to positively expose what happened to his older brother (Peyton). She said that my purpose is sharing our experience about the boys and that Peyton will be my biggest cheerleader. She said that there are individuals in the court system and law enforcement that covered up Peyton's case. These people know what they did and that it was political. These people were more concerned with their careers than doing what was right. She explained that one of the captains tried to bring light to Peyton's case but that they realized it was political and that their career could be on the line. This captain also realized that if they exposed Peyton's case, that there would be other things that would come out and they just couldn't do that. Melissa said this new baby will positively expose those that covered up Peyton's case. Spirit kept saying to her, "karma".

Spirit talked about how Jeremiah adores me and is always focused on how I'm doing emotionally. They talked about how last year after Tayden he knew I was in a really bad place but he never said anything to me as he felt like I was trying not to talk about it. The new baby will teach me lessons that I didn't even know I needed to learn. Many people in my family have spiritual gifts. I am gifted as an empath; I can feel energy in a living body or feel energy in Spirit form. When I feel Spirit I feel prickly and almost goose bumpy like. She said the energy I pick up from Spirit in times of stress when they're trying to console me causes me to experience anxiety-like symptoms.

This is pretty much the gist of it all. We talked so much and it was awesome. I texted her when I got home as it was midnight. She texted back that Tiny Grandma wanted me to know that, "I know that you know I am always here to protect and guide you. You are doing an awesome job as a mommy and wife. Yes, we all have bad days but don't get down on yourself. Some days our heads are literally spinning on our bodies, but that doesn't mean it has to overwhelm us." Best message ever ♥

Nobody Told Me This

10/31/2016

Today at work I started bleeding....I went to the bathroom and a chunk of tissue came out. I looked down and my gut just dropped, "I'm losing it....this baby." I stayed as calm as I could. I went out and talked to my co-workers and told them what was happening. I called Jeremiah and told him...he told me I needed to go home. I went back to the bathroom hoping that somehow this was just a fluke but now I had more blood and was starting to cramp. I am starting to panic...I talked to our bookkeeper and told her I had to leave. On the way home I kept hearing the phrase "sit in the calm" over and over in my head. It was like Spirit was with me trying to calm me. Once home I grabbed my I-PAD and pulled up my Pinterest account. All over the front page were the numbers "444" and in that moment I felt surrounded by the most loving energy that down to my soul felt like angels. I was surrounded by Spirit all around me and I knew they were trying to comfort me. I was told I was having a baby but now I was losing it.... What is happening? This can't be happening? In my messages it was never mentioned that I would be miscarrying...

It was Halloween evening and I was afraid to be on my feet too much so Jeremiah took the girls himself. I kept hoping that maybe this wasn't really happening but deep in my gut I knew I was losing this baby.

11/01/2016

The bleeding has picked up as well as the cramps. I went to work because I knew I couldn't just stay home and wait why this all was just happening. By Tuesday night I was passing bigger clots and bleeding more heavily. I became very scared as I felt like this miscarriage was so much worse than my other two. I contacted Malia and just explained that I was scared about what was happening to me. I am terribly afraid of dying due to a pregnancy after losing Tayden and becoming so sick myself. The clots were big tonight and the bleeding was heavy...

11/02/2016

I continued to bleed and called the doctor's office. They did a sonogram and the tech explained that she did not see a pregnancy...which is what I was prepared to hear. And again, I tried to sit in the calm and accept what was happening.

I was just so confused because I was told by Melissa and Malia separately that I would be getting pregnant. It was never revealed by either of them that I would be miscarrying. I was told about the pregnancy and Peyton coming back and I was prepared for that. I was never prepared for this and it almost felt like a twisted game....where I am briefly given what I want and then it's taken away. I know that's my ego brain talking and I also believe there's got to be more. There has to be a reason...I have to have faith and sit in this calm. But I don't get it....

Malia sent me a message asking about my sonogram. After I explained that there was no pregnancy any longer she told me that had it gone to term this baby would have been a girl. She explained that Peyton decided he wants to come back as a boy and he is saying, "I'll see you soon mommy". It just clicked when she said this. It made sense to me and helped me to understand what was going on. She explained that she saw me pregnant at the beginning of the year. She asked about how I was doing emotionally.

11/15/2016

I am struggling this week....like a lot. I have to go in every week to make sure my HCG levels are going down. But emotionally I am really struggling....my hormones are all over. While I believe what Malia told me about the reason I miscarried, for some reason I am emotionally struggling.

11/22/2016

I talked to Malia this afternoon. She explained in more detail that Peyton's soul prefers to be a boy. Had this baby gone to term it would have been a girl, hence why Peyton decided not to re-incarnate. She encouraged me to go see the woman that did my Reiki session the first time as that had really helped to clear my energy before. She also emphasized that getting pregnant again is still my decision. She also said January, February and March still look like good months for me as far as pregnancy."

She said, "Tiny grandma is here now and she is saying that your mom...she's not doing well. It's getting bad, really bad. She is saying that you need to be prepared for the end. I am sensing that it will be soon that she will no longer be here. It's going to be bad. I am feeling pain in my right side and something with her head, it's almost unbearable. Her left kidney has already stopped working. Tiny grandma does not want you to carry this burden of responsibility when your mom passes. There was nothing you could have done to change this. These were your mom's decisions, that you were just the kid. Tiny grandma is saying that when this happens that there will be a balance. You will have a loss but you will also have a baby again around this same time. She is saying to focus on your family and this new life and don't let yourself get sucked in to the would've, should've, or could've with your mom's decisions in life or that you somehow were responsible for those. Your mom's addiction made her more selfish. She is saying that she is so happy that you are more like her and have a lot of her own characteristics of giving."

I just sat there...this was heavy...really heavy. But once again, I wanted to hug Tiny Grandma for guiding me, protecting me and ultimately knowing what I need. I trust her and I know that as my guide she is trying to guide me in the best way possible. My whole life I have been pulled to her. I met her when I was little but I don't remember meeting her. I would have been nine when she passed. I would always hear family talk about her and I've always been drawn to her. I have always felt like I came from her. The more I learn of her I believe that more than just my short stature came from her. Malia told me that Tiny grandma called me "Her firecracker". For those that know me I have always had a feistiness about me. I believe my pull to her my whole life has to do with the fact that she is working with me tirelessly, and I know that is no small task.

I also felt comforted about being given a heads up about my mom's ending nearing. I know I will be devastated when it happens, but I imagine I will feel relief that her suffering is over. I think my devastation will come from the reality that I will never get that opportunity to have a regular, normal relationship with my mom. Like her death will solidify that small hope inside of me that that can never happen. For 20 plus years I have lived with a small hidden hope that maybe she will stop drinking, maybe she will want to be in my life, maybe she'll want to make up for all she missed out on, maybe she'll want to get to know her grandkids. But, I know she can't do this. Every time, by myself, as I did my own mini interventions to her and questioned her drinking and begged her to let me set up treatment, she refused. I always thought that maybe I could get through to her. Maybe I could say it in just the right way that she could accept help...but to no avail, it never worked. I would hear of criticisms from others outside our family who questioned why we weren't doing anything or helping her. I would just sit there and think, "If you understood addiction you wouldn't be saying this, be grateful that you don't". My mom's addiction has affected all of us in different ways. I am the one that is still here to see it and experience it. Even before Malia came today I have been feeling that my mom's life is coming to an end. I mean feeling it very strongly. I have tried to drop hints to my siblings that I don't believe it will be long in a way to try and prepare them. Now I need to decide how to tell them what Malia said or if I should tell them. Malia also said that normally this is not a message she would deliver to someone but that Tiny Grandma said I needed to know. Tiny Grandma said that I cannot have one more unexpected death from someone close to me. She said I needed to be prepared so that I could start to digest and deal with this happening. Many people may not be able to handle this kind of news but for me, I need this. She's right, I couldn't handle one more unexpected death...

12/09/2016

I saw Malia tonight!! She gave me a little box and it had a bracelet in it. Upon looking closer I realized it had five hearts dangling from it. She said," I saw this and I had to get it for you. It represents the four full term babies you have had thus far and the one that you will be having." She got teary eyed as she said this.

She also talked about how my healing is inspiring others around me. She said that she has also done her own healing with her husband who passed years earlier.

She told me I had been on her mind all day so that is the reason she wanted to meet. I told her how I had talked about her the day before to a friend of mine. This friend lost a loved one the month before Peyton died. We have sort of shared this unspoken "death bond" as both of our lives were forever changed so close in time together. For the year or two after our loved ones died we couldn't even look at each other, let alone talk to each other. The pain was just so raw for both of us and maybe we couldn't talk to each other because deep down we knew that the other really knew how miserable we each were. After so long society expects the grieving to stop, like there's this silent "get over it" code. She and I could each feel this and so we tended to survive in this world by moving forward and acting like we were ok. But, when we looked at each other, we remembered how broken we really were. It's so interesting as so many people told me I was so strong and for fear of letting anyone down, including myself, I kept moving forward. But moving forwarding meant stuffing all of the hurt, the pain, the trauma and giving up hope towards ever living a peaceful life again.

I know what the black hole feels like and how it can sneak up and suck you back in out of nowhere. That's the thing...since meeting Malia the black hole isn't really around me anymore. I mean I still grieve for my boys but my perspective on their lives is different now. I now have learned that I still get to have a relationship with them, just not in the original way I imagined. When I get sad now it's like a selfish sad where I just miss holding them and I miss what our family "could have been". But, the black hole hasn't sucked me back in like it did before my spiritual awakening. I still have bad days but, they're not as bad as they were a short time ago. That is a pain that makes me cringe to remember it and it makes my stomach turn to imagine someone else feeling it.

When I was talking to my friend she mentioned that she is struggling with going to church. Out of nowhere I said, "I too, initially struggled with church and the "you just have to believe mentality". To me, church and the Bible are great ways to teach morality but I also believe there's more to Spirit than what they teach. I enjoy going to church as it helps me reflect on how I can be a better person. To me, that's what church is about.

01/22/2017

Another "angelversary" gone by.

Yesterday marked five years since Peyton died. Five years...how can that be?? It's crazy how time has gone by so fast, yet that moment remains frozen in time. It's one of the most unnerving feelings I've ever felt. I now know why when I asked a woman at a grief group for lost children, "how much longer will this last?" she just bowed her head and cried. What she knew as a grieving mom was that it never ends, it doesn't go away, it doesn't shut off...ever. She saw my broken, desperate soul and it pained her that she could not give me the answer I so desperately needed. Oh, how I had no idea the storm that had embarked upon us.

I had great intentions this year...I wanted to take a more positive spin and celebrate Peyton's death date as like a second Birthday. You know, a celebration of peace from pain for him. That's what I intended to do. I did...but somehow, through some forgotten back door the "heaviness" snuck in. It tip-toed in and it just sat on me very heavy. It pulled at my heart strings and it robbed my eyes of tears. It took my good intentions and threw them in my face. It tried to make me feel like it was coming back, that I couldn't keep doing all the good work I have been doing. It made me feel weak because I didn't feel any better than I did last year at this time. It tried to negate all of the work I've done. I know this now.... But, I'm ok. I struggled yesterday, I hurt for what could have been. But I am finding my peace again today. My bad days don't have to win anymore. They just show me how much love I have for my son. The tears, the sadness is just love...shown in another way.

What I do know is that my soul chose this lifetime with these circumstances. I can't waste this opportunity... I chose it with the hopes of overcoming it. There were certain lessons my soul needed to learn. To make this lifetime count I have to find a way to learn what I was supposed to. I have learned about compassion and I also know I have to learn forgiveness. I'm not there yet....and maybe this will take my entire lifetime...but someday I have to forgive the person that killed my child. And in the end, even if I hadn't of chosen this outcome, the end result is the same.... I was dealt a trauma and I have to find a way to heal from it.

Her soul must be so broken...to carry this deep secret of what she did to my son. Her husband must be so broken as well,

> "Hurt people hurt people. That's how pain patterns get passed on, generation after generation after generation. Break the chain today. Meet anger with sympathy, contempt with compassion, cruelty with kindness. Greet grimaces with smiles. Forgive and forget about finding fault. Love is the weapon of the future."
> ~Yehuda Berg

https://www.google.com/search?q=hurt+people+hurt+people%2C+that%27s+how+pain+patterns+get+passed+on&tbm=isch&ved=2ahUKEwilvIfe_LvrAhUVUc0KHev_D3sQ2-cCegQIABAA&oq=hurt+people+hurt+people%2C+that%27s+how+pain+patterns+get+passed+on&gs_lcp=CgNpbWcQAzoCCABQ3sYBWKv_AWC6hgIoAnAAeAOAAewDiAGNT5IBCzAuMTguM-TQuNi40mAEAoAEBqgELZ3dzLXdpei1pbWfAAQE&sclient=img&ei=J_ZHX8iM-FZWitQbr_7_YBw&bih=576&biw=1366#imgrc=WpNk_G0sidDbkM

to know what she did to Peyton. These burdens are theirs to carry. If I continue to hate them I remain tethered to their pain. Forgiveness is the only way to cut my cord to them, the only way I can be free from them. I have to forgive them for me because holding on to hate for them only pulls me deeper into their negative spiral of a life. For ME, I have to believe and accept that they will have to account to God for their actions. For my soul growth in heaven I have to forgive and not allow this life to harden me.

I believe that Tayden visited me in my dreams on Thursday night. I dreamt of Peyton Friday night and when I woke up Saturday morning I found a dime by my bedroom door. I know they were with me yesterday, I felt it all day. 🖤 🖤

My friend who is also clairsentient and claircognizant like me sent me a message out of nowhere saying, "Praying for a healthy baby boy. I hope this doesn't sound totally nuts!" I text her back and explained that I ovulated last week and that I feel like I am in the process of getting pregnant but obviously it would be too soon for a pregnancy test! She explained that out of nowhere yesterday she had this strong feeling that I was pregnant and she had to tell me!!! She said it is one of the strongest feelings she's ever had! I do feel like I am working on getting pregnant....We'll see what the next couple of weeks will bring. 👼

02/01/2017

My mom called me today. Mom asked if I, my brother and she could sit down to go over her will and legal documents. She explained that she thought this was important and wanted us all on the same page. She said that her health is good and she is a baby boomer so she will live forever. She asked if I would contact my brother and figure out when it is a good time. She repeated this multiple times. I felt like without admitting it, she had a feeling that she wouldn't be living that much longer and that she wanted everything lined up and in order. I felt like her soul was trying to prepare.

"To my angels, guides, loved ones-

Please help me....Please allow me to release this heaviness. I have such anxiety about losing my mom. I am scared for her and about her. I know that my mom's time is winding down. Please let it be the most peaceful way that it can be for her and for us. I need a little reassurance from you. Thank you for always helping me."

03/02/2017 & 03/20/2017

I am 7 weeks pregnant! I saw Malia tonight. She said she just wanted to reassure me that this baby is "sticking" and not going anywhere. She wanted this message to help ease some anxiety that she says I have been feeling (which, of course I have). I talked to her quite a bit about how Trinity's gifts seem to be opening even more.

Trinity has commented about seeing Peyton and Tayden a few times and them telling her they love her. She said she saw Peyton holding Tayden. She said Peyton was a little boy and Tayden was still a baby. She told Peyton she has been praying to God that her mom will have a baby. His response was "that might happen Trinity". When she told us this she said, "Mom, he said that might happen. So maybe yes, maybe no." What she didn't know was that I thought I was pregnant and this sparked me to take a pregnancy test which was positive.

For the next few weeks Trinity would ask if I was pregnant, which I would stammer I didn't know. I didn't want to tell her until I had been to the doctor but her questions persisted. I knew that she knew something. Finally, after my 7 week appointment we sat down with her and told both girls and showed them the sonogram picture. Trinity was so happy jumping up and down and said, "Mom I told you so!"

I am just trying to support her so that she doesn't feel so afraid. She asked me the other night if there came a time if she didn't want this gift anymore, could she pray to God to make it stop? Then she commented that she wouldn't want that yet because then she wouldn't get to see Peyton anymore.

Trinity came home from school last week and said how she had to write a paragraph about something personal about herself. She wrote about how she sees Spirit and has seen her brothers Tayden and Peyton. I tried not to act shocked but inside I was like, "oh shit". We've talked to her about how our family knows about her gift but that she probably shouldn't tell other people because they may not believe her. I explained that her eyes are "special" and she can see what most cannot but most people don't believe what they can't see. I explained that if she tells people about her gift they may not believe her and that's ok because her mom and dad do. She said, "Mom, I'm afraid that my teacher may not believe me." I explained that if that happens just to say, "It's ok Mrs. Engel if you don't believe, my mom and dad believe me." I am trying to be realistic with Trinity for future interactions that I'm sure will happen but yet let her know that her family believes and supports her.

Malia also talked to me about helping/guiding me and Trinity as time continues on. For that guidance, and ALL the guidance she has given me I adore that woman. She holds a very special place in my heart!!♥

It has taken me three weeks to finish this post. I would sit down to journal before bed and then get interrupted or just be too tired to finish. So there, now I'm caught up! Guess what?! I am now 11 weeks pregnant!

03/27/2017

I feel like this baby is a boy. Actually, it is more of a knowing. I was lying in bed the other night and was going over a conversation I had with another intuitive friend. This friend had told me that this baby will be a boy. As I was thinking about this the bathroom scale that was up against our bedroom wall lit up. I knew immediately that this wasn't a coincidence but instead a message and validation from Spirit that this baby is a boy. Our scale is a high tech one that lights up in the middle when you stand on it, except no living person was on it. This was Spirit getting my attention and validating my inquiry! 👍

04/03/2017

This afternoon Jeremiah and I met with the at-risk doctor to take measurements of the baby on the ultrasound. I was really nervous as just going back to that office brought back so many scary moments with Tayden. It was almost like a facing of fears for me. It was like I would know how far I have come in healing by how I dealt with going back into that office. Surprisingly, I felt ok, like I had a peace about myself. The nurse took my vitals and then I was escorted back to the sonogram room. The technician took measurements as she moved the wand all over my belly. Jeremiah and I didn't say a word the entire time as we both just sat there in anticipation. Unfortunately, we've become accustomed to bracing ourselves for the worst. The doctor came in and took some additional measurements. He was looking for certain soft markers for Down syndrome due to Tayden's diagnosis. After looking around he felt everything looked good thus far and guessed that we would have a very low risk for this baby having a chromosomal abnormality. I opted to do the blood test just for some additional peace of mind. Pray for good results. The doctor asked if we wanted to know the gender of the baby if he could see it and jokingly I told him yes but that my mother's intuition already knew! He informed us the baby is a boy, which I knew! ☺ I could feel this rush of excitement come over Jeremiah. My heart strings tugged for him as I know how bad he wants this. ♥ Now, prayers for good blood work!

04/11/2017

The specialist doctor's office called today. As I recognized the number and answered the phone my insides dropped to the floor. I recognized the nurse's voice and immediately tried to assess her tone. After greeting me she went on to tell me that my results came back and they showed "a very low risk" for any type of genetic abnormality. I sighed the biggest relief and thanked her for calling. I know the blood test isn't 100% accurate but it gives me extreme peace of mind. I sat at my desk while tears filled my eyes. I felt grateful, really, really grateful. So many people take for granted just having a healthy baby. 👶

I know that what Malia originally told me from Spirit is all coming true. This baby is a miracle from God, with the help of Archangel Gabriel and my loved ones on the other side. I am so indebted to all of them and have such a profound appreciation for their love and support. Thank you to all of you for EVERYTHING 💖!

I'm thankful for all of it. The highs. The lows. The blessings. The lessons. The setbacks. The comebacks. The love. The hate. Everything.

https://www.google.com/search?q=i%27m+thankful+for+all+of+it&tbm=isch&ved=2ahUKEwjozcLy_LvrAhXbF80KHZNcB8IQ2-cCegQIABAA&oq=I%27m+thankful+for+all&gs_lcp=CgNpbWcQARgAMgQIIxAnMgI-IADICCAAyBggAEAgQHjIGCAAQCBAeMgYIABAIEB4yBggAEAgQHjIG-CAAQCBAeMgYIABAIEB4yBggAEAgQHjoHCCMQ6gIQJzoFCAAQsQM6BA-gAEEM6BwgAELEDEENQ-ZcsWPzRLGCG4ixoAXAAeASAAY8EiAHaMZIBCzAu-MjMuMTAuNS0xmAEAoAEBqgELZ3dzLXdpei1pbWewAQrAAQE&scli-ent=img&ei=UvZHX-jcD9uvtAaTuZ2QDA&bih=576&biw=1366#imgrc=AOzLT-lvYa9_6pM

04/21/2017

I posted this on my Facebook account this morning:

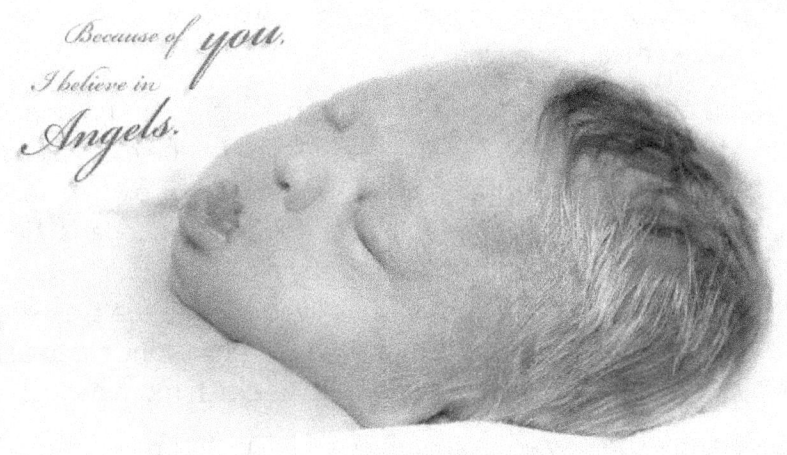

Happy 2nd birthday in heaven to our littlest light Tayden Joseph ♥ I've always felt that Peyton's death "broke" me and Tayden's death "saved" me. I was forced to dig deep and self-reflect on who I am, who I'm not, what's important to me, what's not, and what I believe on a deep spiritual level. I feel his presence often and know our tiny beauty saved my life!!😊

I can't believe it was two years ago that we lost him and then I had all of the complications. I find myself often saying that.....

I saw Malia tonight. We hugged, she rubbed my belly and we quickly started catching up. She told me about some current things going on with her. Then she told me the following things:

Malia said that Peyton was "promised" to me in this lifetime. I told her how before I met her I thought I was done having children after all I went through with Tayden. She smiled and said "he would have come back anyways"!

She also talked about my family. She said that there are many people with spiritual gifts in my family and that as time moves on we will be able to consult with each other and use our unique abilities and senses to help each other. She said that my awakening will open up many of my family members who haven't quite awakened yet or realized their hidden gifts.

She talked about my mom and how she has just given up and is ready to be done with this life. She said it won't be the most pleasant when it happens and that her soul will leave her body before physical death. She said I will be able to tell when that happens. Tiny grandma forbids any of us from feeling any type of guilt or responsibility from mom's death as mom has lived her life the way she chose. That message was really important for Tiny Grandma to tell us. Malia thought maybe it will be springtime when mom passes.

Malia said that she saw a vision of my delivery with Broen. She said the C-section went fine. She saw him being born and then swaddled. She saw the nurses place him in my arms while they were still sewing me back up. She said when I held him he touched my cheek as if to say "I'm here". She said the moment that happens his spiritual memory of all of this will be gone. He will have no leftover memory of any of this. She said he will be a more balanced blend of Jeremiah and me and will be a more serious child then he would've been as Peyton. He will be very curious and focused on what his life purpose here is. She said she knows he is moving all of the time now trying to let me know he's inside of me and ok. 👶

05/09/2017

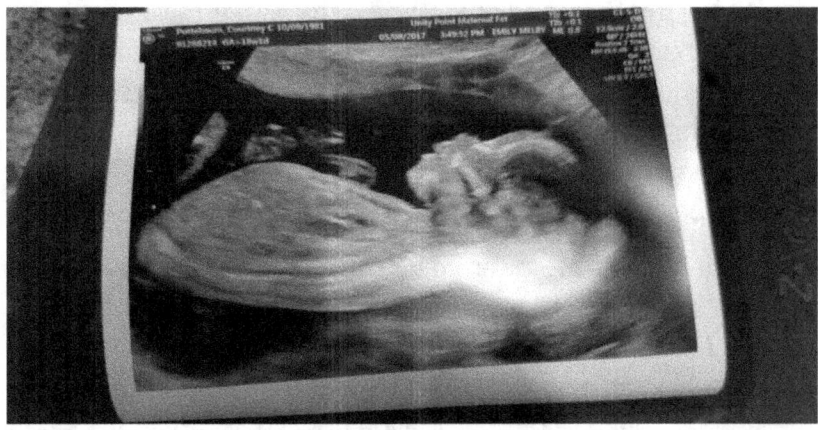

Tonight I posted the following post on my social media page as well as the above picture. The response to this post was overwhelming and I could feel how many people are truly excited and happy for us. Most people want a happy ending!

> "Jeremiah, Trinity, Tenley, our two angel babies Peyton & Tayden 👣👣 and I would like to make it "official" that we are expecting a baby boy in the beginning of October! 👶 Please join us in praying for a healthy baby to complete our family. We feel extremely blessed that God is giving us this opportunity one more time. 💕👣"

A friend posted that it looked like God's heavenly hands were cradling our baby and keeping him safe.

05/15/2017

I heard back from my doctor's office this afternoon and they verified that the last of our genetic testing for Broen came back negative. That felt so good... just to be able to relax a bit and mark that off of our mental checklist. It's like Jeremiah and I have this stored up post-traumatic stress type of response where we are just waiting... afraid to be too happy or expect too much. While I say that I also completely, totally believe what Malia has shared with me about Petyon's soul, this baby and our journey. I have been given the hope and explanation that most in traumatic times don't get. Know that I realize that and feel indebted to my family on the other side for giving me answers and the inspiration I have needed to live the genuine life that I now can live. But in order for them to do this we have also been open to BELIEVING and RECEIVING.

It's interesting how now, after going through my spiritual awakening, I crave to be around those people who think like I do. I crave peace and find myself needing less "stuff". Clutter and useless stuff all over feels like it is heavy to me. I crave to live more minimally, with just what I need right now. Maybe now I have an appreciation for just being here, alive right now in these moments. Just make the best of each day and notice in all of the positive or negative times what it is I am supposed to take away from it. For me, knowing that this life here and now is just part of the journey somehow calms me. I know that I have to appreciate and learn from everything in this lifetime so that I can ascend when I get to Heaven. I will get to see my close friends and family in Heaven and those lessons I don't learn in this lifetime will be learned in my next lifetime. This journey is only part of my entire soul's journey and to make the most of it is the absolute best thing I can do! Blessings on your journey!

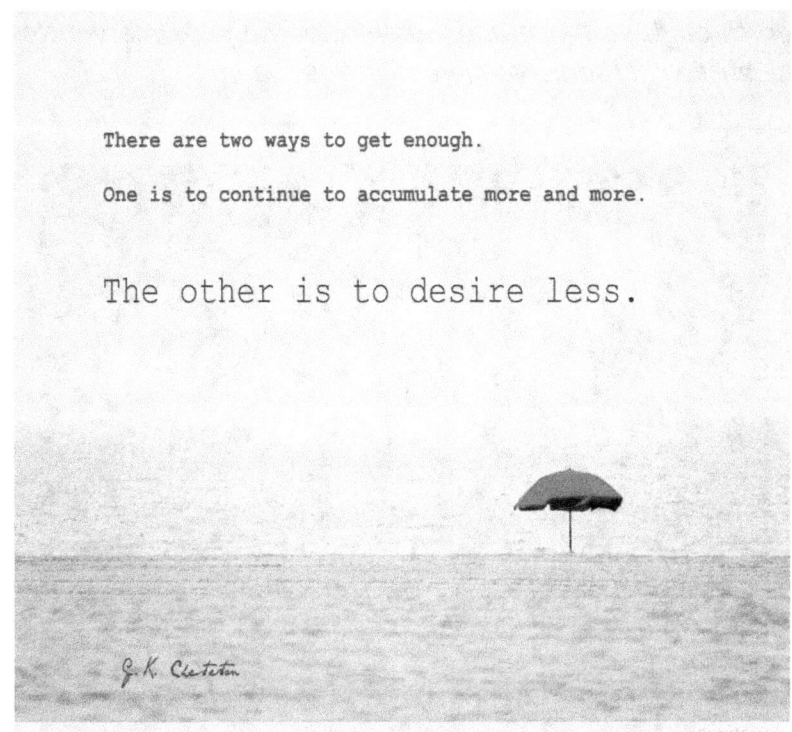

https://www.google.com/search?q=There+are+two+ways+to+get+enough&sxsrf=ALeKk01oeYfQJfFYNV-vogKaCR5o8qkrYA:1592513600196&tbm=isch&source=iu&ictx=1&fir=TET4ug1NtzkPiM%253A%252CLRHv5JlnC41RHM%252C_&vet=1&usg=AI4_-kTVK1nbNf-HebuXP8yLBFQ7H9luxKw&sa=X&ved=2ahUKEwj1_cC7n4zqAhUQac0KHVhYDMIQ9QEwBXoECAoQFg&biw=1366&bih=576#imgrc=TET4ug1NtzkPiM:

06/20/2017

I posted this message on my social media page today. Happy anniversary to us!!!

"Happy Anniversary to us!!! 11 years of marriage, 16 years of companionship, 1 newborn death, 1 infant homicide, 3 miscarriages, 2 beautiful SPUNKY girls and a precious baby boy to arrive. We've

been through so much and I thank God he gave me you to go through it with! I adore you Jeremiah Pottebaum."

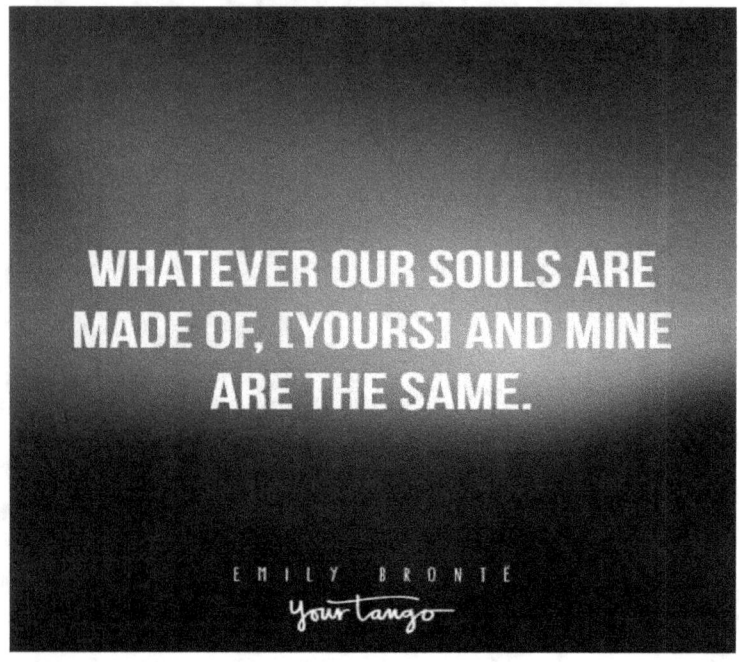

https://www.pinterest.com/pin/230035493448232346/

07/03/2017

Today I had a Reiki appointment at 10:00 a.m. I hadn't had a session since after I had the miscarriage and felt like it was time. I remember Malia telling me that I should go about once a month as it would be good for me. I think I feel guilty spending the money on myself even though I know it is extremely healing to me. Malia had at one point told me that I would be especially emotional this pregnancy. But, that's the thing... I really haven't. It's weird because I feel these deep emotions inside but it's like I can't get the emotions out, like I won't let myself. Like these emotions are trapped inside of me... and maybe I am terrified to face them. I knew that I needed to have the session and see if she can help me release these built up emotions.

Right when I showed up we chatted quickly to get caught up from last seeing each other. I updated her as far as what has happened since I last saw her and the messages I have since received. Some of the stuff I repeated to her from last time, but I tried to get to the new messages that have been passed to me. I have told her really everything that Malia has shared with me.

We didn't waste much time and got started on my session. I laid on my side this time as it felt more comfortable. I tried to relax as much as possible and talk to my angels and guides asking them to come in and allow for the greatest healing for me to occur. The soft music played in the background. I chose to be covered with a blanket. There was some type of incense lit in the background and the practitioner used some type of essential oils as she began. I kept my eyes closed the entire time and just fell into a deep relaxation as she worked above me. She started at my head and face and worked her way down my body placing her hands on certain parts of my body as she meditated. I felt more relaxed in this session than I have in any other session. It seemed to go by extremely fast.

The practitioner talked about part of Peyton's soul coming back and how this happening really has nothing to do with me or him. She said that I am being used as a vessel right now in spreading love and light. By what she explained I got the impression that part of Peyton's soul coming back and me talking about it would inspire many people and pull many people to God, his light, love and belief. She made it sound like it would be a type of spiritual movement or spiritual embracement by many people.

I cried...like a real, genuine, deep down release cry. It felt really good emotionally and it just reinforced to me that I have to heal and deal with all of this as healthy as I can so that one day I can inspire and help others. Malia has told me that once I have Broen that his birth will spiritually unlock me. I look forward to that happening and being able to spiritually become what I'm supposed to become.

07/24/2017

I had my at risk doctor's appointment today and ended up bringing Jeremiah and the girls. We thought it would be exciting for them to get to see their brother up on the screen of the sonogram. The technician was so good and made sure to try and get as many good shots as possible for us to see as much as we could. The doctor thought everything looked great and that Broen was growing along just fine. They sent us a bunch of pictures of him and even printed out a color one of his face. I saw so much of Jeremiah in this picture but I'll let you be the judge! Broen Gabriel makes his appearance below:

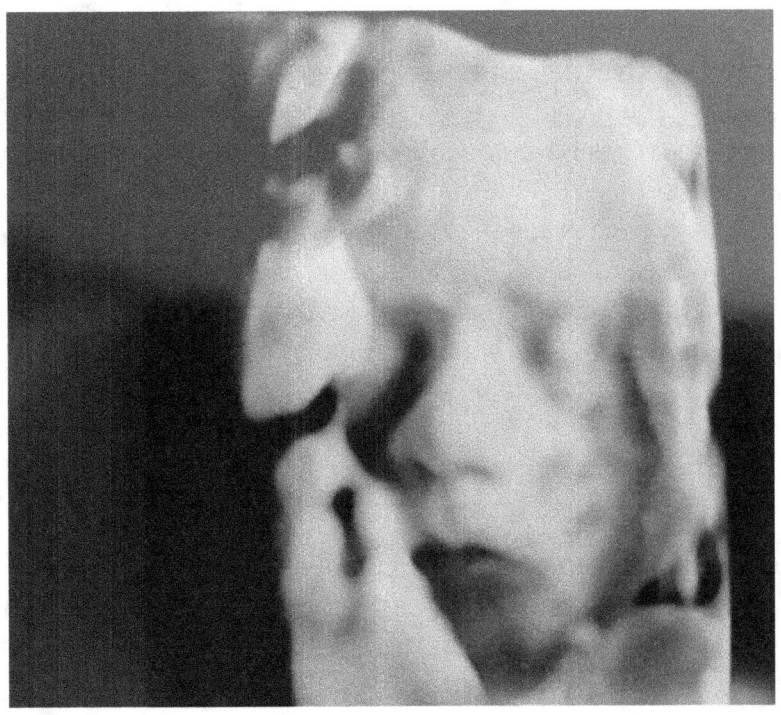

08/23/2017

I had a dream the other night... I don't know if it was Peyton's soul visiting me in my dreams or a message from Spirit. I had given birth to Broen and in certain angles I saw Petyon clear as day and he had tears in his eyes ... but it was the feeling of tears of joy like he was so happy to be there with me in person, so happy to be back with me. I felt like maybe that was a message about how happy he is to be coming back to me. It was right before I woke up so I remembered it clearly. Whenever I have Spirit messages or dream visitations they are always right before I wake up so that I remember them.

I am now 33.5 weeks along. I am huge and feeling really achy, tired and extremely exhausted. I can't believe I will be holding our awaited for son soon. At the same time, it feels so much time yet to be pregnant. As miserable as I am pregnant with each baby, I have felt it to be such a magical event. Watching my belly grow each week and feeling the baby move is an amazing experience as a mother. To think that I will have gone through this five times just blows my mind. Five bundles of love that Jeremiah and I created together and I got to carry each inside me and grow them. I know someday that I will look back and miss these special moments of being pregnant as hard as it is for me to imagine now. I do worry though about being able to still give the girls enough attention or be a "doting" mom to all three of them. I want all of them to always feel like they have a special bond with me. I want to be the kind of mom that when they start their own families some day they think, "I want to be as loving as my mom was".

As closer as it gets to delivery, I pray that my surgery will go well with no complications. After my C-section complications with Tayden there is a hidden fear or reservation that I have concerning another surgery. *Please God, let me have no complications and let it all go smooth. I want to have as easy surgery and recovery as possible so I can concentrate on our new blessing and family.*

Jeremiah put a special alert or ring tone on his phone in case I call for him. I have prepared my mother in law and father to have their phones handy and charged in case I need them. I spoke to a good friend and asked her to be my back up in taking me to the hospital and being in the operating room in case I went into labor early while Jeremiah was away coaching at a volleyball game. With my history of early deliveries, I feel like I have to have some options just in case I don't make it to my scheduled C-section.

So much has happened for me spiritually in the last 20 months. I just hope that even after Broen is here that my spiritual experiences continue to be rich and driving. I hope that I still receive signs, am given messages and am directed in my daily life. These spiritual moments have saved my soul and helped me to align to who I really am. I just don't want to lose those experiences or that connection. I pray that what Malia said is true, that this baby will spiritually unlock me. I look forward to that happening as a connection closer with and to Spirit feels like the exact fitting for my soul. It feels right for me and for my life purpose. Please allow my spiritual gifts to continue to unravel and allow me to have an even closer bond to Spirit on the other side that walks in God's white light.

I feel blessed. There is so much anticipation for this next chapter of my life that will soon be starting! I feel excited for the first time in a very long time. And I owe it all to Spirit. *Thank you... all of you.*

A New Chapter

09/21/2017

I am now 37 weeks and 5 days pregnant. I feel so huge and my whole body is starting to feel exhausted! Today is Thursday and I am feeling like our baby boy will come sometime in the next two days.

I called my sister to inquire about what it is like to start labor with contractions happening first. For some reason I feel in my gut that contractions will come first and progress into labor where they have to take him. I have never gone into labor this way. With Trinity and Peyton my waters broke first and then contractions started. My sister gave me information about her experience with my niece, which seemed to help me feel more relaxed and prepared.

After school I felt like getting a pedicure, which is something I NEVER do. As I pulled up to Tenley's school this strong feeling inside of me was adamant I get the pedicure now so I continued to drive by and went to the salon next door. It felt really good having my feet and calves worked on. I felt relaxed and left to get Tenley. We got home around 5:00 p.m. and I started dinner. I noticed that I felt extremely achy in my lower back and lower abdomen. I had this gut feeling again that real contractions might be starting. I downloaded a contraction timer application and started timing them just in case. They were pretty sporadic and not much consistency to them, but something told me these were different then the Braxton Hicks I normally experience. Jeremiah got home around 6:30 p.m. and by this time my contractions were getting closer but still all over the board. Around 7:30 they were stronger, so I called my dad and step mom to come down and watch the girls for us.

At first presentation in labor and delivery the nurses hooked me up to the monitors. Although the contractions were strong, they still weren't predictable and the nurse made the comment that the doctor will probably just let me go home after being monitored for a little bit. My gut told me that if that happened I would be returning later. Somehow, I knew Broen was coming soon. By 9:30 p.m. my contractions were now coming every 1-3 minutes and they were very strong. The doctor on call from the practice I go to came in to monitor me. He read through my chart and said that with the way the contractions were coming we needed to take Broen so that nothing bad would happen to him. Just like that the nurse went into full preparation mode and she had me prepped for surgery in no time. Jeremiah notified our family that Broen would be coming soon.

I was so scared inside. I was afraid of the surgery because of all of the things that went wrong with Tayden's surgery. Inside my head I kept praying that God would guide the doctor's hand so that I would not have any additional complications from the C-section. Although I had been waiting for this moment to have my son for what seemed like forever, I also was secretly terrified. I have lost two little baby boys and with the messages of Peyton's soul, or parts of his soul coming back through Broen I am terrified of losing him again. I couldn't go through that pain again. So while I am extremely excited to have another little boy, deep down I am anxious.

The nurses finished prepping me and scooted me into surgery where they gave me the epidural and did all of their preparations. I can't believe it's really time. The nurses brought Jeremiah in and I instantly felt better. I felt an energy shift where I knew I could move any worry or anxiety on to him. They numbed me up and started the surgery. It seemed like it took the doctor longer this time but I noticed how calm and "light" his spirit was. He talked and joked during the surgery and his whole aura was very peaceful. I felt calm because he felt calm. I couldn't help but feel like 'Spirit' was there in him. Soon enough I heard the nurses getting excited and could hear them excitedly talk about the doctor pulling our baby boy out of me. I heard them exchanging that he has hair. Even though I couldn't see him I was overtaken with emotions, to know he was finally here and safe. The doctor kept working on me and eventually one of the nurses brought Broen over to us and laid him on my chest. He immediately placed his right hand on my face. If you remember, one of the earlier messages Malia passed to me was that she saw my delivery and that the nurses would place him on my chest and he would touch my face.

Jeremiah snapped a picture as Broen's hand was coming down my cheek. Jeremiah was a little late in his picture but you can see the end picture of his hand on my cheek. As he lay there snuggled on my chest I felt an overwhelming sense of reunion and familiarity. He and I... we have been here; we have done this before.

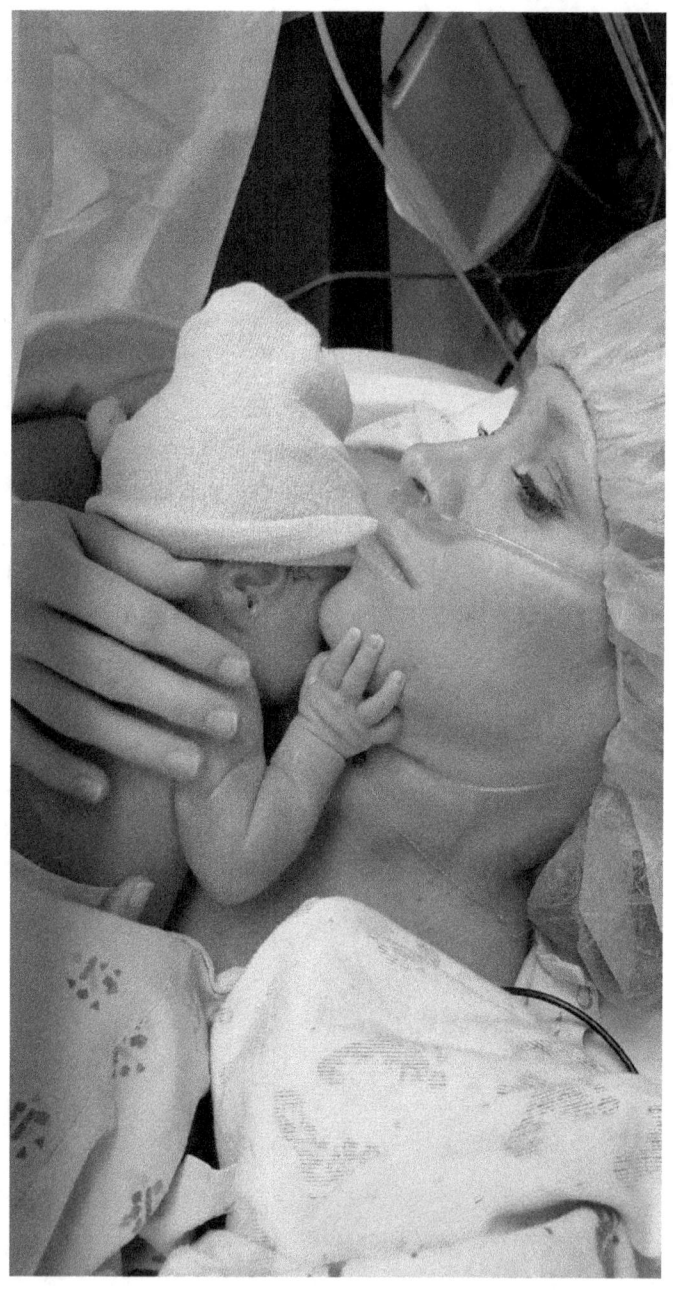

12/19/2017

I came back to work three weeks ago... My dad and step-mom watched Broen my first two weeks back to work. His first week of real daycare was last week. Of his first six days back I kept him home for two of them due to sickness. My anxiety has been through the roof. Right in the morning when I wake up my stomach just knots up and I get sick in the bathroom. My stomach remains upset all day while at work and I find myself constantly trying not to worry about him. All of the trauma and loss with Peyton and I'm sure Tayden as well, has come flooding back. It's almost like a PTSD where I am having flashbacks about what I went through with Peyton. Being here at work has been rough. I am constantly wondering if I should find a way to move around our finances so that I could stay home and care for him. That way I could protect him... protect him from other people, from so much exposure to sickness, from anything that I view as negative.

A good friend of mine at work just looked at me as I told him that I wanted to quit my job. His response was, 'no that's not best for you or for him'. He pointed out that Broen has his own path and that I have to allow Broen to take root in this world and that I can't shield it from him. He pointed out that maybe this is forcing me to deal with deep emotional wounds that haven't really healed or that by being put in this situation is the only way they could heal. He also pointed out that my career choice is part of what makes me, me. By staying home he feels like I would be losing that social part of me that connects with people. I see his points and the logical part of my mind can agree with what he says. The emotional part of me clings to Broen in an attempt to shield him, love him and keep him safe. The other part of me thinks that even if I stayed home I would still hold on to this anxiety as every sniffle he has or every time he's sick I go on high alert that the worst is going to happen. I can tell I am already doing that now. I've taken him to the doctor two times in the last week, once for impetigo and once for a cold. I constantly check on him at night making sure he's breathing even though I have a monitor on him when he sleeps. I am constantly checking his diapers to make sure he's hydrated and analyzing every bowel movement he has. It's not quite fair to say I am "just" worried about someone else caring for him. While that is a HUGE part, it's not ALL of it. I am worried about losing him and so I am hyper vigilant about caring for him and making sure he's ok. My coping at this point goes to the worst case scenario. That is something I have to work on changing. Once Broen hits 6 months of age I wonder if that will change for me since at that point I can no longer compare anything to when Peyton was here?

Dear God, Please help this very blessed PTSD momma cope with the anxiety and fear of losing him. Help me to trust again and have hope and peace that all is well. I didn't anticipate all of this nervousness and anxiety. I know how blessed I am but I am so afraid that I will lose this boy too.

12/20/2017

Sunday night I had such strong anxiety about going to work the next day that I texted Melissa, my gifted family member and asked her if she would help me with some guidance from Spirit. Our conversation went something like this:

My Message to her: "Hi, I am wondering if you can help me... I know you are extremely busy which is why I've been hesitating to text. I'm wondering if you could reach out to Spirit for me as I am a "hot mess"! I went back to work three weeks ago. My stepmom watched Broen the first two weeks and he started daycare a week ago. (Tenley goes to the same place for full time preschool.) Basically I am a hot mess going to work and having him away from me in daycare. My anxiety is through the roof and I feel like I have small anxiety attacks every morning. I have even debated quitting my job, even though I don't know if that would be financially possible. I feel I need guidance or I am going to have a meltdown. All of my trust/trauma issues from Peyton have come flooding back. Am I on the right path by continuing to work or should I be figuring out how to stay home? What can they tell me about these extreme fears, anxieties, so forth? Melissa, I would so appreciate any guidance/connection you can give me. I feel so pulled to you for guidance. Thank you for reading my novel!"

Her Responses: "I have been debating calling you or just showing up- I do have a lot to tell you- as a message from above-and have been waiting for the right time to deliver the messages(nothing bad at all!!) But they told me I would know when the right time would be-. Please know that your anxiety is totally normal for what trauma and heartache you all have gone through- to be honest Jeremiah has some too (he just doesn't voice it) as he wants to be strong for you- These emotions are going to be hard to let go, but you will be able to- it's the unknowing that is so scary. Your Tiny Grandma is telling me to tell you- you are a fighter, and this is one you are going to have to fight through, it's going to be hard at first, but you will get through it- Take it day by day-breathe- and write down your emotions- have you been journaling? She says to bring your journal with you and when you start to feel your heart in your throat to start writing everything- You have and have had tons of support around you- I think that's why I haven't seen too many lately-not that you need it- but they are protecting you- ahh, I can see a huge bubble-like a half circle around you and it's like a bright light. She said they have left signs here and there for you- and when Broen was first born you could feel them? But not so much anymore? She says, 'No worry my darling, we are still here, you just not need to look so hard at times and when you don't get the answer you want right now doesn't mean it's not going to happen- but that we are trying our best up here to see what they can do-

The message I have for you is one I wanted to tell you in person-but I feel that you need it right now- Broen is a gift from God himself- Your body can no longer carry babies anymore- and I'm pretty sure your doctors were shocked and surprised with how well everything turned out with Broen- please know he was hand-picked from God and you had the best of the best guardian angels looking over you- Broen is not a replica of Peyton, but you already know this- he does have a lot of his tendencies- I see a golden glow all the way around him- and I've never seen this or heard of this-

Me: "I haven't been journaling since he was born but I will start doing it again. (I had journaled on my iPad since Peyton died, then when Tayden died, then through my spiritual awakening with Malia coming and your messages.) That gives me some confidence that maybe I can do this but just focus on each day at a time so it doesn't seem too impossible/overwhelming. Lately I have been talking to Tiny Grandma out loud asking her to help me get through this. I didn't anticipate how hard this would be so I think it overwhelmed me when all of these emotions came flooding out... yes, just breathe."

Her- "God hand-picked his child to help heal you- it's what you, yourself needed. Period. It's what you needed emotionally, spiritually, and physically- to help go on day by day and not feel that huge gouge in the pit of your stomach- that kept you keep going back and holding on to those feelings and wondering what if, or why didn't I? Or couldn't I have done this? Peyton wants me to tell you this- Broen was not put on this earth to replace me and my brother, we know this- we were part of the team who went to God to send Broen to you. You are an amazing mommy, please don't doubt your thoughts, actions, or teachings- you and daddy did everything you could for me, and I am forever thankful for God sending me to you both while I was still on this earth."

Me- "Oh my gosh Melissa... hand-picked by God... I wanted to say, what did I do to deserve him? I knew my pregnancy with him wasn't "normal"... I knew there had to be more going on because it was so "easy". I feel so indebted, so grateful to God for blessing me... so is there a part of Peyton's soul in Broen? Is Broen like an angel? I'm crying and showing Jeremiah these texts too."

Her- "This was one of the things God was so worried about when he chose Broen for you, the strong emotions that haven't quite healed yet- however, you have some pretty persistent angels up there looking over you all- they told him it would be hard yes, but nothing that they all know you will be able to overcome- just remember you have a strong support system on this earth and up above-if you ever need to text me-

There are parts of Peyton in Broen, yes, but it is not his entire soul- and even though I haven't seen or held him- I feel he is like a golden child from God- he's got a golden glow all the way around his body- I can tell you this, I have never met anyone on this earth who has so much spiritual glow like Broen has- so I've never asked this question before and I just point blank asked-is Broen an angel sent down from above- and I got yes and no- how they explained it is this: To you and I, Broen is an angel sent down from above because of all the healing he will provide- he will move mountains they tell me, but to God he is another one of his children. To God they are not angels until they graduate and have earned their wings.

Me- "I know Tiny G'ma said they've been around me... Is there a reason I haven't felt them lately? Good tears I promise! Needed tears! Is Trinity still seeing Spirit?"

Her- "Because you've been looking too hard she says- "Hunny, in order for us to help you through this, there will be times you will think you feel we aren't around. We are not to be your security blanket. (Man she's straight to the point). And that was a strict rule! We are here to help guide you darling." Sorry did that answer your question about them not being around?"

Yes, Trinity can still see Spirit, lately she hasn't tho- and I'm not sure if it's because Broen is around? She feels a huge level of comfort around him- It's like they have a connection, no words needed between them."

Me- "Yes, I see that connection already... when she holds him it feels magical to me. They adore each other already... Yes, I need that from Tiny G'ma! Blunt and to the point... maybe where I get it from. What is Tenley's gift?"

Her- "Lol your uncle said her gift is going to keep you all on your toes ;) lol, he loves her- said she's got a lil wild side".

How amazing is all of this??? I feel so lucky that I have some very spiritually gifted people that are helping me through this. If my loved ones on the other side feel like I can do this then I have to trust that I can! One day, one breath at a time.

01/13/2018

Tonight I was in the shower with Tenley and I had Jeremiah hand me Broen too. He has been really congested so I have been taking him in the showers with me to try and help thin the mucus he is experiencing. When I felt he had been in there for a sufficient amount of time I called to Jeremiah to come get him. Tenley also decided to get out with him. Jeremiah started his normal routine of getting his diaper on, putting lotion on him, putting his foot monitor on for bedtime. I was still finishing my shower and heard Broen just start wailing and Jeremiah scolding Tenley. I quickly got out to see what was going on and heard Broen continuing to cry what sounded like a painful cry. Jeremiah proceeded to tell me that Tenley was lying next to Broen while Jeremiah was getting him clothed and Tenley yanked on his arm. Broen kept crying and nothing Jeremiah or I did seemed to soothe him. I was worried that maybe she pulled his arm out of the socket or something and asked Jeremiah to take him up to the hospital. I was so scared. I was upset at Tenley for messing with him. I scolded her about Broen not being a baby doll and that you have to be careful with him. I know she is just a little girl but I am always terrified of Broen being hurt. I decided to get Trin and Ten ready and take them up to the hospital as well.

As we were driving there in the darkness I heard Trinity sniffling and getting emotional. She said, "Mom, I know you're not in the mood... But, Peyton is talking to me. He wants me to tell you that this was an accident mom. Tenley didn't mean any malice by what she did. She didn't mean to hurt him and that accidents happen. He's saying that you're so overprotective of Broen because of what happened to him. You need to let go of your fear of something bad happening to Broen. He says that you have been talking or listening to someone who talks about being positive. He says that you need to focus on being more positive. If you keep fearing the negative things with Broen, more negative things will happen. You need to focus on the positive. He says he loves you but that you have to start thinking differently. Broen is ok, he is in one of the rooms at the hospital with dad and he is fine.... I think that's all. I don't hear him anymore."

Then she looked at me, as by now tears are streaming down my cheeks and she says, "I'm sorry I started crying mom, I just got really emotional when he started talking to me. I wasn't expecting to hear from him and then all of a sudden I just heard his voice and he was telling me to tell you."

In that moment I was so proud of Trinity. Here is this little girl delivering such profound messages. Messages that I desperately needed to hear. Messages that I could only hear and accept from my dear son Peyton. Tiny grandma couldn't have delivered it... no other deceased family member could have delivered it because I would have been defensive, I would have felt the need to make an excuse for why I felt as I did. This message HAD to come from my dear boy Peyton. Spirit on the other side knew it... Peyton knew it... I knew it. He was right... I was overprotective of Broen because of everything I went through with Peyton. Of course, I am that way ...

BUT, for the sake of myself, my family and for Broen I have to learn to step back. I have to let those emotions from so long ago... the ones that I THOUGHT were gone ... go. I have to be positive and I have to have faith and trust that if God was blessing our family with Broen that he has a purpose and I have to step back and let him live that purpose. If I'm being really honest... I don't want to do that. That terrifies me. I just want to keep him in a protective bubble but I know I can't do that either. I will listen to my baby boy on the other side and put one foot in front of the other and be as positive as I can. I can't waste this wonderful miracle that God has given me.

03/10/2018

Broen will be 6 months old on the 21st of this month... Peyton died on the 21st of the month at the age of 6 months. For me, the 21st will be a sort of monumental day... like a hump that we will have gotten over. I've had all this fear about Broen being safe and find myself subconsciously comparing him to Peyton. But, after the 21st I can't do that anymore, because that's all I had. Six months... that's it. And yet, somehow it seemed like a lifetime to me. How can 6 short months have such a hold on my heart and my life now 6 years later? My love for him I just can't explain... I can't even describe my pull to him even to myself. As I write this tears just naturally pour out of my eyes. It's not a sadness that leaves me entirely depressed like it used to but it's a sadness that creeps out after so long and reminds me of what I had and will always wonder what could have been. But I know from all of my spiritual learning and guidance that was Peyton's path... He was here to teach us lessons. I know that he chose this lifetime, including the path of leaving at a young age. But gosh, even though I'm learning... Some days it's still really hard. And deep down all of the enlightenment and spiritual growing doesn't take the place of just having my boy. I often imagine him and I together, now he would be 6.5 years old. I imagine how our family would be different... the joy he would bring us.

Maybe with Broen and with knowing that there are parts of Peyton's soul in him. Maybe I have felt like in a small way I have gotten some of my time with Peyton back. But I know that Broen is Broen... he's not Peyton. He will continue to grow and be his own person. Please understand I feel so blessed and happy about this. But, maybe in a way it will also be validation that Peyton is really gone, if that makes sense. I know that sounds really confusing and I'm struggling to find the words to match how I'm feeling. The closer we get to this six month mark brings about some sadness from me, which sounds crazy. Maybe also fear as it was this six month mark when my life was turned upside down six years ago and I've never been the same since.

I know that there are going to be some amazing, happy, exciting and healing moments ahead with Broen. I know that. But Broen doesn't replace Peyton, nor should he. You know, I think of the message I got from Melissa where she talked about how there was a team of loved ones on the other side and they went to God to ask him to send me Broen. And how God responded with some reservation about the deep emotional wounds that haven't quite healed... To me, that message validated how deeply Peyton's death affected me.

I know there is so much healing that will happen moving forward. And I have many good days but today, tonight, is not one of those days. I just get to remind myself of the deep love I have for my family members, my kids, my babies... all of them. I feel love on such a deep level but I also feel pain on such a deep level. This is the journey of grief...and I don't think it ever ends. But really, do I want it to? With my grief I also get to remember the deep love I had, the beautiful feelings that I got to experience. This is life, the wonderful emotions of joy, excitement, inspiration, depression, sadness, hurt, and pain. But most important of them all, LOVE♥.

Transition

04/21/2018

Today is Tayden's birthday. If he were alive he would be three years old. That doesn't even seem possible...

Yesterday Broen had to have surgery to get tubes put in place. Today he has a high fever and is miserable. I had his ENT doctor paged since it is the weekend to inquire about if he needs to be on antibiotics as yesterday when he had the procedure his doctor said his ears were really infected and filled with pus. He wasn't put on an antibiotic but with how he is feeling today I feel like he needs one.

I had just gotten off of the phone with the doctor to let him know about Broen's continued fever. All of a sudden the phone rings right before I put it on the charger. I answer it and it is my mother's husband. He says that they were going to go to the grocery store and my mom went to open the truck door and somehow missed. He proceeds to say that she slid along the truck and ended up hitting her head on the curb. He said it knocked her out cold and there was blood coming out of her ear. He said he called 911 and the ambulance was taking her to the hospital. I told him I was on my way and hung up the phone. I looked at Jeremiah and told him I had to go.

On the way to the hospital I called some family to let them know what had happened. Once I get there I am allowed into the Emergency Room where they are working on her. I see that there is blood coming out of her ear and the back of her head. She was conscious. The doctor and nurses had just brought her back from having a CT scan done. There is a doctor next to her who starts to explain what he saw on the CT scan. He introduced himself and my gut instantly dropped. He was the doctor that operated on my dear son Peyton.

This neurologist goes on to explain that my mom has a fractured skull and subdural hematoma. My gut drops even further... I have heard of these injuries before too. Peyton had a fractured skull and subdural hematoma as well. This all seemed so ironic. I have done this before. I have been here before. After the doctor was done talking I asked to meet with him in the hall. I explained to him that my mom is an alcoholic and has always denied it. I explained to him that I know mom's head injury is of most concern but that I am sure there is much more going on with her body as well. They eventually move mom up to a room on the stroke floor where two nurses monitor two to four patients. Mom is conscious but starts to sleep a lot.

The next few days they are correcting mom's electrolytes and monitoring mom's head with additional CT scans. They have her hooked up to IV's. After a few days on that floor the doctor and nurses decide to move her down to the rehabilitation floor. They are wanting her to start to work with the physical therapists and the speech therapists. I notice that now she is a lot more confused than she was in the beginning. She seems to have lost twenty years of her memory.

After a few days in the rehabilitation unit mom started to have seizures on the right side of her face. The doctors immediately moved her up to the ICU unit. They started her on anti-seizure medications in an attempt to get them to stop. Now, she was in and out of consciousness. When she was awake she really couldn't speak or move. I felt like when I looked into her eyes she was still there but I felt that she couldn't show that she understood. I almost felt like she was trapped in a body that wasn't letting her respond.

This journaling has explained the last two weeks with mom in the hospital. During these two weeks I have been working full time like normal and caring for all three kids. Jeremiah is in track season so once he gets home from practice in the evenings I am running up to the hospital to be with my mom. I feel exhausted and emotionally numb. Deep within my soul I know that my mom isn't coming back from this injury. I have been trying to "keep it together" for two full weeks and my shoulders are feeling heavy. *How did this all happen? Is this the end as Malia had mentioned?*

05/05/2018

Today a team of doctors wanted to meet to come up with a game plan for my mom's care. They explained how at this point they have her on the highest dose of anti-seizure medication and still can't get the seizures to stop. She was now sleeping most of the time. When she was awake she didn't seem to be able to move or communicate. As the doctors met with us we were prepared that they would give us the "hospice" talk. They did mention this being an option but wanted to try one more thing. They suggested putting mom in a medically induced coma for a short term to try and let the brain heal. We agreed to this as long as it was only short term as mom never would have wanted to be on life support for any amount of time. And so for the next six days mom was on life support.

After they got the machine hooked up to her we were allowed to enter...I walked back into the room and *that* smell came flooding back. I remember the smell of the equipment from when Peyton was on the ventilator. I was thrown back into those days with my dear son....six years ago. And now, mom lies here with similar injuries and a deep gut feeling that she may have the same fate. So much loss...so much love with nowhere to go. That's what grief is...it's just the love that we have that has no physical place to go.

For the next six days mom lies still while the machine keeps her alive and she is put in a deep sedative state. This is our last effort to save her, if that is part of her path. She is still getting fluids, tube feedings and vitamins to nourish her body. As I see her this week I feel like her body feels lighter... like maybe she's not inside there anymore. I've felt this before as well...even though at the time I didn't know what it was. I don't feel her soul anymore...just like when they brought Peyton's body out of his craniotomy and deep down I knew he was gone, the vessel was empty. Her soul is not inside her body anymore.... That much I can feel.

This Sunday is Mother's Day. Will we lose her on Mother's Day?

05/11/2018

Tonight they took mom off of the vent. She's breathing on her own but not conscious. Our goal now is to just keep her comfortable until her body passes. *I can't believe I just wrote that...*

Here we are....sitting with her. Country music is playing in the background to make her feel comfortable. Her chest raises up and down. I've been here before...two times before. I should be comfortable with this....but, it's still different. This is my mom...her body is failing. Her soul between here and up there.

"Mom, it's ok to go. I just want you to be at peace. I want you to be happy. I want you free of the misery you have felt here. I don't want your soul to be trapped anymore. I don't want you to feel any more pain. You drank because you felt pain, you hurt. Please know, I forgive you for who you couldn't be. Please forgive me for any feelings of hurt I may have caused you. I love you and do not hold any anger towards you. I want to have peace with you, peace about our past. Maybe I grieve for what never was...I think I always had hope for what could be and I now grieve for what I never had, what we never had. Hurt people, hurt people....and I know you were hurting so terribly inside. I love you and thank you for teaching me what you needed to, what our souls agreed to so many years ago before we came here."

I sit watching her...knowing that my uncle is by her side in Spirit. We never die alone. My boys are waiting for her above. How blessed that she will get to see them soon. As I say that my eyes tear up...how for just a moment I wish I could watch that reunion and feel that embrace. I wish I could have a "heaven" pass just for a moment....get my fill of love and happiness and comfort. As said in many quotes, I wish heaven had visiting hours.

Please let her transition comfortably.

Tonight I contacted Malia and asked her if mom is afraid to leave. She responded that she's "reluctant". She said there's things unsaid by her...

Dear God, What does she want to say?

05/12/2018

Today I spent almost the entire day at the hospital. My brother came back last night and is staying with us. Today there's not much change with mom. She's still holding on... We're making her as comfortable as possible. She's getting morphine and Ativan to keep her calm. We just sat with her all day trying to comfort her that all is ok. She is loved and everything that has happened in our life is what it is. I don't bear any ill feelings anymore. But why does it take death for most of us to "get there"?

"Mom, I love you and I don't hold anything against you. You were struggling and I know you couldn't be who you wanted to be for us. I know you're holding on because there is so much you wish you would have said and done. I know mom... its ok. I just want you to finally feel peace and its ok for you to transition to the other side so you can finally feel this. I am so sorry for my judgment of your suffering and that I couldn't always understand it. Please forgive me. We also know there's so much left unspoken about your story. We know."

05/13/2018

Happy Mother's Day....

Mom seems the same today. Her vitals really haven't changed. She has been here in the hospital now for three weeks as of yesterday.

Towards the evening I go home to see the kids and help Jeremiah with the evening routine. My brother and his wife stay into the evening. They keep the country music playing, letting her know that she isn't alone and that it's all ok.

Late into the evening they show up back at the house. They look tired, drained and ready for bed. I feel exhausted from the last three weeks.... of spending time at the hospital, working, taking care of the kids, and keeping the household running while Jeremiah has been gone coaching track. It's been so busy, so exhausting, so draining...

My head hits the pillow and I am out.

I wake to the phone ringing. It doesn't seem that I have been asleep that long. I look at the clock. It's 9:50 p.m. and I've only been asleep for about 25 minutes. I hear an upset voice on the other line. It's my mom's husband.... "Courtney, come she's going. Come now" his voice crying. I run downstairs and wake my brother and sister-in-law and tell them mom is failing. They jump out of bed and we are out of the house in minutes. Now we're off to the hospital.... for the last time. But this time there is urgency...

That's the thing.... We were all there for two days straight, someone always by her side. But now, we were gone and now she is leaving. This was the way my mom preferred it. She was very private in the living so why would we expect her to be any different in dying? She was waiting until my brother left to leave and let her physical body go.

I called my sisters to let them know what's happening and that it's time to be at the hospital.

We get to the hospital and head straight to her room. I prepare myself for what I will see when I walk in. Unfortunately for me death has been a long lost friend, a familiar voice in my head. I walk into the silent room and there her body lays. Her body, still and silent. Her body, her shell is all that remains. She is gone...

I've known about this moment for quite some time. Malia delivered the message to me some time back that my mom would be leaving this earth soon. She even told me it would be something with her head and her liver. She was right about all of that. I have been preparing for her death for quite some time but yet, the reality of it really happening seems overwhelming. This small part of me feels relief for her soul, that maybe now she is free. She doesn't have to hurt anymore... She doesn't have to worry about judgement anymore.... She doesn't have to live with the guilt eating her. She can finally let all of the battles inside of her go.

But as her daughter, it hits me that my mom is gone.... forever from this lifetime. A pain in my stomach aches as I realize that so much of my grief rests on the fact that any opportunity for a real relationship with her is gone. Deep down I always had hope that maybe I could still have "a mom". Like maybe someday she would admit her addiction, she would get help, she would get better and I would have the relationship with her that I so desperately wanted. For me, the fact that my mom has just died means that the hope I've always held on to is now also dead. For me, it's over. All possibilities are over....in this lifetime.

I sit on her bed beside her and just hold her hand. I sat there and stroked her hand trying to indent into my memory the feel of her skin, the feeling of her in my head. This is the last time I can touch her. I remember this feeling so vividly as I experienced it also with the boys. This feeling of not wanting to leave because once I leave I can never have this back. Once I leave, it solidifies that this person is gone and that my life will now drastically change. So I sit and try to soak it in.... For some people this part is the hardest part; to sit with a dead body. For me, this part is the part that is preparing me for the weeks and months to follow. I kiss her forehead, I stroke her temple, I lay my head on her chest and I squeeze her hands.

After some amount of time and the realization that we've said all of the goodbyes we can we get ready to leave. I get up to walk to the door and then stop. That haunting feeling that I've also felt before stirs in my soul. I turn around and give her one more "goodbye" touch and kiss and then I breathe deep and walk out of the room. No goodbye is ever the right goodbye.

It's 11:45 p.m. and today was Mother's Day. Weeks ago when this journey started I had a gut feeling she would leave this earth on Mother's Day. How ironic that she struggled being the mom I needed yet passed on Mother's Day. I can't help but believe that there is a deeper meaning in this... She was telling us that although she couldn't be what we needed that her desire had always been to be our mom. Her addiction won that constant battle.

I received a text from Melissa, my gifted family member, a little after midnight, who I have not yet contacted to let them know that my mom has died. She goes on to say that, "They showed me that your mom transitioned to Heaven. Your uncle walked beside her and your grandparents led her through Heaven's gates. Your boys were waiting, jumping up and down, excited to get to greet her. As she walked through the gates they ran to her with their arms outstretched and she bent down and embraced them both. She looks so beautiful...tall, slender, beautiful blonde hair, her cheeks roses pink, she's glowing. She is free of any burden or pain or suffering. She is truly free."

I read this text and just bawl as I imagine this scene. How I wish that I was there to witness this reunion...that I could see both of my boys and my mom healthy and happy and thriving. I just laid in bed and cried and cried.... and cried. And for a split second I feel envious that she gets to hold my boys as that's all that I've ever wanted to do. I just want it to be me. And then I feel comfort for her that she is truly free of all of this pain that she has carried for so long. For twenty years I have just wanted her to feel happy and finally she gets to feel this. But oh, for such a moment I wish I could be up there to see this gathering....and be with some of the people I love the most.

08/06/2018

Broen was baptized today. This is such an interesting place to be. The church that we attend is amazing, they are. But they don't quite match up to the beliefs that Jeremiah and I now have. I go and basically pick apart the pieces that fit me. I take what works and I leave what doesn't. Maybe there isn't anywhere that would be "perfect" for us. I like going to feel inspired and uplifted even though it might not totally align with us. And deep down, I don't think they would accept us if they knew what we really believed.... We believe what they teach but we also believe in so much more.

COURTNEY POTTEBAUM

09/21/2018

Broen baby is 1 year old today!!!!!!How is that possible???

In the fall of 2016, Melissa, my spiritually gifted family member channeled a conversation with a deceased family member on my mother's side. He told me how I would be having a baby in the future and that the healing this baby will provide will "move mountains". While at the time I believed, it was hard to grasp that this would all indeed happen. Three months later I was pregnant. And now two years later with my baby being one year old I finally comprehend what my grandfather was telling me.

The amount of healing that Broen's presence has brought our family has been amazing. We have all been provided with such a pure form of healing through love and appreciation of our baby boy. Broen doesn't replace Peyton or Tayden but he completes the cycle of their losses. He completes the emptiness that took place when the boys' losses hit us. The part of my soul that left with Peyton was given back to me through the love I have experienced with Broen.

Broen's coming has provided so much hope and belief to our family and indirectly to everyone else we know or who are impacted by us. Our story, our struggles, our losses and blessings give hope that there's so much more going on that most of us aren't tuned in to. The other side is real and they support us all of the time. Our struggles are not meant to debilitate us but instead advance us into a new state of being. The contrast we experience is to enlighten us and to elevate our soul growth. That is so hard to understand in our earthly physical bodies. It is so hard to understand why we are going through what we are or why others are going through what they are.

Through my gifted friend and gifted family member I have been able to learn and connect with Spirit. It it important to note that we all have different religious and spiritual beliefs yet that has not interfered with our ability to deliver and hear Spirit. I have been given the proof I needed to have faith that God and Spirit exist. I have been blessed for an explanation about a lot of the pain in my life. There are so many more gifted people in this world than we know.

But because of taboo or judgement they remain silent about their gifts for fear of judgement. If we could open our eyes and minds and embrace all of our gifts we could get the biggest healing ever imaginable. Unfortunately, modern religion hasn't done the best job at portraying the messages of Spirit.

Churches, parishes, priests, pastors and even the bible are all from man. They are man's best attempt at capturing the message of God and Spirit. But as "man" we fall short with our interpretations because the other side/heaven/whatever you want to call it is so much more than we could ever verbally describe. Unfortunately, in an attempt to reach people modern religion has also judged people in a way that God/Source never would. It has debilitated some people to the point that they think they are terrible people or feel like God won't accept them. When hardships have happened it's trained us to believe that God is punishing us or that we somehow did something wrong to deserve this. NONE of that is the case.

God/Source/Universal energy/whatever you want to call it loves us and supports us on this journey. Our souls, along with God and our guides for this lifetime chose to come to this life to experience different things. We chose our life circumstances and the big things for universal soul growth opportunities. The smaller details we iron out along the way while living. We did not choose these things to punish or cripple ourselves. We chose these things to help us give ourselves experiences and different perspectives to grow our soul to be more like God. From what I gather we came here to learn a few "big" lessons in this lifetime with smaller ones scattered about. For example, I believe that one of my big lessons in this lifetime is to learn forgiveness. I've had a lot of pain and hurt in this lifetime and plenty of people I could be angry at for causing this. Those negative emotions won't help serve me in this lifetime. While understandable for me to feel that way towards those people, those negative emotions will not help my soul to grow or evolve, which is the reason we came to experience life. Whatever lessons I do not or cannot learn in this lifetime I will then live in another lifetime. Many call this reincarnation. Call it what you want but most of us have lived many lifetimes, "wearing" many different identities all with the opportunities for expansion and learning lessons with the intent to grow our soul to be more like God.

For me, I know forgiveness is one of the big lessons I have to learn here in this lifetime. I've always tended to be a "grudge-holder". If someone wronged me once, I never allowed myself to get close to them again. I have to learn to forgive. Peyton and Tayden made such sacrifices for me to come to earth and leave early with the intent of helping me to dig deep and be forced to do some serious soul work. I will not have their sacrifices be in vain. I will not waste the opportunity they gave me. It is true that out of our deepest pain can be our greatest growth opportunities. In some way I will find a way to genuinely forgive the person that murdered Peyton. I cannot even fathom that now, but on a soul level, I have to. And not just a task to be completed but a true deep-down forgiveness of my soul. I came here to evolve.

It would be great if we could learn out of opportunities that bring us happiness and pleasure. And maybe in some ways we can. But I do believe it is out of the pain, the hurting, and the suffering, the trauma that we are then broken open and our layers stripped off. It is by "standing naked" in front of the crowd that we are given an opportunity. We can choose to do the work and evolve, which often is hard and involves working through the pain. Or, we can choose to shut down, be angry and give excuses for all of the reasons we are justified in feeling how we do and not moving up or beyond. Believe me, I get both paths... I truly do because I did both. But, at some point we have to realize that our intent was never to stay paralyzed from this life. The hurt was not meant to devastate us forever. It was meant to get us moving, to start asking questions about why we are here, what we are supposed to be doing with our lives. It was an opportunity to see what really is and realize why we are here. It is an opportunity to take our greatest, most debilitating pain and connect with others and evolve. It is through heartache that most of us are then able to open up. When things are going well we often aren't good at self-reflecting so maybe it takes the traumas to help us just stop and start asking the questions that our soul needs us too. At the same time there may be truly debilitating things and traumas that weren't part of a "plan" that happen to us but the only positive power we have is to start healing ourselves.

A change in perspective really is the most important thing we can do. It changes everything. Somehow that change in perspective makes it understandable or at least "doable". It helps us to recognize that there really is a reason, even if we can't understand what that might be. And if there isn't really a reason or a lesson, it's still vital that we work to release the trauma and start doing the work to HEAL.

Happy 1ˢᵗ Birthday To Our Special Boy!

This is what I posted on my social media page:

"This sweet boy is 1!! We actually celebrated his birthday yesterday ONLY a month late 😊 This milestone is a huge blessing for our family. Many of you know about the tragic losses of our sons Peyton and Tayden. After losing Tayden and struggling to take one more of life's "hits" a very brave woman that I did not know took a risk and approached me. I wore the mask on the outside that I was doing "ok" but I was drowning inside. This woman explained that she was spiritually gifted or what's better known to most of us as being a "medium". She connected me to my relatives on the other side including my sons. She gave me the answers that nobody else could. She gave me the healing that nobody else could. She told me that Jeremiah and I would have one more baby (which we did not think could medically happen after some complications after having Tayden). She told me this baby would be a boy and was a miracle from God. She told me that my loved ones on the other side said that we needed this baby boy and that the healing that he would provide would "move mountains". Now with Broen being 1 year old I can assure you "they "are right. Our family has been given the biggest blessing and we are so thankful to God for it all!"

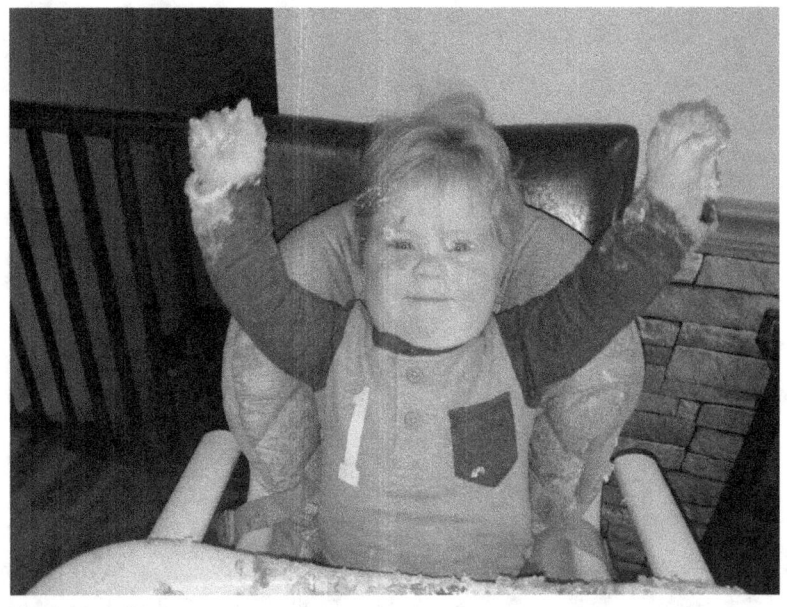

10/31/2018

Happy Halloween! We took our "Super Kids" around trick or treating with our costumes on. Jeremiah was such a good sport wearing spandex even though I think he was silently humiliated!!! Anything for the kid's right?!

12/25/2018

Merry Christmas from our family to yours!

02/09/2019

It's 4:00 a.m. ...... And I finally got to see him in my dreams!!! I was *JUST* with him....

In my dream Jeremiah and I are looking at buying/moving into a new home. We are walking through this home, an older home deciding if we want to buy it. It has a lot of natural rustic woodwork throughout the home. I go down into the basement to look around and there is a door in the basement that leads to someplace else, almost like a secret passage. I go through the passage which takes me to a huge underground area that is set up with benches, almost like pews in a church. There are people who are there to play many musical instruments, coming and going. It is a place where all of these people come together to play together and somehow I am the orchestrator of it all, by it being underneath my house. This boy comes up to me. Immediately I recognize who it is. It is our sweet son Tayden!! He presents himself as a young teenage boy, maybe 12 or 13 years of age. He has very blonde, short, wavy hair. He has red cherry lips. His skin color is porcelain like Trin and Broen's. He is small but muscular for his stature. I can see the slight Down syndrome presentation in his eyes and his face but it is ever so slight. He tells me, "My teacher said I should tell you that you were my mommy before. Mommy, your purpose isn't to write a book, it's to make a movie." He felt good, happy, peaceful and I didn't want to leave that feeling with him. And then the next scene I see is me telling Jeremiah above inside of the house how I spoke to Tayden and what he looked like. I watched Jeremiah's reaction play out. And then I woke up...

I looked at my phone which said it was 4:00 a.m. and I sat there replaying what just happened. I got to see my precious boy. He was beautiful... absolutely stunning! He was so handsome and so calm and peaceful. I told him thank you in my mind for letting me experience him. Five days earlier I was just talking to my sister telling her I would give anything to see him. I guess he felt I was ready.... And his message....? My purpose is to make a movie? *Dear son, you're really going to have to line up a lot of things and the right people to make this happen!*

I went back to sleep knowing I would be getting up for good in a little over an hour. When I woke up for good I couldn't wait to tell Jeremiah. As I told him I could hardly hold back my excitement and I couldn't wait to explain what Tayden looked like. I could feel a sense of wishing that was him, that he could see his boy. My gut dropped as I too wished he could have this experience. This reaction from him is exactly what my dream showed me in his reaction, which felt like "de ja vu". After I told him what Tayden said about my purpose Jeremiah responded, "Wow, that's deep."

Later that morning I texted my sisters to tell them what had happened. Their responses were that of pointing out that many movies first begin as books which made me feel like publishing my book is first and the movie will follow. My sister stated that she could imagine it on the big screen, being very dramatic, if done correctly. My hope is that it would be healing....

Holy crap, I got to see my boy! He was beautiful... Thank you, thank you, thank you. This was a true visitation .... So different from a normal dream. All of my senses could feel him. And he felt AMAZING and he was absolutely STUNNING. My heart feels so full and so thankful for the opportunity to see and talk with him. THANK YOU TAYDEN! I love you, oh so much! Tears of joy stream down my face.

06/23/2019

We had family pictures today! We haven't had them taken since before Broen was born. Our good friend took them for us and she was amazing. It was great conversation, great love and just a genuine love for our family. She and her husband are 'real' people and we are blessed to know them.

Photo Credit Carolyn Goodwin Photography

Photo Credit Carolyn Goodwin Photography

These boys....They're in every part of what we do.... They just are.

12/25/2020

Merry Christmas! How lucky are we to have three beautiful physical living children to share this day with! They are the reason my wallet is empty and presents are galore around our tree. I know I have once again bought too much for them but the joy it brings me when they open each present is the best feeling in the world!

01/06/2020

So here I am.... January of 2020! I don't get to meet with you so much anymore. Three kids, a husband, a household to run and a full-time job leave me with early mornings and exhausted evenings. I am just too tired at night to meet you with my pillow, my ear plugs in and emotions ready to be spilled out onto this tablet. What a blessing to have so much to be tired about! Broen turned 2 in September and he is ALL BOY. He is in, under and on top of everything. Literally, ON TOP of everything. He is so wild and rambunctious and full speed ahead. Trinity is maturing... she's 11 now. She does well in school and loves sports. She is very protective of her siblings and is an excellent big sister. Tenley is 6 now and she is such a dual sided girl. She is the sweetest and loving girl but she is also a mixed bag of feistiness and fire. She knows what she wants and she is determined to get it! Tenley is my true empath as well. She has a deep love for everything and a yearning to help all.

We still have Cojo, one of our miniature wiener dogs and our lab Lady. Cojo is fifteen and a half and Lady is nine and a half. We put Bailey down in July. She had been suffering for the last year. She had lost a bunch of weight, she was shaking all of the time, she was losing control of her bladder all of the time. Her personality had changed and she seemed in pain. Her bloodwork came back normal but I knew she had something major going on. I was debating getting a sonogram of her abdomen to try and find out what was wrong, but I was hesitating because I didn't know if she would make it out of the anesthesia. One night Spirit spoke to me in my sleep and told me to "get the scan, you'll feel better." I woke up that morning and called the vet's office and scheduled the scan. After the scan Bailey completely stopped eating and drinking and I put her down two days later after trying to feed her through a syringe. Two weeks later the vet called with Bailey's results from the radiologist who confirmed that she had nodules on her liver and that it was likely liver cancer, which would not show up in blood work. In that moment I thanked Spirit for intervening and helping me make the decision that I needed for what was best for her and for me. I was able to have peace that I did the most humane thing for her by putting her down. She was really sick and really suffering. Even though just a dog to most, to me, she was one of my first babies. Bailey and Cojo took me through some of the most traumatic nights after both of my boys. I know Bailey's purpose was to be there for me when I was too broken to talk to anyone else. She could give me the love that I needed that I didn't know how to ask for ... she sensed it. I didn't have to explain myself or rationalize why I felt the way I did. She just nestled into me and told me through her vibes that she was there and she loved me and in those moments that was enough.

"Bailey, you served your purpose well and you took care of me in ways that nobody else could. Thank you for being my faithful companion. I hope you felt loved and doted on and feel grateful that you got to be part of our family. We love you baby girl and thanks for making me a mom first!"

Here was hours before we put Bailey down. A picture with me and one last sleep next to her brother.

PEYTON'S PASSING

"Fly high baby girl. So much love and appreciation to you for walking and wagging part of this journey with me. To me, you were always more than a dog. I will miss your companionship tremendously."

Our lives are so full now and busy as we're running kids from activity to activity and managing work and a household. So much has happened to our family in these last few years. I meet with a few spiritual friends every month to talk about "Everything to do with Spirit". At this point every member of our family has had a spiritual experience and this group of friends provides support and guidance for all of us. Once you have your own experiences you believe in a way that nobody else can understand.

So many people in our society are awakening to Spirit at this time. But there is still this taboo or judgement that someone is crazy or delusional if they are open to experiencing Spirit. I am so happy that we came to a place of openness and acceptance and that we have allowed these experiences for they have transformed our lives. I can't imagine it ever being any different. Spirit has given us hope, passion, compassion, empathy and peace. We have been given answers and guidance and I can't imagine doing life without them. I have people constantly seeking me out to talk to me about my experiences since losing the boys as many people have heard of our story. I know that Spirit is using me as a vessel to teach others and help others to connect to Spirit like we have. For those that don't believe like we do or think its nuts, that's ok, we're never offended. It's not our responsibility to make anyone else believe. I wouldn't want that kind of responsibility! We just realize for those that might take judgement against us...this just isn't their journey and that's ok. We wish them well and send them on their way. We have a few family members who don't believe in this and we just know this isn't their thing and we try to steer clear of the topic around them. But, if it happens to come up we also don't feel like we need to panic or make them comfortable in our world of belief. That's their job.... to figure out how to accept us just the way we are. We're all a lesson for each other!

In a few weeks it will be approximately 8 years since Peyton's death and the complete devastation of everything Jeremiah and I were.

Although our struggle and trauma didn't end there and Tayden had to step in and help to break us completely open. By being broken down we could finally open up enough to be who we were really meant to be. Jeremiah and I are EXTREMELY spiritual, but we couldn't get there without being completely broken open and raw. We had to dig ourselves out and allow our natural spiritual connection and abilities to take over. We had to yearn for meaning and purpose so much greater than needing to be accepted. For us, we finally became WHO WE ARE and WHO WE WERE ALWAYS MEANT TO BE! But, we wouldn't have gotten there without going through what we did with the boys. Looking back, I can now understand why things took the turns they did. All along the way our spiritual guides were loving us and calling us forward to evolve and connect and find our purpose. We took the leap and it was the best decision we have ever made. Not that I ever wanted *ANY* of this tragedy but by finding my spiritual connection I am able to live a more connected life for the rest of my life! It happened early enough that I get to live more of life in this type of appreciation for what I now understand.

Life is rushing by and I am getting pieces of my life puzzle answered. Here's to more understanding, more growing, more learning and MORE connection with my spiritual team on the other side. Most importantly, here's to MORE connection to my own source energy!

01/21/2020

8 YEARS.... How has it been 8 long years since our first boy was killed and our lives were forever changed? The holidays this year seemed difficult for Jeremiah. He struggled, he was removed but he tried so very hard to be ... normal. We always get a little distant during the holidays because we know that once they're over it is the dreaded anniversary of Peyton's passing. It's so interesting because so much healing has taken place these last four years but even with all of that healing and growing and connecting there is still this place inside of

us that is still hollow. It hides and stays mostly out of the way these days. But every once and awhile it seeps up to the surface to let us know that it's still there, that we are still human and that there are some pains that don't completely leave....

This was supposed to be the year, the anniversary that I could genuinely, calmly state and feel that I had forgiven Anna. I thought about it off and on in 2019; that was my goal. I wanted to be at a place of true forgiveness to her. But, today creeped upon me and I stood here looking at myself in the mirror saying, "You're just not there Courtney". I want to be so bad. But, I'm just not and I'm frustrated that I'm not. I see these people on TV who go through like tragedies and they are in court forgiving the person who killed their loved one weeks or months before. Here I am 8 years later and I'm just not there.... I can't fake much; I never have been able to do that. What you see is what you get. I've never been able to hide how I feel about anything which makes me too much for some people. And today on an important day, I still can't hide the fact that I'm just not there. I'm close... I have been climbing this wall for what seems like forever.

What I do know is that my loved ones and guides in Spirit wrapped my broken self up in their arms and protected me 8 years ago. They saved me and forced me to find some will to live. They had big plans for me... Maybe deep down I know all they have done for me and how they have protected me. Maybe I want to make them proud and forgive her so that they feel like all of their efforts weren't wasted. But, I know that they love me... and no matter what they have always and will always love me. I wish I could see beyond the veil and hear the conversations they've had these last 8 years. I know it's taken a team of them to support me and I'm sure they've banged their head a few hundred times against the wall as I stubbornly miss their signs or guidance. When I think about my team I am overcome with such extreme gratitude.

I also think about Jeremiah. He has gone through all of this alongside me, experiencing as much pain as I have and yet there is something more solid about him. I feel like he is constantly in a state of wanting to make me happy. Not just the kind of happy superficially but he's always very concerned with what makes my soul happy. I wonder if before we chose this life, did he agree to go through this with me and agree to be my life-float?

To the situation that transformed my life and broke me down. I don't know if I should forever be enraged at you or embrace you for the awakening that was brought into my life. What I do know is that I wouldn't be in a state of spiritual awakening if I hadn't had lost my son to murder. I wouldn't have had a reason to understand. It's easy to say you believe when life is going great. But, when your life is stripped piece by piece away from you, you look for answers wherever you can get them. Maybe that's the point.....

To 8 years ago...

PEYTON'S PASSING

When I got home today from work the girls had this display all set up on the kitchen table to surprise me. How thoughtful is that? The fact that they knew it was 'Peyton's day' but that they wanted so bad to make me feel loved. Again, I don't have to say a word but they can FEEL everything. They can feel when the grief creeps in. Their aunt sent the flowers but the girls made the signs and set it all up. What great sisters.... What great girls. And just maybe the boys were whispering in their ears, saying, "Tell mom, she may not see us, but we're always by her side."

01/25/2020

Today I took a class all day to get certified in Reiki Level One. It was a great experience and something that I have been pulled to for quite some time. I have had my own Reiki sessions done for the last four years. They have been so beneficial for me that I have just felt so compelled to get certified. I can't wait to take the Level II class and then eventually the Master class.

I got to meet with Malia and some other spiritually gifted friends. Some of the information that I learned from different sources is summed up here:

I was told that my loved ones are saying that I need to just take a leap of faith and finish my book. They said it is time to start this finish, which I have been putting off for some reason. Maybe I have been waiting for some perfect ending but is there ever a perfect ending? While alive we are always evolving, whether we realize it for not. They also told me that they saw Anna apologizing to me at some point for what she did to Peyton, in an attempt to clear her conscience. They also validated that the movie that Tayden told me about last year in a dream visitation is a real thing. They said that it will bring healing to many people and this is why I need to finish my book. And this alone.... Is the very reason I have ever wanted to share this. Of course, all of this is information that very gifted people are picking up now and maybe things or paths will change, people will make different decisions that will change outcomes but either way for me, it's a path of clarity.

The way I understand when mediums see projections of future events or things happening is that based on that moment in time this is what they see happening. If certain decisions are changed or made differently after the reading that could cause the path to change, and maybe the outcome no longer matches the original message. We all have free will and we get to choose so much.

It was a great night, with lots of messages and learning of Spirit with other incredibly open-minded friends. We give each other love and support and positive vibes to do this thing called life! Here's to the learning... may we never stop!

02/08/2020

Spirituality does not come from religion. It comes from our soul. We must stop confusing religion and spirituality. Religion is a set of rules, regulations, and rituals created by humans, which were supposed to help people spiritually. Due to human imperfection religion has become corrupt, political, divisive and a tool for power struggle. Spirituality is not theology or ideology. It is simply a way of life, pure and original as given by the Most High. Spirituality is a network linking us to the Most High, the universe, and each other.
Haile Selassie

https://www.facebook.com/FractalEnlightenment

This is it! For me, this hits home. To all of our leaders in religion, whoever you are and wherever you are. You help your people the most if you can teach them that they don't need you to have a relationship with their own source! That connection already resides inside of them. Instead, use your teachings to inspire them, to lift them up, to encourage them to their own power. That vibration feels better and it will make you more genuine and uplifting to all who work with you. If you're trying to grow believers, grow them to have their own power to connect to their own source. That's influence.... That's God Force!

COURTNEY POTTEBAUM

02/17/2020

This is it:

> I don't want to fix you, and I can't heal you, but maybe I can help you see just how beautiful your broken is. Each cracked piece fits into the masterpiece of who you are right now And, right now, I see a beautiful soul.
> LK Pilgrim

https://www.facebook.com/FractalEnlightenment

We're just people... trying to figure out this life thing. We've all experienced pain and we ALL have a story. We come from a thousand different backgrounds with a thousand different belief systems. But, at the end of the day we just want to feel relief, joy and purpose. We just want to feel LOVE. When we've lost someone and the grief is so unbearable we have to find what brings us peace. It doesn't matter your religion. It doesn't matter your belief system. It only matters what you do to healthfully find peace. If going to a church and listening to a pastor brings you a sense of closeness to your loved one, then great. If hanging out in the solitude of nature brings you the comfort and connection to peace, then great. If talking to a medium, like I did, brings you peace, then great. Call "God" or "IT" whatever you want but whatever it is, I believe we're all talking about the same thing. You don't need someone else to connect you to that wellbeing, to your loved ones. We are all capable of doing that ourselves on one level or another. Every single person can sense energy in some shape or form... that's what everything is. Some of us are Empaths or Clairsentients and we FEEL energy. So, if I'm in the most positive place I can be, I can tune in to feeling my loved ones or the energy around me. Maybe your strongest area is that you're Clairaudient so you hear energy, so maybe when you're at your most positive you can hear the internal or external messages from your loved ones or guides. Claircognizance is the ability to just "know" things. Its things that nobody tells you but somehow you just know information about people, places and events that you've never been told by other living people. Clairvoyance is the ability to see Spirit either with your physical eyes or pictures, visions and symbols in your mind's eye. The ones I mentioned are the most common "Clair" gifts. There are other spiritual gifts that I'm not as versed with. We all have something and could access it if we believed it and allowed it. Negative emotions like fear and grief can prevent our ability to tap into our unique gifts or to sensing energy around us. Staying miserable really has no benefit. Abraham Hicks and the Law of Attraction teach us all about using our emotions as our guidance system. When our loved ones die, we may not be able to sense them in the same way we're used to physically touching them or talking to them. But, if we're gentle and positive enough, we can learn to sense them in the way that is easiest for each of us to tap in to. All of this takes raising our vibration... which means we have to pull ourselves out of grief the best we can.

If thinking about energetic gifts makes you uncomfortable you can always focus on the "gifts" that you provide this physical earth such as your ability to be of service. Gifts such as compassion, empathy, genuineness, truthfulness, helpfulness and positivity all shape this world in amazing ways and helps to lift the vibration of all.

There is no one way.... There is no right way. There is only YOUR way... and that is all you need.

04/15/2020

We've been home from the quarantine for the last four weeks due to the COVID-19. Many people are panicking and are really scared. But, for some reason, I'm not. Being home for me the last four weeks has been wonderful. I am more of an introvert or outgoing introvert and I LOVE being home... it's my favorite place to be. I don't mind social distancing because I often have empathic overload when I'm out in public. I send so many condolences and have so much love to the people who have lost and will be losing loved ones. Although out of terrible circumstances I have appreciated the break with my kids, the stillness and quietness of being home and not rushing all over the place with work and kids' activities. I feel safe being home. I always joke with co-workers that I'm not the "fun" one but I sure will be the one to listen to you, hug you and try and help you feel heard and loved.

Last night before bed I spoke out loud to my mom and told her that I was ready for communication with her in Spirit. I can tell she's been visiting us often. I feel her energy and we've had an awful lot of cardinal visits in which Trinity yells out, "It's Grandma"!

Tonight at dinner Jeremiah looked really "spacey" as if he was in deep thought. I thought maybe at first that he didn't like what I had made as he was eating really slowly. After dinner when I was rinsing off the dishes he said, "I have to show you something" and went and grabbed his phone. My stomach dropped and I asked "Is it bad?" and he said, "No". He pulled up a screen on his phone where this was typed, "10-16 Epic". He then looked at me and said, "Last night in a dream, I heard your mom say, "Tell Courtney, 10-16 Epic". He said, "I heard her clear as day. I woke up and typed this into my phone so I wouldn't forget. I tried to research this today to understand what this might mean but I have no idea." I stood there, with my mouth hanging open and tears in my eyes. I asked my mom to speak to us and she did. I guess time will tell and in the meantime I will be on the lookout for a reference to 10-16 Epic! No matter what I'm so happy she reached one of us and that Jeremiah got to experience what he did. Although some people may not want to hear messages from their deceased loved ones, I am NOT one of them. I want to hear from them ALL, ALL of the time!

04/23/2020

We are now finishing our 6th week of being at home during the quarantine of COVID-19. I feel immense empathy for the people and families directly affected by this virus. This time for me has caused me to go inward and explore my spirituality even more.

All of this learning has taught me that stillness and peace are really the best place to be. In order for my world to be wonderful and my personal life thriving I have to come into my own space where I am as positive as possible and my personal vibration is high no matter what is happening around me. I can't cling to perfect conditions in order for me to feel happy. I have to feel happy despite the condition. Abraham Hicks talks in depth about this in their work on The Law of Attraction. I have always understood their teachings but struggled with practicing them as I am such a science minded/practical/logical thinker. But I am learning that my inner peace has to be MY peace, not the peace that some other condition is giving me. Therefore, I cannot help but to think of all of the time I have wasted on hating Anna for killing Peyton. Although ALL of that hurt is still justified in my 'logical' brain, it doesn't serve me to believe that. By taking her out of the equation, focusing on myself and finding my OWN unique connection to SPIRIT I have finally discovered that I can feel peace inside. And that peace is something that feels free and light and joyful. I cannot have both. I cannot continue to hate her and simultaneously want the feeling of freedom. To be quite honest, I almost have an "un-feeling" about her, meaning I don't have any feelings towards her. I am indifferent towards her because my peace cannot hang on her actions or behaviors. If you would have tried to tell me that 8 years ago I would have come unglued. But now, after time and after all of this spiritual exploration I am finding that my inner peace and stillness can only exist with that connection. But, I would have never found this place had Peyton's murder and death never happened. So for that, I have to thank my first son Peyton. He left so I could learn all about pain, happiness and what forgiveness really is. He left so I could learn how to find my own true, real inner peace and my OWN connection to GOD/source energy/non-physical energy/ and to my own spiritual gifts. There were certain lessons I could only learn through his traumatic passing. I've always said his life and death had a purpose.

So I guess, to any of you suffering and in deep despair… There is hope after and through pain. But, it also takes work and it takes courage for you to connect to who you really are and to what you really believe. Every single person reading this has your own connection to God/Source Energy/ Non-Physical beings. We ALL have spirit guides to help guide us through life and they're always speaking to us. We ALL have angels who are there to protect us until we leave our physical bodies. There is so much non-physical energy focused on every single one of us right now. We are loved dearly and our non-physical source energy guides, angels and loved ones want nothing more than for us to grow, learn and find happiness. But, we have to be willing and go inwards and connect with our own being and discover what really makes us happy. Every single one of us has a spiritual gift and each of us has to discover what it is and how to use it for the highest good of ourselves and others. My dream is that every hurting person can connect to who they are, your own 'source energy' and the soul that stirs inside your body. I hope you can connect to the non-physical source that surrounds you and is trying to help you. My hope for all of us is that we can learn how to be the observer of our own mind and emotions and learn to keep our vibration high, all the while letting others worry about their own vibrations. Go inward and ask your angels and guides for guidance and then STOP and LISTEN to what they're trying to tell you! We need to start working more on ourselves and spend less time judging others. Peace within and around is my hope for all of us! Love to you ALL.

05/21/2020

I have had trouble stopping writing as I'm always wanting to update you on my most recent spiritual message. My gifted cousin's wife Melissa contacted me tonight about a random run in with a close friend of mine. I told Melissa how I am writing a book and publishing some of my journal entries in an attempt to gain the TRUE picture of grief. I told her that my hope is to help someone else that is struggling like I was. I told her I always felt alone with not much hope and if reading my story helps someone else to feel normal in their grief then 'all is right' with the world! Here is a gist of our conversation:

Me: "Spirit has 'been on me' to finish this journaling for the last 6 months as I have dragged my feet. There were 6 weeks left blank when I got Tayden's diagnosis and I didn't want to have to go back and relive that time. They told me I had to and that this would be one of the last chapters of my healing to complete so I've used this quarantine time to do that. Another gifted friend of mine recently saw/talked to Peyton who said both he and Tayden will be helping with this endeavor. I just want to make them both proud and hopefully give somebody else hope when they're struggling. I am trying to give somebody else something that I didn't have... which was hope."

Her: "They are so proud of you Courtney. They just said, 'Our mom rocks, doesn't she?' As in you are truly amazing and as they say, a rock."

Me: "Tayden told me over a year ago in a visitation dream that my purpose was to make a movie. I know this sounds crazy so I haven't said this to many people. I believe I will publish my book and then a movie will come from that. I just want to make sure I'm delivering it the right way with guidance from all of our loved ones on the other side."

Her: "Do you remember the night we sat in your car after the Theresa Caputo show? And I told you that you would be doing something that would advocate for your boys? And the main push will be from Peyton? At the time you were kind of stuck and I told you your purpose was to go out and share your guy's story? And no, that doesn't sound crazy at all! The boys say, 'This is what you were meant to do- to share what you've gone through. Even though we are not here on earth physically- you are advocating that this does happen. Terrible things happen that we may never ever get answers to, nor be able to blame someone for, or legally have them be held responsible- but that as much as we are terribly missed, and our lives here on earth were super short- our family that are still here physically need to still LIVE- they need to live for our grandparents, our sisters and brother, the rest of our family and friends- and as much as we may or may not believe, there is a book already written- it's not our book, but God's. It is incredibly hard when you feel like you have had one blow after another- but to learn to grieve and keep going-one foot in front of the other- even though it may feel like sludge- you keep going and finding your purpose so you can fulfill your duty as to the reason why God put you here on the earth and hasn't taken you yet. You're right mom, you do have to have hope, faith but most importantly, trust- that you are doing the best you can, with what you know how here on this earth without being able to go straight to God yourself and ask, Am I doing this right?' "

Me: "I do remember most of what you channeled that night. I remember you talking about a push from Peyton so that all makes sense to me. Thank you so much for the messages! Maybe it's encouragement or validation that "ok, I'm doing this ok". My biggest thing is I just want to be as tactful but, yet transparent as I can be."

Her: "You're right. I believe I said Peyton would be your biggest cheerleader or something similar? Courtney- your grandpa just told me- Courtney, you've hit the nail on this one- with a side grin and his blue eyes twinkling- I don't feel any negative pull back or caution at all and if at any time I do, I will be sure to reach out. Going back to your validation to make sure you are being tactful and transparent- I am to tell you that this is your story- and you tell it how you want to- I have been told that- Are there times when you start writing and you just can't stop? Or you write something and then erase, write again then erase? They want me to tell you to listen and feel with your gut when writing- you will know your answer as to if it's tactful or not or too transparent or not- Does that make sense?"

Me: "Thank you for that additional guidance! I get teary hearing from the boys and my grandpa. I think of them often and am always hoping they're proud of me. Please, if any time in the future if they give anything else please send it to me. I am a really transparent person and I know that makes some people uncomfortable. My book will literally be a collection of my journaling which will be raw, emotional, honest and again, offensive at times to some. But, it will be REAL and THAT is what I wished I could have picked up and read myself. People who hurt will "get me"... they will resonate with me. If they could finish it with a little hope then I feel everything I went through with the boys and even my mom were "worth it". "

This was the end of our conversation. Again, each message I get only cements inside of me the belief and faith in Spirit around us. How lucky am I to be surrounded by a handful of very gifted people who are willing to use their connection to help steer me? That's the thing, everyone is gifted in some way. Maybe it's time we find out what our main gifts are and start using them for each other. Maybe it's time that there isn't a taboo on working with Spirit. Maybe it's time we start accepting each other just as we are with all of our uniqueness and all. Maybe it's time we start drawing on each of our own unique talents and abilities to help heal each other and this world and stop expecting everyone to fit into some cookie cutter mold. Can we praise differences and uniqueness and use it as an opportunity to learn from each other and grow?

With ***LOVE*** and ***ACCEPTANCE*** from me to all of you. Let's start healing, growing, learning from each other and accepting each other with *LIGHT* and *LOVE*. May you embrace your trials and march forward soldier!

07/04/2020

Happy 4th of July! We had a small group of close friends over to help us celebrate this day, as we do each year. Due to COVID this year's gathering was smaller. There was a small parade in town in the morning and we took the kids. It was nice because we were able to still social distance as we sat in our chairs and watched.

Later into the evening as dusk was approaching, we all made our way to the front yard to watch the fireworks that were going to go off at the local park. Our house was the perfect location as you can see the show from our street. I was talking to one of our couple friends and the man mentioned something about his deceased father. I was covered in goosebumps or what I call "Spiritual Chills" and I said to him, "well he's with us right now". I became extremely emotional and felt such love.

For me, when I sense Spirit near me I get goosebumps all over. I feel emotions that aren't mine at the time, I feel a heaviness or tightness in my chest and a flutter in my stomach. Sometimes I feel ear pressure in one or both of my ears. I also experience spiritual chills when

Spirit is validating a truth that I just heard or that I just said. For example, if I was to say something to someone and break out in goosebumps then I know that Spirit is validating that what I just said is a "spiritual truth". Vice versa, when someone else is speaking and I break out in goosebumps, Spirit is validating to me that what the other person just said is a spiritual truth. I use this tool often for clarification.

Right before we sat down to watch the fireworks, I was talking to one of my other friends there. This friend is also an empath like me and experiences Spirit and spiritual chills in much the same way as I do. I mentioned that deep down I still struggle with guilt that I couldn't "see" the danger that I was placing Trinity and Peyton in by taking them to that particular daycare provider. That deep down I still struggle with anger at myself that I didn't "see" what was happening. My friend looked at me and said, "Courtney, maybe your last job isn't forgiving Anna. Maybe, it's finally forgiving yourself." In that moment she broke out in spiritual goosebumps all over her body. She lifted up her arms to show me and said, "You know what that means". In that moment tears came to my eyes as now I was covered in goosebumps as well. In that moment I felt them say, "It's time to forgive yourself for what you didn't know and what you didn't cause. Mom, it's time to move on and LIVE." Just like that....

The firework show started and as I sat watching the beautiful lights I was so overcome with love. I knew the boys were with me watching the show with the rest of us, as they always are. I was just given my most important message yet and it was all because a great friend of mine was able to listen to her intuition to give me the most important message that I needed to hear. And I was so thankful that my ears were open to receive her message.

Spirit uses **all** of us as vessels and they communicate with us through the most able way they can. Some of us can see Spirit, some of us can hear Spirit, some of us just "know" what Spirit is giving us and some of us can feel Spirit. By using our unique spiritual gifts we can help each other out. This is our life to live with certain lessons weaved into it. We each have different things to learn and build on. Rather than condemning each other, could we encourage each other in the battle that we are each fighting? And maybe, we could start loving ourselves and looking at life differently. I have experienced a lot of death, trauma and grief. But because of those experiences I understand pain. With an open heart I am able to experience Spirit and empathize with others.

I was a young mom doing the very best I could. I loved my children dearly and would never have purposely put them in harm's way. At the time I didn't recognize any signs that may have been present, to show that something was wrong with the person watching my babies. In fact, I wouldn't even have known what signs to look for. At the time, I dearly loved the person that was watching my children. I thought the world of her; I adored her. I don't believe her entire being is dark as I experienced many moments with her that were enjoyable. But deep down she was struggling with life in a way that I didn't see. She was good at hiding her own pain. Stresses overtook her that morning and my dear Peyton was her target. She doesn't admit it, but I know she has had to live with this guilt for the last 9 years. I can't imagine carrying this guilt and how it tears her insides apart. I don't hate you anymore. I forgive you Anna... for what you did and for what you didn't do that you should have.

But more important than forgiving you, I forgive ME... **Do you hear that self?** I forgive you for doing the very best through all of this that you could. Let me cut this last pair of shackles. I am free. I can feel full of love. I have grown and expanded. I have learned and I have felt deeply. It's time for me to LIVE.

TO ALL OF YOU-

It's time to forgive the situations that hurt you. It's time to forgive yourselves. We're all here to learn. Let it go. Stand up and be the warrior that you really are. It's time to step into your true power. Try *and find the light in your dark situation. Take it day by day, step by step. One foot in front of the other. Forgive the bad days and let them come. Have faith that you have the power and a spiritual team that is trying to help pull you through this. You **CAN** do this. Let light and love embody your being. Keep marching forward!*

With Love Always~

07/23/2020

Happy 9th birthday in heaven to our dear Peyton James!!

This last week I noticed that Jeremiah was a bit "off". He was kind of moody and just pulled away. I asked him several times what was wrong and in the car one night he adamantly stated, "I don't know." I felt his answer wasn't that he didn't want to talk but that he really didn't know.

After my chiropractor appointment I stopped at the store to grab cupcakes to celebrate Peyton's birthday tonight. I called my sister and we talked about it being Peyton's birthday. I got home and updated Jeremiah on my talk with my sister. As I now told Jeremiah about this conversation tears welled up in his eyes. Then it hit me.... He has been "off" the last week because Peyton's birthday was approaching and he was grieving. Nine years out and you would think I have this grief thing all figured out. But we both grieve differently and at different times.

We all deal with things differently and that's ok. It's ok to feel "off". It's ok to feel sad. It's ok to not know why you feel the way you do. But whatever you feel, whenever you feel it... let it COME OUT so that it can flow out and you can start to move past it.

"Feel your pain, experience your pain, see your pain.... But then.... Come back to LOVE."

The End

It seems appropriate to end what I've shared with you on Peyton's birthday. Peyton's death broke me; Tayden's death saved me. Forever from then we deal with their losses in the best way we can.

We can all do this but it is a lifetime journey. Peace, love and strength on your journey. Let the valleys come and feel them. But then, pick yourself up and strive back up. Find purpose, find joy, connect to your spiritual self, forgive others, forgive yourself and learn how to be everything to do with LOVE. You've all GOT this.

LOVE to ALL of you on your journey!

"A little less judgement, A LOT more love"

~Courtney

"Maybe the goal isn't to just 'get through it', but to get through it with LOVE, scars and all. To see your scars with love; that's when you know you've healed. "- Courtney Pottebaum

Contact: peytonspassing@gmail.com

@Photography By Nichole

Resources That Helped My Spiritual Awakening

Websites:

Amanda Linette Meder- Medium & Spiritual Development
https://www.amandalinettemeder.com/blog

Delores Cannon- Hypnotherapist of past life regressions
http://dolorescannon.com/

Dr. Joe Dispenza
https://drjoedispenza.com/

Dr. Katharina Johnston- Medical Intuitive & Energy Work
https://drkatharina.com/

Esther Hicks- Channels Abraham Hicks and The Law of Attraction
https://www.abraham-hicks.com/

Kelli Miller- Medium & Spiritual Development
https://psychickelli.com/

Lori Ladd- Ascension Teacher
http://www.lorieladd.com

Tara Arnold- Channels St. Germain
https://www.youtube.com/channel/UCecwwx-YPNGHcLjOi_HVHU_Q

Books:

Anita Moorjani, "What if THIS is heaven?"

Anthony Williams, "Medical Medium: Secrets Behind Chronic and Mystery Illness and How to Fully Heal".

Anthony Williams, "Cleanse to Heal".

Brian L. Weiss, MD. "Many Lives, Many Masters".

Dr. Bradley Nelson, "The Emotion Code."

Eben Alexander, M.D., "Proof of Heaven."

Esther and Jerry Hicks, "The Astonishing Power of Emotions".

Esther and Jerry Hicks, "The Vortex".

John MacARTHUR, "Safe in the Arms of God."

Matthew McKay, PhD., "Seeking Jordan".

Theresa Caputo, "Good Grief".

Theresa Caputo, "Good Mourning".

Theresa Caputo, "There's More to Life Than This".

Theresa Caputo, "You Can't Make THis Stuff Up".

Thomas John, "Never Argue With a Dead Person."

Walter Makichen, "Spirit Babies".

William P. Young, "The Shack".

Movies:

"A Dog's Purpose"

"Breakthrough"

"The Shack"

Songs:

"A Drop in the Ocean" by Ron Pope

"Down" by Jason Walker

"Everything's Right" by Matt Wertz

"From Where you Are" by Lifehouse

"Headlights on The Highway" by Ron Pope

"Higher Love" by Kygo

"Home" by Michael Buble

"I Won't Give Up" by Jason Mraz

"It is Well" by Bethel Music and Kristene Dimarco

"Let it Go" by James Bay

"Missing You" by Tyler Hilton

"Please Don't Go" by Stephanie Rainey

"Outnumbered" by Dermot Kennedy

"Rise Up" by Andra Day

"Sea Breaze" by Tyrone Wells

"See you Again" by Carrie Underwood

"Small Bump" by Ed Sheeran

"This is Me" by Kesha

"Time After Time" by Boyce Avenue

"The Longer I Run" by Peter Bradley Adams

"Underdog" by Alicia Keys

"When a Heart Breaks" by Ben Rector

"You Are the Reason" by Calum Scott

"10,000 Reasons/What a Beautiful Name" by Caleb and Kelsey

Healing Practices:

Acupuncture

Aromatherapy & Essential Oils

Chiropractor Therapy

Counseling & Therapy

Herbal Medicine

Hypnotherapy (clinical/spiritual)

Involvement in Faith Based Groups

Massage Therapy

Meditation

Mediumship

Physical Activity

Reiki & Energy Healing

Sound Healing & The 9 Solfeggio Frequencies

Traditional Western Medicine

Yoga

www.ingramcontent.com/pod-product-compliance
Lightning Source LLC
Chambersburg PA
CBHW071802080526
44589CB00012B/645